The Historical Atlas
of Montgomeryshire

(Combining a history of the county with maps, diagrams and photographs)

PUBLISHED BY THE POWYSLAND CLUB

Edited by
David Jenkins

For the Millennium
Published November 1999

THE POWYSLAND CLUB

Instituted 1867

Registered under the Charities Act 1960, Reg. No. 501303

The Powysland Club is indebted
for financial support with the publication of this volume
to Powys County Council

ISBN 0 9503613 7 2

Editorial Support Group:-
P. M. Davies, R. G. Gilson, E. R. H. Gent, D. W. Hall, G. T. Hughes, D. W. L. Rowlands
and D. Woodhouse

Printed in Times Roman 12 point

Designed and printed by WPG Co. Ltd, Severn Industrial Estate,
Welshpool, Powys, SY21 7DF

Foreword

I am delighted to present, on behalf of the Powysland Club, this book about Montgomeryshire.

The Powysland Club is the senior county historical society in Wales, having been founded in 1867. Most years since then it has published the *Montgomeryshire Collections,* reflecting the latest research on the history, archaeology, and genealogy of Montgomeryshire. Recently, it has published a number of books, chiefly on the history of individual towns in the county, but this work, covering almost every aspect of the county as a whole, is our most ambitious project yet, the scope of which may be grasped by looking at the table of contents.

The atlas has its origins in the publication in 1988, by the *Cymrodoriaeth* of the Powys Provincial Eisteddfod, of *Atlas Hanesyddol Maldwyn hyd at 1966,* edited by E. Ronald Morris. The Powysland Club is deeply grateful to the *Cymrodoriaeth* for allowing them access to the original material produced for the Welsh-language atlas; this publication draws heavily upon that material.

This atlas represents a tremendous amount of voluntary work by many of our members and other individuals who have given of their time to write contributions. This work has been edited by Dr. David Jenkins, Senior Curator of the Department of Industry in the National Museums & Galleries of Wales. He has been the grateful recipient of the support of many members of the Club Council too numerous to mention individually. Many of the maps were drawn by Helen Riley and Brian Williams, whilst most of the modern illustrations were taken by Windham Hime, Robin Hughes, Brian Poole and David Hall. Other illustrations have been drawn from the archives of the Museum of Welsh Life, St. Fagans and the Department of Industry of the National Museums & Galleries of Wales, Cardiff. The Club is grateful to the National Library of Wales for permission to use the Speed map on the dust-cover.

I commend this book to anybody with an interest in the history of our county.

D. W. L. Rowlands (Club Chairman)

Contents

Foreword by D. W. L. Rowlands (Chairman of the Club)

† Indicates the author is deceased.

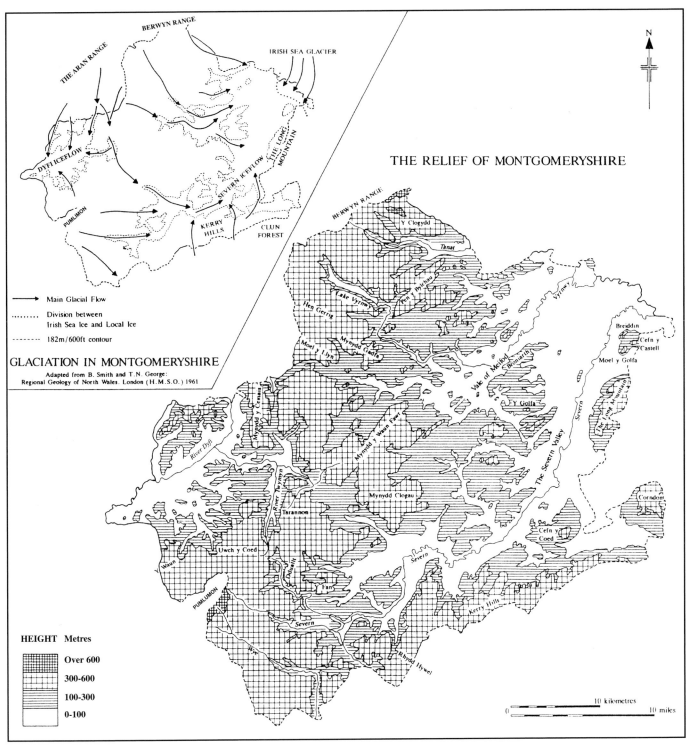

THE RELIEF OF MONTGOMERYSHIRE

GLACIATION IN MONTGOMERYSHIRE
Adapted from B. Smith and T.N. George:
Regional Geology of North Wales. London (H.M.S.O.) 1961

Main Glacial Flow
Division between
Irish Sea Ice and Local Ice
182m/600ft contour

HEIGHT Metres
Over 600
300-600
100-300
0-100

Relief

Montgomeryshire, like Wales as a whole, comprises an upland mass with lowland fringes in the east and west of the county. The lowlands by extending up the river valleys, penetrate the higher land. About a quarter of the county area is below 600 feet O.D.; nearly half of the county area reaches 1-2,000 feet O.D. A very small proportion (mainly in the Pumlumon and Berwyn uplands) is over 2,000 feet O.D. There are no spectacular, rugged mountains within the county limits, as in neighbouring counties, although on the northern and south western borders such scenery marks the county boundary.

In general, Montgomeryshire can be divided into

three relief zones: (a) Lowlands (below 600 feet O.D.), (b) Hilly Country (600 to 1,000 feet O.D.) and (c) High Moorland (1,000 to over 2,000 feet O.D.).

Lowlands are most extensively developed in the east - in the Vales of Severn and Meifod. In west Montgomeryshire the Dyfi Valley constitutes an important lowland element. In the Severn Valley the lowland penetrates westward as far as Llanidloes. Similarly, a tongue of lowland reaches westward from the Vale of Meifod to Llangadfan. A lowland area also extends up the Tanat Valley into the Berwyn Hills.

The greatest extent of hilly land occupies nearly a third of the county, between the Severn and Tanat rivers. This is broken country with many steep hillside slopes which has been carved up by the numerous tributary streams of the Severn system. Similar scenery lies between the Dyfi lowland and the Pumlumon upland to the south.

High moorlands are found over nearly all the western half of the county. These have been cut into by many headwaters of the larger rivers. The land surface (once this altitude has been reached) is gently undulating and it is possible to see for many miles across the peat bogs, which lie in the shallow depressions, and the green patches of the drier slopes. Because of its altitude, this is a land of cloud and frequent showers at most seasons of the year.

The present relief features of Montgomeryshire are the result of the long and complicated geological history of mid-Wales (see Geology p.9). The nature of the rocks alone has not been responsible for the present relief. Considered generally, it may be noted that the relief of Montgomeryshire has a northeast-southwest 'grain' which reflects the Caledonian trend of the ancient rocks beneath the land surface. This has been further emphasised by erosion of the land surface - hard, resistant rock bands stand out as hills, ridges and steep slopes (for example, Moel Pentyrch, two miles west of Llanfair Caereinion); softer rocks have been eroded more easily into depressions and valleys. The more rugged scenery of Corndon Hill, the Breiddin Hills, the Berwyns and Pumlumon Hills, however, has resulted from the erosion of

resistant, volcanic rocks which do not break down easily.

The larger valleys and vales of Montgomeryshire are wide with flat fertile floors and are usually bounded by steep sides. Such features, although originating as river valleys, are the result of widening and straightening during the last Ice Age which ended about 10 thousand years ago. The main glaciers all arose beyond the county limits as the Inset map shows (p.7). They flowed gradually through the county from ice centres on the higher ground to the north (the Aran Hills, Berwyns) and to the south (Pumlumon, Kerry Hills and Clun Forest). In the west, several minor tributary glaciers merged into the Dyfi Glacier, in the east into the great Severn Glacier. The effect of this glacial action was to convert the pre-existing, narrow river valleys into the wide beautiful vales of our landscape today.

W. T .R. PRYCE

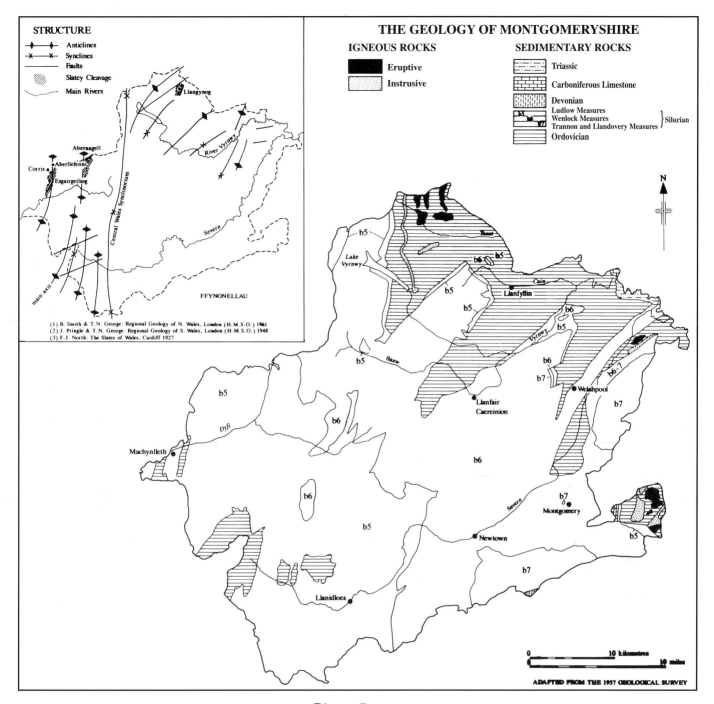

STRUCTURE

- Anticlines
- Synclines
- Faults
- Slatey Cleavage
- Main Rivers

Llangynog

Aberangell
Corris • •Aberllefenni
Esgairgeiliog

Central Wales Synclinorium

main axis

River Vyrnwy

Severn

FFYNONELLAU

(1) B. Smith & T.N. George: Regional Geology of N. Wales, London (H.M.S.O.) 1961
(2) J. Pringle & T.N. George: Regional Geology of S. Wales, London (H.M.S.O.) 1948
(3) F.J. North: The Slates of Wales, Cardiff 1927

THE GEOLOGY OF MONTGOMERYSHIRE

IGNEOUS ROCKS

- Eruptive
- Instrusive

SEDIMENTARY ROCKS

- Triassic
- Carboniferous Limestone
- Devonian
- Ludlow Measures
  Wenlock Measures } Silurian
  Trannon and Llandovery Measures
- Ordovician

Lake Vyrnwy

Llanfyllin

Cain

Vyrnwy

Welshpool

Llanfair Caereinion

Machynlleth

Dyfi

Banw

Severn

Montgomery

Newtown

Llanidloes

0   10 kilometres
                        10 miles

ADAPTED FROM THE 1957 GEOLOGICAL SURVEY

Geology

The history of Montgomeryshire begins with the formation of rocks. By 350 million years ago the most ancient ones had been laid down. Older rocks than these lie in Merioneth, Caernarfonshire and Anglesey. To the southeast of the county, the rocks are generally of more recent formation. Grits, shales, mudstones, poorly developed limestone, red sandstones and the various types formed by volcanic activity are the main rocks of the county, but newer types are generally absent.

In Ordovician times a great ocean lay across Britain, with its deepest parts lying along a northeast-southwest line. Somewhere to the northwest was a vast continent in the place where the modern North Atlantic occurs. At that time, modern Montgomeryshire formed the floor of this sea. Geologists think that this ocean had a sinking floor and shrinking sides which allowed large quantities of sediment (brought in by rivers and streams off the land) to be poured into it. In southeast

Montgomeryshire a fossil shoreline has been located which marked the limit of this sea. The earth's crust must have been very unstable for a number of active volcanoes stood on the floor of this Ordovician sea, some with their peaks above water. From these centres of eruption great clouds of fine cinder and ashes arose to drift across the waters. Huge volumes of molten lava poured over the ocean floor. Although the volcanic vents have not been accurately located, volcanic rocks occur today in the Aran Mountains and the Berwyns in the north, the Breiddin Hills in the east, and Corndon Hill in southeast Montgomeryshire. Near the Breidden Hills bomb rocks have been found which must have been hurled into the air when violent explosions happened. However, by the end of the Ordovician Period the volcanoes were extinct. Many geologists contend that the volcanoes themselves were not actually located in Montgomeryshire and that the lava flows reached the county area from centres of eruption further north in Merioneth or even from as far away as Caernarfonshire.

The Silurian Period, which followed, lasted for about 30 million years. The sea which had existed in Ordovician times remained, but during Silurian times it became narrower between the northwest and southeast shore, and deeper in the central parts. Fossil shorelines have again been located along the possible southeastern margins of this Silurian sea, in the neighbourhood of the Berwyns in northeast Montgomeryshire. Rock deposits in west Montgomeryshire suggest that here the ocean was very deep - too deep, in fact, for living creatures in abundance, for the green-blue-black rocks found near Llanymawddwy and Machynlleth have very few fossils except for graptolites. Near Meifod similar rocks have been located as deposits in hollows on the floor of the Silurian sea, suggesting that in this area there existed lagoons not far from a coastline.

From the start of Silurian times minor earth movements happened and these became gradually more intense as time passed on. The sea floor was being pushed up in some places and depressed in others. Around Lake Vyrnwy in north Montgomeryshire gritty bands of rock alternate with shale layers, resulting in rugged, picturesque scenery today. Ludlow Beds occur in the east and southeast parts of the county. The study of these rocks has indicated that while these were laid down on the sea floor, the material was brought into these areas by submarine currents from regions to the south and southwest of the county. Was there a great landmass with northward flowing rivers somewhere south of the Silurian sea? Few active volcanoes existed during this Silurian Period, but it appears that certain hills like the Berwyns and Breiddins had become islands before the end of this time, due to the developing earth movements.

At the close of the Silurian Period the great ocean which had existed for many millions of years was changed by the Caledonian Orogeny. The floor of this ocean was squeezed from the southeast margins so that it buckled into upfolds (anticlines) and downfolds (synclines). This mountain-building period occurred 320 million years ago. The older, more resistant rocks did not fold easily with the result that they cracked (faulted) and cleaved into slaty formations. Throughout the county these folds were orientated in a northeast-southwest direction - the Caledonian trend. The main fold in Montgomeryshire is the Central Wales Syncline, which extends from the north of the county southwards to Pembrokeshire. There are many associated folds in west and northeast Montgomeryshire (see inset map). Besides influencing the modern relief of the county it resulted in slaty rocks being formed at Corris and Aberllefenni. In southwest parts of the county, and extending into Cardiganshire, lead, zinc, copper and other minerals of economic importance were formed in the faults and fissures of rocks affected by the forces of mountain building. In other parts of the county volcanoes again became active as at Llanyblodwel near Oswestry and in the Berwyns.

After this period of mountain building the great ocean of Ordovician and Silurian times disappeared from central Wales. Sediments from the floor of this ocean formed land where previously a sea had been. The Devonian Period now began. In north Wales this was a time of great deserts - like those of central Asia at the present time. The rocks formed at this time are mostly red sandstones, but geologists think that most of these have been removed by erosion from Montgomeryshire. The only remaining deposits are today in the southeast of the county in the vicinity of Clun Forest.

Although extensive Carboniferous and Permian rocks occur not far from Montgomeryshire, with the exception of a small outcrop of the Carboniferous deposits in the Llanymynech area, none remain within the county itself. A time-gap of 90 million years, therefore, exists between the Devonian and the Triassic rocks in our county. Did the missing rocks once lie over Montgomeryshire? Had they been worn away before those of the Triassic Period were deposited in the northeast of the county? These are questions which, at present, are difficult to answer.

The Triassic Period lasted for about 30 million years. During this time a lake or inland sea existed east of the county. This is thought to have been a desert sea for it contained few living creatures. Sediments deposited there are generally red in colour (a sign of aridity), with streaks of darker materials. These facts suggest that seasonal floods brought the darker sediments from a nearby landmass - the red deposits occurred in the dry season.

Although rocks are still being formed at present in Montgomeryshire - mostly along the floors of river valleys - Triassic rocks, laid down 160 million years ago, formed the last major deposits in Montgomeryshire until the Ice Age.

W. T. R. PRYCE

Moel-y-Golfa from Severn Valley

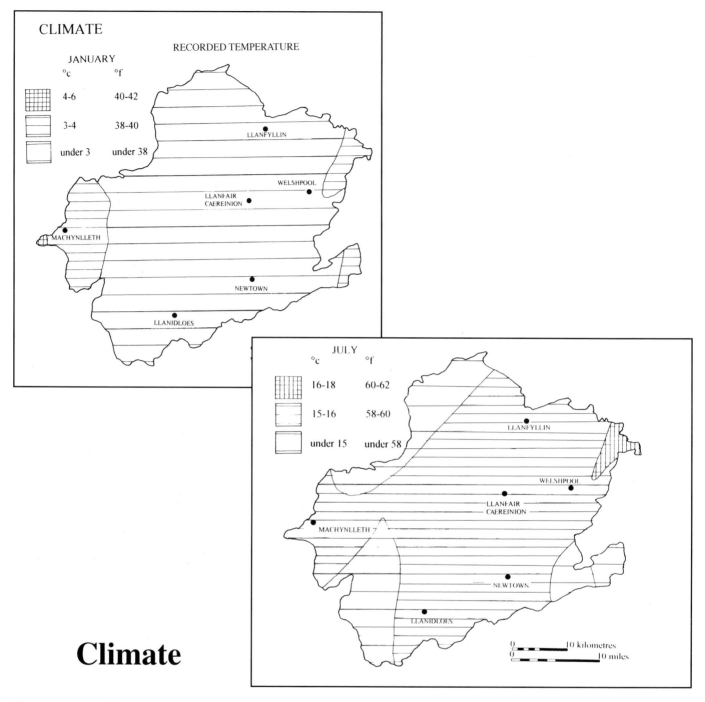

CLIMATE

RECORDED TEMPERATURE

JANUARY

°c	°f
4-6	40-42
3-4	38-40
under 3	under 38

JULY

°c	°f
16-18	60-62
15-16	58-60
under 15	under 58

0 ___ 10 kilometres
0 ___ 10 miles

Climate

The seasonal distribution of temperatures over the county is largely governed by the following factors:

a) Altitude: temperatures fall approximately one degree Fahrenheit for every 300 feet of ascent above sea level.

b) Distance from sea: land surfaces warm and cool more quickly than the sea. Therefore places on the coast may have higher winter temperatures than inland stations because of the warming influences of the sea.

The resultant effect of these influences can be noted from a study of the maps showing the seasonal distribution of temperatures in Montgomeryshire. In January highest temperatures are recorded in the Dyfi Valley because warm air is channelled inland from Cardigan Bay. In July the warmest parts of the county lie in the lower Severn Valley - a lowland area, sheltered from the cooling effects of the sea in the summer season. Over the greater part of Montgomeryshire, however, altitude exerts a stronger influence on actual temperatures at all seasons of the year. In January the coolest parts are the high moorlands. These uplands also prevent warming influences from penetrating further eastwards. In July the High Moorlands - extending from the Berwyns to Pumlumon Fawr - are the coolest areas. Much of this land is 1,000-2,000 feet O.D., resulting in a significant fall of temperatures. Locally, temperatures may be greatly affected by aspect - the direction in which a site faces. Consequently, as the north sides of valleys face southwards, they enjoy higher temperatures.

The rainfall map also reveals the influence of relief in determining the geographical distribution of the average rainfall, which is received over the county area. Much of this rainfall occurs when warm, moist air is forced to rise over relief barriers; cooling takes place and rain or snow is precipitated. The prevailing winds over western Britain come from a south-westerly direction and since they have to cross the High Moorland in west Montgomeryshire, the heaviest rainfall occurs in these localities. A comparison of the relief and rainfall maps shows that most land over 1,000 feet O.D. receives upwards of 60 inches per annum. On the other hand, the annual rainfall reduces eastward of the High Moorlands. Lowest aggregates have been recorded in the east low-lying river valleys where less than 30 inches is received in a typical year. All land east of the High Moorlands, therefore, is in a rain shadow area. It is interesting to note that rainfall increases over the higher ground in this eastern part of the county. Thus the Long Mountain and Corndon Hill receive over 35 inches, while the surrounding lowlands have less than 35 inches per annum.

The incidence of sunshine and snow coverage further illustrate the influences which have already been described. Lowest total sunshine hours (fewer than 1250 hours per year) occur over the high moorland - an area, as we have seen, of heavy rainfall and extensive cloud development. The eastward drift of clouds which have been formed over the high moorland results in reduced sunshine (fewer than 1300 hours) as far as a line joining Llanfyllin and Newtown. Further east, and also in the lower Dyfi Valley, sunshine conditions of up to 1350 hours prevail.

Similarly, snow can be found lying on the high moorland extending from the Berwyns south to Pumlumon Fawr and over the Kerry Hills in southeast Montgomeryshire on more than twenty mornings in an average year, associated with the lower seasonal temperatures which result from increased altitude. Less than five mornings with snow are recorded for the Dyfi Valley, especially for the part below Machynlleth where the mild influences of Cardigan Bay can penetrate inland. The lower Severn Valley has an average of 10-20 mornings with snow. This region is low-lying and sheltered by hills and high moorlands to the west and therefore lies in a snow-shadow zone.

W. T. R. Pryce

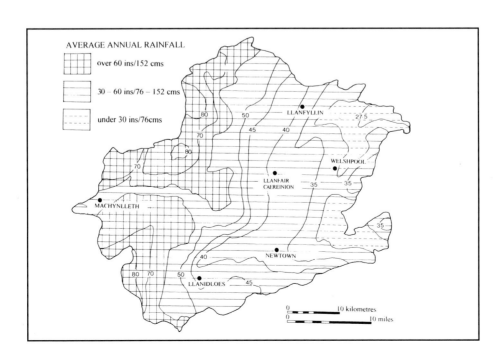

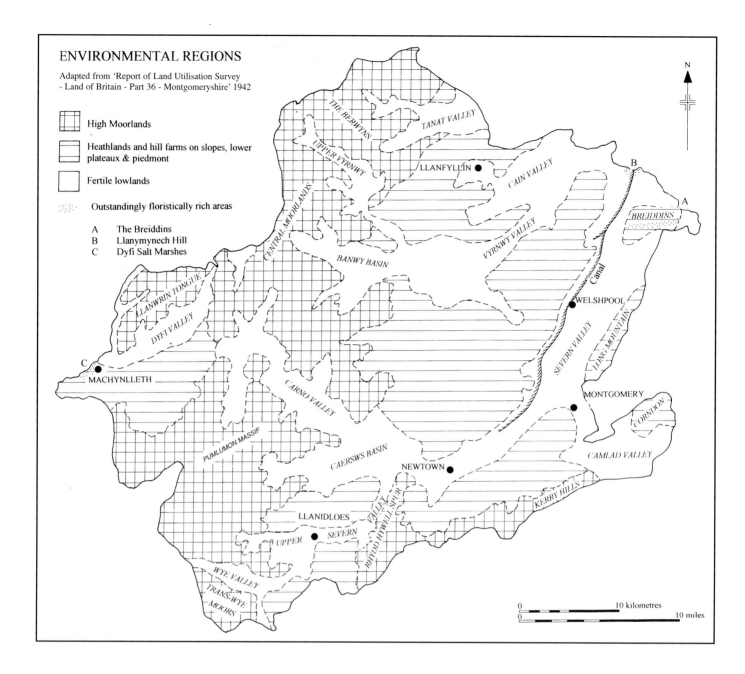

ENVIRONMENTAL REGIONS

Adapted from 'Report of Land Utilisation Survey
- Land of Britain - Part 36 - Montgomeryshire' 1942

High Moorlands

Heathlands and hill farms on slopes, lower
plateaux & piedmont

Fertile lowlands

Outstandingly floristically rich areas

A   The Breiddins
B   Llanymynech Hill
C   Dyfi Salt Marshes

Flora and Fauna

The often tranquil, sometimes grand, scenery of
Montgomeryshire is a result of its geological history.
Its resistant, ancient rocks, first folded then
peneplained, uplifted and tilted, form mountains
rising to over 2,000 ft. on its northern and western
flanks, which drop by a series of plateaux to the
lowland of wide river valleys in the east. By
contrast, the valleys on the western flanks are deeply
cut, soon reaching the tidal waters of the Dyfi
estuary.

The mountains rising in the path of the moisture-
laden westerly winds are drenched by heavy
rainstorms, while the eastern lowlands bask in the
drier conditions of a rain shadow. The gateway from
England is guarded by Llanymynech Hill composed
of the newer Carboniferous Limestone on the west
and the higher eminence of the Breiddens, an
intrusion of igneous rocks on the east.

Such contrasting relief and scenery has given rise to
different environments, which in turn support varied
assemblages of wildlife. The contrast in elevation
and climate between east and west has resulted in

marked differences in the flora which, being the base of the food chain, is reflected in the fauna.

The thin soil of the summit plateaux of the Berwyns and Pumlumon, saturated by heavy rainfall, gives rise to an accumulation of peat where sphagnum moss, the insect-eating sundew, cross-leaved heath, cotton grass and bog asphodel are the dominant plants, while the shy-flowering cloudberry and the tiny lesser twayblade occur as rarities. The emperor moth and large heath butterfly breed on the heather and cotton grass respectively and such ground-nesting birds as the curlew, ring ousel and meadow pipit appreciate the peace of these sparsely populated areas. They in turn attract such predators as the buzzard and raven.

On the slopes of these moors, where quick drainage carries away the nutrients, the thin acid soil supports heathland, with heather and gorse and some bilberry and cowberry dominating the higher levels. Here wheatears and skylarks make their home providing prey for the merlin and hen harrier, two birds for which Montgomeryshire is nationally important. So too is the peregrine falcon, which breeds on the rocky outcrops of these slopes.

The lower slopes were formerly wooded but, being cleared gradually for farming, now present bracken,

heaths or grassy slopes where the dominance of sheep rearing limits the regeneration of trees. It was in the remnants of these acid woodlands that the red kite survived in its last stronghold in Britain and active conservation methods have now helped it back from the brink of extinction. On the grassy fields, the locally developed Montgomeryshire red clover was once an important fodder crop, though it is little used today. It is still grown in New Zealand from where seed is exported under the name of "Monty Red". The large and small skippers and the dark green fritillary are butterflies of this zone, and bees thrive on the heather.

As the ground has a low economic value for farming, much has been planted with conifers but the large plantations, being of alien species, support few indigenous invertebrates. Rosebay willowherb, foxgloves and ferns flourish in the lighter areas beside the rides, while badgers, foxes and voles take advantage of the shelter of the dark interior.

The lowlands of the river valleys vary in character according to their exploitation by man. The most floristically rich areas are old unimproved hay meadows where cowslips, vetches, dog daisies and other flowers form a colourful blanket in early summer, but the development of economic farming methods have wiped out these meadows in all but the poorest or most remote areas, replacing them with monocultures of rye grass.

Similarly, the old woodland management by coppicing which encouraged the flowering of primroses, violets, bluebells and yellow archangel when light was let into the woods, is largely now discontinued, and many deciduous woods have been felled decimating the numbers of fritillary butterflies, particularly the pearl-bordered fritillary, which breed on the violets. The woodland wildlife now finds refuge in the hedges which, as a habitat for primroses and violets, blackbirds, thrushes and a host of other small songbirds have an importance far beyond their original use. Particularly attractive in the Severn valley are the fragrant hawthorn hedges planted at the time of the 18th century enclosures, while in the Cefn Coch area laburnum hedges are equally picturesque. Butterflies abounding in the flower-rich meadows and hedgerows include orange-tip, peacock and small tortoiseshell, while many of the small songbirds are preyed upon by sparrowhawks and tawny owls.

The hilly ramparts of the Breiddin and Llanymynech Hill are floristically the most interesting areas of the District; the Breiddin, with its base-rich igneous soil, was for long a Mecca for herbalists and botanists since its unusual flora was highlighted by the finds of Edward Llwyd of Llanforda, Oswestry. The three rarities he recorded in the late 17th century, rock cinquefoil, spiked speedwell and sticky catchfly, still survive today, happily now protected by the quarrying company working the hill for roadstone.

Llanymynech Hill owes its interesting flora to its dry limestone soil tolerated by such unusual plants as salad burnet, wild clematis, yellow-wort and nine species of wild orchids, together with a host of more common varieties such as wild thyme, cowslips, wild strawberry and quaking grass. The abundance of flowers attracts a similar wealth of lepidoptera including green hairstreak, dingy skipper, grizzled skipper and brown argus butterflies and the mullein shark moth. Swifts nest in the rocky crevices high on the quarry face.

The wetlands of the county include the contrasting clear lakes of the mountains, with few nutrients to support plants, and the overgrown lakes and pools of the lowlands fed by waters from the well-fertilised surrounding fields. These are often flanked by dense stands of reeds, bulrushes and yellow iris, building up reed swamps in which, occasionally, rarer plants like water violet in the Flash at Welshpool may be found, and in which sedge warblers make their nests.

The canal and the slowly flowing rivers support their own typical flora and the earliest county record made in 1663 by George Bowles was the rare touch-me-not balsam which can be found on the banks of the Camlad near Churchstoke. Along the canal bank flowering rush, bur-marigold, gipsywort and several species of polygonum may be found and grass snakes are not uncommonly seen slithering across the tow-path.

To the naturalist perhaps the most interesting feature of the Severn and Vyrnwy valleys is the survival of the otter here, when it was vanishing, almost to extinction, in other areas. Modern sympathetic management of the river banks, with advice from the Vincent Wildlife Trust, is now enabling it to make a welcome revival.

The most unusual assemblage of plants in what is virtually an inland county are those of the salt marsh at the head of the Dyfi estuary where such coastal species as sea milkwort, thrift and sea aster thrive. Coastal birds seen here include several species of duck and waders and the red-breasted merganser. Snipe feed on the salt marshes of the new Morfa Dyfi Reserve of the County Naturalists Trust.

Miss E. M. Hignett

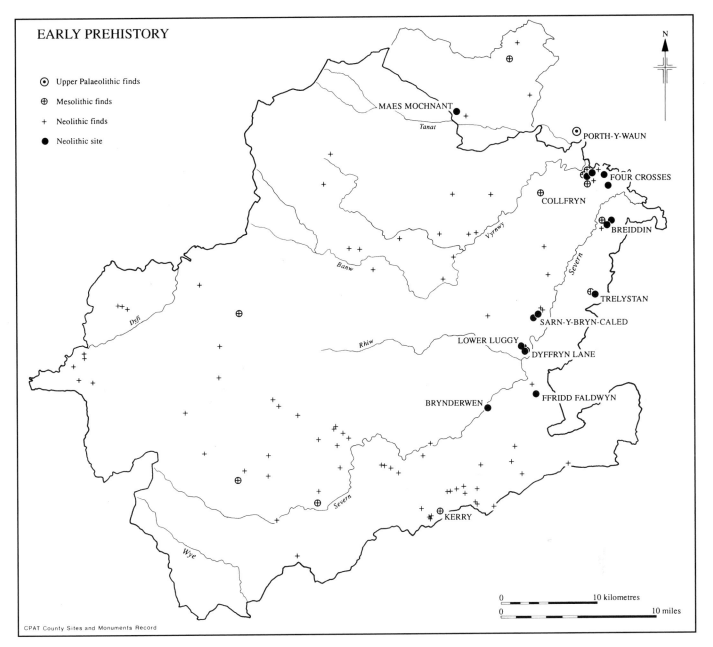

EARLY PREHISTORY

⊙ Upper Palaeolithic finds

⊕ Mesolithic finds

+ Neolithic finds

● Neolithic site

MAES MOCHNANT

Tanat

PORTH-Y-WAUN

FOUR CROSSES

COLLFRYN

Vyrnwy

BREIDDIN

Banw

Severn

Dyfi

TRELYSTAN

Rhiw

SARN-Y-BRYN-CALED

LOWER LUGGY

DYFFRYN LANE

FFRIDD FALDWYN

BRYNDERWEN

Severn

KERRY

Wye

0   10 kilometres

0   10 miles

CPAT County Sites and Monuments Record

Early Prehistory

The first humans to visit the county following the last glaciation are likely to have been nomadic late Upper Palaeolithic hunters from the south and east of Britain setting up temporary camps in pursuit of migrating herds of horse and reindeer as well as smaller mammals, birds and fish. Little direct evidence of human activity has yet been found in the county during this cool climatic phase, but a barbed bone point forming part of a typical hunting spear of this period, found at Porth-y-waun in the lower Tanat Valley, just across the border with Shropshire, and dating to about 12000 BC, presents the first clear evidence of human activity in the region.

More permanent settlers, depending upon hunting, fishing, and gathering wild fruits, are likely to have started coming to the region during the Mesolithic period, from about 8000 BC onwards, during the gradual amelioration of climatic conditions. Recent studies of ancient pollens preserved in waterlogged sites in several parts of the county are beginning to reveal the kind of environment exploited by these early settlers. From about this time the landscape would have been fairly densely covered with birch woodland, with some pine and elm in probably all but the more mountainous areas. The presence of hazel, willow and initially some juniper pollen

17

suggest areas of scrub. This, together with areas of grassland, would have provided grazing for herds of wild ox and red deer which are likely to have been hunted for food. From a date of about 6800 BC there was a notable expansion of oak woodland, and from about 5500 BC a rise in the proportion of alder, accompanying a gradual decline in birch and hazel and the virtual disappearance of pine. This corresponded with a climatic phase that had changed to being slightly warmer than that of today, which was to last until about 3500 BC. Radiocarbon dating of plant and animal remains, as in later prehistoric periods, provides the essential chronological framework for understanding these climatic and environmental changes and the associated evidence of human activity. Settlements of the Mesolithic period in the county still await discovery, but some activity, albeit on a limited scale, is clearly represented by small flint points (microliths) belonging to hunting and fishing implements. Examples characteristic of the later Mesolithic period, after about 6000 BC, have been found at a small number of both upland and lowland sites in the south and east of the county, as for example near Kerry, in the valley of the Vyrnwy, on Long Mountain to the east of Welshpool, and in the valley of the Clywedog.

The period between about 4000-2500 BC was one of dramatic change that witnessed the gradual eclipse of the early hunter-gatherer economies in favour of arable farming and pastoralism throughout the greater part of western Europe. Agricultural techniques were gradually adopted and adapted to suit local conditions. Native forests began to be cleared to provide arable land for the cultivation of cereals and legumes, and for the creation of pasture for herds of domesticated sheep and cattle. New tools of Neolithic type were adopted, including polished axes, adzes and chisels of polished flint and stone, which were used for tree-felling and carpentry. Flint arrowheads were used for both hunting and warfare, and pottery was being made for the first time.

The rate at which these new ideas were adopted in mid Wales is still open to question. The pollen record shows only slight indications of the impact of man on the natural environment in the earlier Neolithic period, and in common with other areas of highland Britain it is possible that population densities remained at a relatively low level. A settled farming economy was evidently adopted either very gradually or at a much later date than in other more favoured parts of southern Britain.

The best general indication we have of the extent of human settlement at this time is given by the find-spots of flint and stone implements. Characteristic types include polished flint and stone axes, flint scrapers and knives, and either leaf-shaped or, later on, obliquely-pointed flint arrow-heads. Their distribution is fairly widespread throughout the county, and although they have mostly been found by chance, there is a clear suggestion that a broad range of different habitats were already being exploited by man, including both the major river valleys and at least some upland areas.

Most of the raw material, for the flint and stone implements, were probably either imported from some distance or arrived by way of trade or exchange. Some of the flint tools appear to be made of material from the chalklands in Wessex or Yorkshire, and a number of the stone axes are of hard, fissile rocks found in the Lake District, north Wales and south-west Wales. The occasional discovery of some larger flint flakes, on Long Mountain for example, suggest some implements other than axes were made from imported raw materials, rather than arriving as completed objects. Similarly, some of the Neolithic pottery from the county appears to be made of clays which originated a reasonable distance away, in this instance suggesting contact with areas to the south-east, coinciding with the present-day Herefordshire borderland.

The earliest certain evidence of Neolithic activity in Montgomeryshire is represented by an earthen long-barrow discovered from the air at Lower Luggy, Berriew. Trial excavations have shown that the oak timbers that revetted the mound of this burial monument were felled in the period between 3700-3300 BC.

The first significant indications of the human impact upon the natural environment began in the middle and later Neolithic period, from a date of about 3000 BC. By this time there are indications that substantial openings were beginning to be made in the native forest cover, possibly for the creation of grazing. Forest clearance in some upland areas may well have caused waterlogging, resulting in the initiation of blanket peats. Although there is still little indication of arable cultivation or the extent of forest clearance, the increasing evidence of human impact on the natural environment during the middle and later Neolithic periods appears to be linked to the increasing number and diversity of types of sites and finds of these periods in the county.

There is still little direct evidence of human settlement, but a pattern of small, thinly-scattered farmsteads belonging to individual family groups seems to be likely. Traces of two stake-walled timber buildings with central slab-lined hearths and cooking pits were found at an upland site at Trelystan, associated with decorated pottery known as grooved ware, dated to the period between about 2900-2500 BC. The buildings were small and insubstantial, and may represent temporary summer camps. Neolithic finds are known from a number of other upland sites such as the Breiddin and Ffridd Faldwyn which became hillforts in the later prehistoric period, and there is the possibility that some of these may have acted as fortified or hilltop settlements.

It seems likely that settlement activity would have been focussed on the lowlands, but evidence for this is very sparse. A pit containing a fragment of Peterborough pottery of middle Neolithic date is known from a valley-bottom site at Brynderwen, Llandysul. Similar fragments of Peterborough pottery are known from the Breiddin and also from a number of lowland monuments associated with burial and ritual activity. The small number of excavated sites of this kind exhibit a wide variety of form. A large pit grave dated to about 3000 BC is known from Four Crosses (Llandysilio) which contained traces of an inhumation burial accompanied by a simple round-bottomed bowl. Fragments of a highly decorated Peterborough bowl were found in the upper silting of an encircling ring-ditch which possibly acted as a quarry for building a low earthen mound or barrow above the burial pit. A small penannular ditch— a circular ditch with a narrow entrance causeway — is known from a second gravel site at Sarn-y-bryn-caled, just to the south of Welshpool, dated to about 3000-2800 BC the entrance of which was marked by two timber posts. Four cremation burials and fragments of Peterborough pottery, were found in the ditch. In this instance it seems likely that the soil removed from the ditch was used to construct a low outer bank rather than a central mound. A large, rock-cut grave found beneath a low stone cairn at Trelystan contained an inhumation burial, possibly within an oak coffin, which is dated to about 3000 BC.

The burial at Four Crosses and both the burial and the houses at Trelystan were subsequently overlain by circular Bronze Age burial mounds of earth or stone. These monuments are fairly numerous and are widely distributed throughout the county, and although they are probably largely of Bronze Age date it is now clear that a reasonable proportion of these sites must have their origins in the middle and later Neolithic period.

Neolithic pit grave at the centre of a burial monument at Four Crosses, photographed from the air in 1982. The earliest burial monument, dating to about 3300-2900 BC, is respresented by the pit grave and the innermost ring-ditch. The monument was enlarged on two successive occasions between the later Neolithic and early Bronze Age.

Photo: CPAT

The broad, circular ditch of the Dyffryn Lane henge monument, Berriew, probably dating to the period between 3000-2500BC, photographed from the air in 1986. The monument had a single entrance about 3 metres wide, visible in the foreground, and was enclosed by an outer bank with an external diameter of about 85 metres. The Maes Beuno standing stones lie on the edge of the road just to the right of the photograph.

Photo: CPAT

The penannular ditch at Sarn-y-bryn-caled forms part of an important complex of burial and ritual monuments of middle Neolithic to Bronze Age date which lie on a gravel terrace just above the flood-plain of the Severn. These include a narrow ditched enclosure known as a cursus, about 400 metres long. Sites of this kind appear to have no utilitarian function but may have been used for ceremonial processions of some kind. The penannular ditch may not have been primarily intended as a burial monument and appears to belong to a class of site known as henge monuments (named after the Neolithic ditched enclosure surrounding Stonehenge) which again appear to have had a ritual function.

Similar dating is likely in the case of a further complex of burial mounds and ritual sites at Dyffryn Lane, Berriew, just 4 kilometres to the south, where a further concentration of valley-bottom sites is known. The focus of this complex is a much larger ditched enclosure with a broad outer bank up to 80 metres across and a single entrance pointing to the west, again forming a henge monument with an outer bank. Parts of a stone circle appear to have been removed from beneath a large central mound within the central enclosure in the 19th century, and it seems possible that it continued in use as a burial mound into the early Bronze Age. The standing stone known as Maen Beuno, which now lies in the verge of the road just to the south-west, may have been an outlying stone associated with the circle.

These developments are paralleled elsewhere in Britain at this period. No doubt the Severn valley, as throughout the county's history, provided a passageway for new peoples, new ideas and materials. Little is yet known about how and where people lived at this time, but the existence of these larger, communal monuments suggests that by a date of 2500 BC, on the eve of the early Bronze Age, human societies were already reasonably well organized. We may already be witnessing the origin of tribal groupings which were to become such a dominant feature of later prehistoric periods.

W. J. Britnell

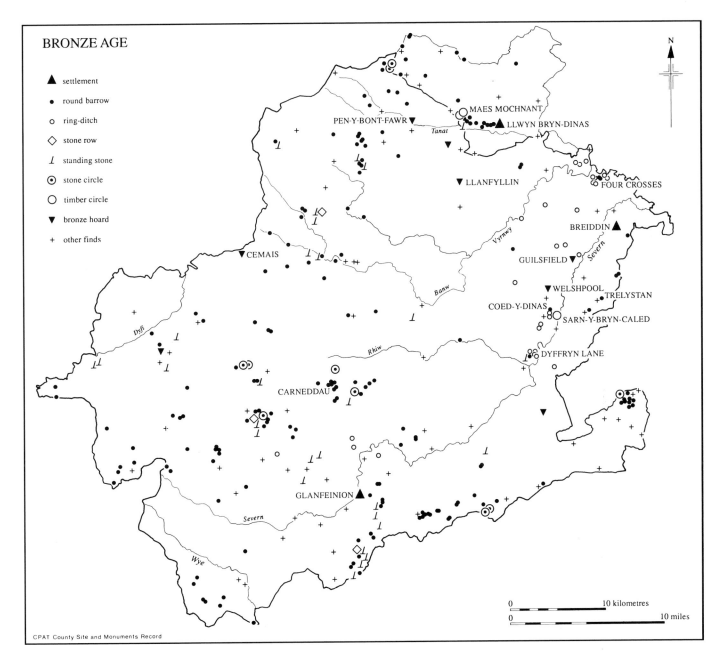

BRONZE AGE

▲ settlement

• round barrow

○ ring-ditch

◇ stone row

⌿ standing stone

◉ stone circle

○ timber circle

▼ bronze hoard

+ other finds

MAES MOCHNANT

PEN-Y-BONT-FAWR ▼ ▲ LLWYN BRYN-DINAS

Tanat

▼

▼ LLANFYLLIN

○ FOUR CROSSES

BREIDDIN ▲

Vyrnwy

GUILSFIELD ▼

▼ CEMAIS

Severn

Banw

▼ WELSHPOOL TRELYSTAN

COED-Y-DINAS

○ SARN-Y-BRYN-CALED

Rhiw

○ DYFFRYN LANE

Dyfi

◉ CARNEDDAU

◉

◉

GLANFEINION ▲

Severn

Wye

0   10 kilometres

0   10 miles

CPAT County Site and Monuments Record

Bronze Age

Copper and then bronze technologies were introduced to Britain from about 2500 BC. Although bronze became widely used for the production of tools and weapons, flint and stone continued to be utilized during the earlier Bronze Age for the production of scrapers, knives and axes. A new form of flint arrowhead with barbs and a tang was first introduced at this time. Wristguards were also used by archers, of which a perforated stone example, dated to 1900 BC, was found beneath a cairn at Carneddau (Carno). A fine flint dagger, similar to early copper ones, is known from Trefeglwys.

Metamorphic rocks near Hyssington (Churchstoke), on the eastern borders of the county, were quarried for the production of shafthole implements known as battle-axes and axe-hammers during the period between 1650-1400 BC; these found their way to various sites in the county, as well as north Wales, the Midlands, and as far afield as Wessex.

Stone technology was thus abandoned only gradually, and the technological innovations represented by metalworking are just one element in a dramatic period of human history which witnessed the continuing evolution of the former middle and later Neolithic societies, rapid population growth, agricultural expansion, and increasing pressures on the natural environment.

Climatic change played a critical role in these developments. Though the climate appears to have begun to cool from about 3000 BC, it would still have been both warmer and drier than today, and enabled greater exploitation of the more marginal upland areas of the county. A decline in oak woodland was partly due to climatic change and partly to gradual and then accelerating deforestation for the use of forest resources and the creation of both arable and pasture. The first significant human impact on the natural environment becomes evident towards the end of the early Bronze Age, from a date of about 1400 BC. The onset of cooler and wetter conditions, from about 1300 BC, will have resulted in a drop in agricultural output, and contributed to the social upheavals and economic changes which affected much of Europe in the middle and later Bronze Age.

Few settlement sites are known, though a single Middle Bronze Age timber roundhouse is known from excavations at Glanfeinion, near Llandinam, dated to the period about 1400-1170 BC, and possibly representing a small unenclosed farmstead. Associated with the building were large quantities of charred naked barley and probable fragments of cattle and sheep bones.

Evidence for the general location and intensity of human activity in the county partly depends upon chance finds of tools and weapons and partly on monument types characteristic of the period which have been identified by fieldwork and aerial survey. Characteristic sites include burial mounds, standing stones, stone rows, ring-cairns and stone or timber circles. Few, if any, settlement sites of early or middle Bronze Age date have been positively identified, but it must be assumed that areas of settlement and farming activity bear some relationship to the distribution of chance finds and funerary and ceremonial monuments. These are widely distributed throughout the county but show notable concentrations in certain areas. Evidence from Four Crosses (Llandysilio) and Trelystan suggests that at least some monuments and cemetery areas which had been established by middle and later Neolithic communities were to continue in use into the early and middle Bronze Age. This continuity of use, lasting for a period of probably more than a millennium, provides clear evidence of social stability.

Likewise, early complexes of ritual as well as funerary monuments at Dyffryn Lane (Berriew) and Sarn-y-bryn-caled (Welshpool) also continued in use

Temporary reconstruction of the Bronze Age timber circle at Sarn-y-bryn-caled, excavated in 1991 in advance of the construction of the Welshpool bypass. A more permanent reconstruction of the timber circle, dated about 2100 BC, has now been built at the Museum of Welsh Life at St Fagans.

Photo: CPAT

as ceremonial centres into the Bronze Age, possibly serving more dispersed communities. As we have seen in an earlier section, the probably Neolithic henge monument at Dyffryn Lane — a large ditched enclosure with a single entrance and an outer bank — appears to have been superseded by a stone circle and then by a barrow, both of which are likely to be of Bronze Age date. Further ritual monuments were added to the complex of Neolithic sites at Sarn-y-bryn-caled which appear to have been started in the period 3000-2800 BC. A henge-like ditched enclosure with two opposed entrances at Coed-y-dinas, just to the north, is associated with Beaker pottery. A double timber circle about 20 metres across was also erected in the heart of the complex in about 2100 BC and is associated with two cremation burials one of which was accompanied by four barbed and tanged flint arrowheads and the other by a simple food vessel. The posts forming the circles were between 30-70 centimetres in diameter, and may have supported wooden lintels, to produce a monument similar in appearance to Stonehenge. An entrance in the outer circle appears to be aligned on the midsummer sunrise, and therefore perhaps emphasising the importance which must have been attached to the seasons of the year in early ceremonial activities. A similar complex of sites is known in the upper Tanat valley at Maes Mochnant near Llanrhaeadr-ym-Mochnant from aerial reconnaissance. Other similar ceremonial centres almost certainly await discovery in the county. Little excavation has been carried out on the stone circles, standing stones and stone rows in the county, but the circles and a proportion of the other sites are again likely to represent Bronze Age ceremonial monuments.

Earthen round barrows, stone cairns, ring cairns and ring-ditches appear to have been primarily funerary monuments. Whilst a proportion of these were constructed in the middle and late Neolithic, a majority of those known from the county are likely to be of early to middle Bronze Age date. Burials were occasionally accompanied by a pottery vessel which was often decorated, belonging to a variety of different types. Belonging to the early Bronze Age are beakers (e.g. Aberbechan Hall, Llanllwchaearn, and Darowen) — a form introduced to Britain from continental Europe — as well as food vessels (e.g. Penegoes, Two Tumps, near Kerry, and Trelystan). Larger food vessel urns (e.g. Garthbeibio and Trelystan), and collared urns (e.g. Caebetin, near

Kerry, Carneddau, near Carno, and Lan Fawr, near Churchstoke), were all developed from indigenous potting traditions of the middle and later Neolithic. By the middle Bronze Age, after about 1400 BC, plainer and less distinctive urn types had evolved (e.g.Four Crosses, Pennant Melangell), which by the later Bronze Age, after about 1000 BC, only appear on settlement sites (e.g. the Breiddin). In the later Bronze Age, as in the succeeding Iron Age, some other tradition for the disposal of the dead was adopted which has left no clear trace. In the absence of settlement evidence of the early Bronze Age it is uncertain to what extent the pottery types noted above were also in everyday use. Fragments of Beaker pottery which possibly come from domestic rather than burial contexts and dated to the period between 2400-2000 BC, are also known, however, from Collfryn (Llansantffraid [Llansanffraid] Deuddwr) and Four Crosses (Llandysilio).

Other types of object accompanying burials are fairly scarce. Two riveted bronze daggers as well as a beaker were found in a mound at Darowen. A cremation burial at Garthbeibio was found with a small stone battle-axe, a flint knife and a food vessel urn. An inhumation burial at Four Crosses was associated with a jet or shale button.

As in the Neolithic period, Bronze Age burial monuments display a wide variety of form and burial practice. Indeed, the few excavated examples in the county show little similarity apart from an invariably circular form to the monument, and evidence that they were often constructed with some care and were frequently added to or enlarged over the course of time. Different materials were used in their construction and will no doubt have depended upon availability as well as upon local tradition. Some earthen barrows were clearly built of turf stripped from the surrounding area (e.g. Four Crosses, Trelystan), whilst others were built of soil quarried from an encircling ditch (Four Crosses). Stone cairns (e.g. Carneddau, Trelystan) were either built of freshly quarried stone or of stone which appears to have been cleared from the surface of neighbouring fields. Larger quarried stones were used for burial cists (e.g. Ystrad-hynod, near Llanidloes, and Carneddau) and for revetting the burial mound (Trelystan). Tree trunks or large timbers were used for coffins, and wooden posts or stakes were used for internal fencing or revetting (e.g. Caebetin, near Kerry, Trelystan, Four Crosses). The only discernible pattern is that over the course of the early Bronze Age, between 2500-1400 BC, a tradition of interring individual inhumation or cremation burials below a mound, and occasionally accompanied by a smaller pottery vessel such as a beaker or food vessel, was superseded by one in which multiple successive cremation burials, possibly representing single family groups, were buried within or beside a single larger monument and occasionally contained within a larger pottery vessel such as a collared urn or food vessel urn.

It is uncertain whether the whole of society would have been buried in this manner, or whether these methods were reserved for certain social groups. Both infant and adult burials are represented, however, even though some special status may have been accorded to the burials of adult males.

At face value, the number and distribution of burial mounds in the county presume the existence of at least three or four hundred family groups or small communities occupying tracts of land extending from valley bottom to upland plateaux. Settlement evidence in both the uplands and lowlands is very sparse however, and it must be assumed either that people led a nomadic or semi-nomadic existence or that settlements were of a kind which have not yet been clearly identified. Upland settlement might be represented by scattered and often isolated circular huts, but few if any of these have been investigated. A characteristic settlement form in the lowland and upland edge during the subsequent Iron Age are banked and ditched farmsteads. Several hundred of these are known, and it is likely that some began life in the Bronze Age. Direct evidence of cereal production and other forms of arable agriculture in the county is slight, and there are suggestions that a number of both upland (e.g. Carneddau) and lowland (e.g. Four Crosses) funerary monuments were constructed on former pastureland, which may stress a dependence on pastoralism. Cattle, pig, sheep and horse are likely to have been reared, but the relative importance of each of these species to the economy cannot be established on the evidence currently available. The only direct evidence of field boundaries for controlling grazing or protecting crops, are lines of stakes found dating to about 2000 BC, beneath two upland barrows at Trelystan.

Excavations at the Breiddin have produced the first certain evidence of defended settlements within the county. Between 1000-800 BC the hilltop was fortified by a timber-revetted rampart; this was probably over 1 kilometre in length and enclosing an area of 28 hectares subsequently occupied by the Iron Age hillfort. Environmental evidence shows a rapid deforestation of the hilltop at this time, probably arising from the construction of the defences. Despite slender evidence of internal timber buildings, it is clear that the settlement was intensively occupied if only for a relatively short period, having produced significant quantities of later Bronze Age pottery and other evidence of domestic activity. Bronze-casting crucibles, a mould fragment and metalworking hearths indicate that the settlement was also an industrial centre. Bronzework from the site includes a socketed axe, sword fragments, a torn fragment, a socketed knife, a spearhead fragment, a socketed hammer, as well as a number of dress pins with expanded heads. Other defended settlements of this period in the region probably include Ffridd Faldwyn (Montgomery), Old Oswestry (Shropshire) and Llwyn Bryn-dinas (Llangedwyn).

Other items of metalwork have been mostly found by chance and are widely distributed throughout the county. The style and metallic composition of the artefacts changed through time, in parallel with developments throughout Western Europe, which allows individual finds to be dated. A wide variety of tools, weapons and ornaments was in circulation during the Bronze Age of which both the range and the numbers that have been found show a substantial increase towards the middle and late Bronze Age. Examples of early Bronze Age metalwork include a number of simple flat axes (e.g. Carno), riveted bronze daggers (e.g. Darowen, Four Crosses) and a bronze awl (e.g. Ystrad-hynod). Middle Bronze Age finds include various types of socketed spearhead and palstave axes (including hoards of these axes from near Cemais and Llanfyllin), as well as a number of dirks or rapiers (e.g. Churchstoke, Llanwddyn). Late Bronze Age types comprise a wider variety of forms, as we have seen from the Breiddin. As in the earlier Bronze Age, many of the later Bronze Age finds have been found singly and by chance, as for example a socketed knife from Llandinam, but two hoards — one containing two woodworking gouges and one containing nine ornamental torcs — were found near Pen-y-bont-fawr, and a hoard of three socketed axes was found near Welshpool. A much larger hoard deposited near

Crowther's Coppice hillfort (Welshpool), the so-called Guilsfield hoard, contained about 120 objects, including axes, gouges, spearheads, ferrules, sword fragments and a sword chape, as well as casting waste and cakes of smelted copper. Evidence of bronze casting in the early Bronze Age is scarce, but is indicated by a stone mould for casting daggers and possibly axes from New Mills (Manafon). The Guilsfield hoard and the finds from the Breiddin indicate metalworking in the later Bronze Age. Although it is likely that sources of copper in the north and west of the county would have been exploited for the production of copper and bronze artefacts, there is as yet little positive evidence for this; analysis of the later Bronze Age material from the Breiddin, for example, suggests the reworking of imported scrap metal.

Reasonably discrete distributions of certain late Bronze Age axe types in north-west Wales, north-east Wales and the Welsh Marches suggest that by the period about 900-800 BC we may already be witnessing the emergence of tribal territories corresponding with those that are historically attested in the succeeding Iron Age — tribes, probably already Celtic-speaking, and possibly with political centres based upon larger defended settlements of the kind evident at the Breiddin. The emergence of fortified settlements, and the broadening range of weapon types in the later Bronze Age may be seen as partly a response to economic recession and social conflict brought about by deteriorating climatic conditions and the abandonment of the more marginal tracts of upland during the middle and later Bronze Age.

W. J. BRITNELL

Bronze Age cairn with surrounding ring-ditch at Trelystan on Long Mountain, photographed during the course of excavation in 1979. The burial monument, built before about 2000 BC, was built over part of a late Neolithic timber house, dating to the period between 2900-2500 BC. Photo: CPAT

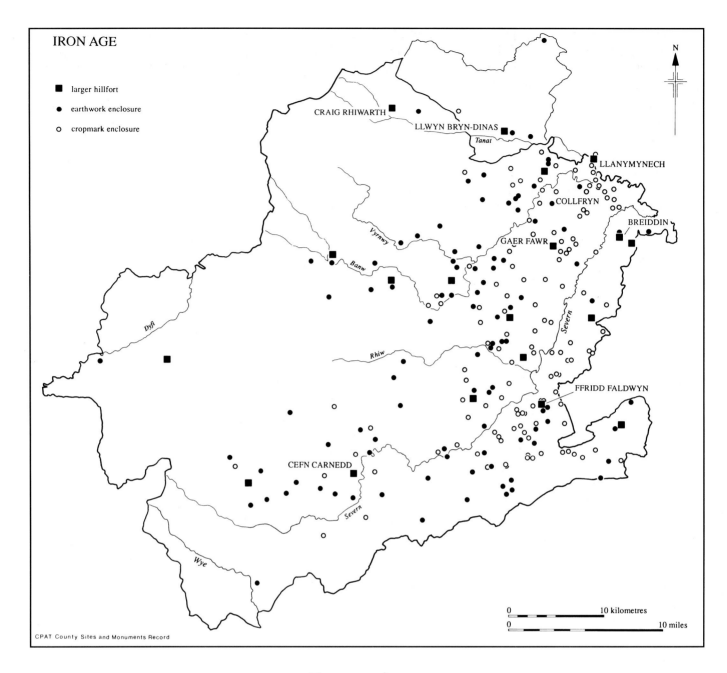

larger hillfort

earthwork enclosure

cropmark enclosure

CRAIG RHIWARTH

LLWYN BRYN-DINAS

Tanat

LLANYMYNECH

COLLFRYN

BREIDDIN

Vyrnwy

Banw

GAER FAWR

Dyfi

Severn

Rhiw

FFRIDD FALDWYN

CEFN CARNEDD

Severn

Wye

N

| 0 | | 10 kilometres |
| 0 | | 10 miles |

CPAT County Sites and Monuments Record

Iron Age

Ironworking technology was first introduced into Britain in about 700 BC, but as in the case of the introduction of bronze, probably several centuries elapse before the impact of this new technology can be clearly detected. The period lasts until the advent of Roman military and civil administration, which began to impose itself on mid-Wales from about AD 70.

By the conquest period the region was occupied by the tribe of the Ordovices, whose territory seems to have extended over the greater part of central and north-west Wales. The first element of the name is British, and derives from Welsh gordd (hammer), the tribal name therefore perhaps having the meaning 'the hammer-fighters', with reference either to a weapon or to an emblem. Rather than representing a single political entity it may have been constituted of a federation of smaller tribal groupings which, as we have seen, possibly emerged during the later Bronze Age. There is uncertainty about the boundary between the Ordovices and the Cornovii, the tribe that occupied the west Midlands region, and it is possible that eastern parts of the county would have fallen within their territory.

This period sees a massive expansion in the number of known settlements. These include a small number of large defended hillforts and a wide range and greater number of small and medium-sized hillforts and other more or less well-defended banked and ditched enclosures. A human population possibly numbering only hundreds in the earlier prehistoric period may well have grown to thousands in the later Neolithic and Bronze Age, and then possibly to tens of thousands in the Iron Age, a density comparable with those attained in the medieval period.

Over 250 defended or semi-defended enclosures of varying size are known within the county, the majority of which probably belong or originated during this period. It is clear that at least some of the larger and smaller sites were occupied simultaneously. This suggests a hierarchy of settlement types which provides an expression of the social and economic structure of society. In broad terms, some of the larger settlements, varying in size from about six to fifty-six hectares, appear to represent tribal centres housing many inhabitants, though not necessarily throughout the year, whilst the smallest settlements, often less than one hectare in extent, denote farmsteads belonging to smaller, extended family groups. A wide range of sites fall between these two extremes, however, which emphasises that in reality the picture would have been much more dynamic and complex than this simplistic model presupposes.

Few if any sites would have been continuously occupied throughout the Iron Age. It is likely that some began life in the later Bronze Age, whilst others continued in occupation into the Roman period. The Breiddin hillfort (Crugion/Criggion), for example, had been first occupied in the later Bronze Age at a date of about 1000 BC, but may have been abandoned before the Iron Age. The defences were only reconstructed in about 400 BC, and it is likely that it then declined as a major centre well before the Roman conquest. The smaller enclosure at Collfryn (Llansantffraid Deuddwr) was first constructed in about 400 BC and may have remained in continuous occupation until about AD 350, a period of three hundred years after the Roman conquest. Despite an underlying pattern of social stability, the abandonment of some settlements and the establishment of new ones will no doubt reflect the fluctuating fortunes of family and tribal groups, as well as occasional tribal hostilities.

Pre-eminent amongst the larger settlements, are the hillforts such as Craig Rhiwarth (Llangynog), Llanymynech, Gaer Fawr (Guilsfield), the Breiddin, Beacon Ring (Long Mountain), Ffridd Faldwyn (Montgomery) and Cefn Carnedd (Llandinam) which must have formed major centres of power and authority. The defensive banks and ditches of many of these hillforts — often set out along the contours of a hill and originally strengthened by timber gates and palisades and stone revetments — are still clearly visible as earthworks. These larger sites are roughly spaced at distances of about 10 kilometres and are normally sited on land above 200 metres above sea level.

Small and medium-sized enclosures and hillforts are more numerous, and in parts of the county approach a density of one site every one square kilometre. They are more often sited on valley sides and bottoms, and normally lie below 200 metres. Their defensive banks and ditches have frequently become levelled by centuries of ploughing and are now often only to be seen as crop-marks from the air. Their defences are again likely to have been strengthened by timber gates and palisades. Some sites, like several of the hillforts, have a number of concentric lines of defence, with outer enclosures or compounds, surrounding central habitation areas, which appear to have been used for protecting stock. Considerable manpower was expended in the construction of all but the most modest of such sites, and in certain cases an element of conspicuous display is evident in their design.

Sites of all categories are largely confined to either the lowlands or the upland margins, a distribution which not only suggests that the population density would have been greater in the eastern valleys of the county, but also that is was based upon an agricultural system that successfully combined arable agriculture on the richer lowland soils with animal husbandry on higher ground. The pattern of exploitation in the uplands to the west is less clear, but there are a number of isolated stone huts which may represent the smaller settlements of shepherds or cattle ranchers. Isolated houses built of timber would be difficult to identify whether in the uplands or lowlands and it is therefore uncertain what proportion of the contemporary population may have lived outside the more substantial enclosure and hillfort settlements at this period, and to what extent the apparently more sparsely occupied upland areas towards the western side of the county were extensively exploited. Despite a lack of settlement evidence, it is significant that pollen records show a resurgence of deforestation in some areas of the western uplands at this period, leading to the creation of new grassland. However, the uplands continued to be less hospitable than they had been in the earlier Bronze Age and competition for good farmland to support the growing population is likely to have continued to be intense.

Evidence from a hill-slope enclosure at Collfryn (Llansantffraid Deuddwr) in the valley of the Vyrnwy indicates that cattle, sheep and pigs were reared, but the relative importance of these species is uncertain. The hunting of wild animals and game seems to have contributed relatively little to the economy. Plant remains recovered from Collfryn and the Breiddin hillfort show that crops of wheat and barley were grown. Fields were probably attached to most settlements; the ancient field-system adjacent to the Breiddin hillfort, is one of the few instances where this has been positively identified. Most of the buildings found within settlements in the region at this period appear to have been of timber, although at some hillforts such as Craig Rhiwarth, buildings had stone footings. Two basic types of timber building are known from excavation, which are known as 'roundhouses' and 'four-posters'. The roundhouses (e.g. the Breiddin

and Collfryn), were between 5-10 metres in diameter. They normally had a single door, occasionally a central hearth, and would originally have been surmounted by a conical thatched roof. The buildings seem variously to have been used as houses and workshops. Four-posters, formed of stout upright posts set in a rectangle about two to four metres across, are thought to represent raised storage buildings, possibly for grain. These have been identified at a number of sites (e.g. Ffridd Faldwyn, the Breiddin, Collfryn). A proportionately greater number of these storage buildings is present at the Breiddin than at Collfryn, which suggests that a particular function of some of the hillforts may have been for the storage and redistribution of surplus grain, possibly levied from the surrounding countryside. Continuing demands for large quantities of timber for the construction of buildings, as well as for the defences and for fuel, would have placed increasing pressures upon the natural environment and is probably a further explanation of the extensive inroads that were evidently made into the surviving natural forests at this time.

As in the case of the later part of the preceding Bronze Age, there is no evidence of burials or burial monuments at this time, or direct evidence of ceremonial sites, religious customs or beliefs. Historical sources, however, acquaint us with the Druids, a priestly class which had emerged and

The circular drainage ditch of an Iron Age roundhouse at Collfryn, Llansantffraid Deuddwr, with postholes of door-posts in foreground, photographed during the course of excavation in 1982. Several large roundhouses of this kind were found inside the multiple-ditched hill-slope at Collfryn.

Photo: CPAT

evidently exerted some influence on native societies at the time of the Roman conquest. Small quantities of finer and occasionally decorated pottery were imported from the Herefordshire region during the middle and later Iron Age but pottery seems to have been otherwise generally little used in the region at this period. A very much coarser ceramic is known from a number of sites which, analysis has shown, probably originated in the Cheshire Plain. It appears that these vessels held cakes of salt produced at inland production sites such as Nantwich and Middlewich, which are known to have been centres of the salt trade in the medieval period. Other items of trade included plain and decorated glass beads and shale bangles. Coinage was not in use by any of the tribes in Wales and it is probable that most goods were traded by means of barter and exchange.

Both iron and copper metalworking were carried out, at a number of different types of site in the region during the Iron Age. Ironworking is likely to have been based on the exploitation of localised sources of ore, perhaps including bog ore, or on imported material or scrap. Ironwork found at the Breiddin includes a dagger, iron brooches and a pair of blacksmith's tongs. Linch-pins for securing chariot wheels found at the Breiddin and Collfryn provide the first evidence of wheeled transport in the county, although it is likely that horse-drawn vehicles were in use from the later Bronze Age onwards. As in the Bronze Age, local sources of copper ore are likely to have been mined and smelted, and the presence of small furnaces, deposits of slag, and bronze-casting crucibles at a number of excavated hillforts, smaller enclosures and undefended sites (e.g. the Breiddin, Llanymynech, Collfryn, Four Crosses, Llwyn Bryn-dinas), is evidence of a flourishing bronze-casting industry probably producing such items as clothes fasteners, jewellery and horse-gear.

Organic materials such as wood, basketry and leather must have been used extensively throughout the prehistoric period, but evidence of this is only rarely found in circumstances where the materials have been preserved by waterlogging. Wooden bowls of several kinds were found during excavations of a pond within the Breiddin hillfort; other wooden finds include a large mallet head, a pestle, fragments of mortised timber, and willow hoops for securing bundles of kindling or thatching materials. A small wooden sword, probably a child's toy, sheds light on other aspects of everyday Celtic life which can only rarely be glimpsed. Stone spindle-whorls and clay loomweights from the Breiddin provide evidence of weaving, a craft industry that was probably introduced during the Bronze Age. Simple saddle-shaped quern-stones for grinding corn are known from a number of sites.

In all likelihood, the advancing Roman military forces in about the 70s AD encountered a mature and densely settled landscape, partitioned into scattered farmsteads, owned by Celtic farmers who bore allegiance to clans which in turn were united into one or more larger tribal groupings. The underlying social and economic structures which developed during this period may well have survived the impact of Roman military authority following the conquest, once the higher echelons of native political power had been eventually subjugated. Traditions of land-use, ownership and inheritance, which had evolved by this time, may have become sufficiently stable to persist, largely unaltered, into the early post-Roman period.

W. J. Britnell

Pen-y-Castell on the hills north of Llanfair Caereinion, photographed from the air in 1979. The concentric banks and ditches are typical of the numerous smaller Iron Age hillforts and enclosures in Montgomeryshire.

Photo: CPAT

29

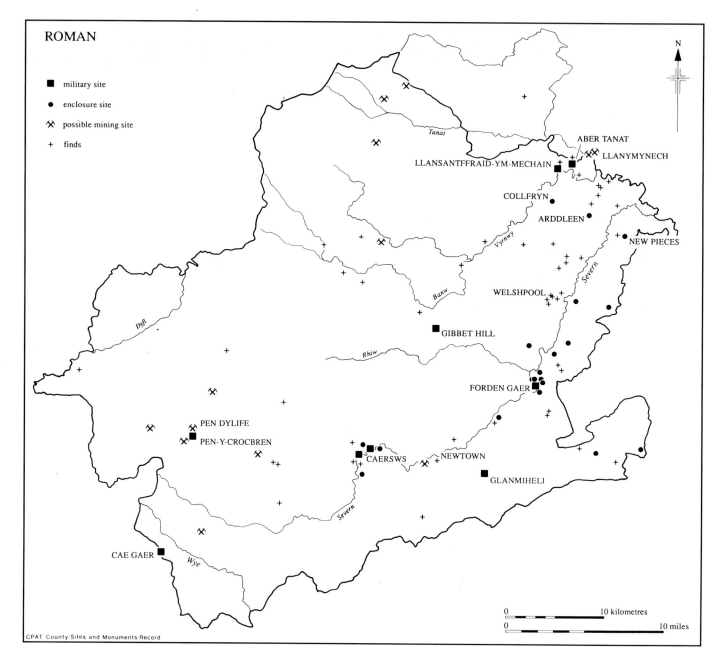

Map legend:

ROMAN

■ military site

● enclosure site

✕ possible mining site

+ finds

Place names on map: ABER TANAT, LLANYMYNECH, LLANSANTFFRAID-YM-MECHAIN, COLLFRYN, ARDDLEEN, NEW PIECES, WELSHPOOL, GIBBET HILL, FORDEN GAER, PEN DYLIFE, PEN-Y-CROCBREN, CAERSWS, NEWTOWN, GLANMIHELI, CAE GAER

Rivers: Tanat, Vyrnwy, Banw, Dyfi, Rhiw, Severn, Wye

0   10 kilometres
0   10 miles

Roman Period

Despite the resistance of certain native British tribes, much of the south and east of Britain was rapidly conquered following the landing of the Roman forces under the command of the emperor Claudius in AD 43. Within four years the invading armies had established a heavily policed frontier to the new and valuable province of Britannia along the line of the Fosse Way and the Ermine Street — stretching from Exeter in the south-west to the Humber in the north. It appears that imperial policy only anticipated conquest of this lowland area. Although valuable mineral wealth lay in the regions beyond, the newly conquered territory encompassed most of the more valuable farmland in the island. Continued aggression by the predominantly pastoral tribes beyond this early frontier appears to have demanded a revision of this policy, and the decision was made to try to subjugate the entire island. Conquest of the west and north of Britain proved to be a more costly and arduous task, and it was not until 40 years after the invasion that the native tribes occupying Wales were finally subdued, following the occupation of Anglesey in about AD 84.

Early resistance to the Roman army appears to have been orchestrated by Caratacus, a native prince who had fled into Wales from the south-east. The Roman army probably first campaigned in what is now Montgomeryshire in pursuit of Caratacus under the governorship of Ostorius Scapula in about AD 51. Tacitus, the Roman historian, tells us of a final battle held in Ordovician territory at a point where Caratacus had mustered a native army on a steeply-sloping hill approached across a treacherous river. The precise location of this battle is unknown, although various sites in the upper Severn valley between Caersws and Llanymynech have been suggested. Caratacus escaped capture on this occasion, however, and although the native forces were eventually overcome by an army of up to 20,000 men, drawn from several Roman legions and various auxiliary units, the army failed to retain control of the territory. Further campaigns were undertaken during the fifties and sixties, until Ordovician territory was finally subdued by about the year AD 78, during the governorship of Julius Agricola.

Physical evidence of the historical account of the conquest and subsequent policing of the Ordovices in the county is represented by large auxiliary forts on the banks of the Severn at Forden and at Caersws. Two forts are known at Caersws, an earlier one at Llwyn-y-brain, to the east of the village, and a later one within the village itself. The forts at Caersws and Forden probably housed cavalry units, and initially lay in advance of a legionary fortress near Wroxeter, before the legionary base policing mid and north Wales was moved to Chester in the eighties. Forden Gaer and Caersws are probably to be equated with the names Levobrinta and Mediomanum which appear in the Ravenna Cosmography, a seventh-century manuscript based on earlier sources. Stamped tiles found at Caersws suggest that at one stage the fort was garrisoned by a unit raised in the Roman province of Iberia.

Major lines of communication were established linking the forts at Forden and Caersws with the fortress and subsequent major town at Wroxeter, forming part of a network of roads ultimately leading by way of Watling Street to Londinium, the chief town of the new province.

Smaller fortlets which assisted in policing the district by the Roman military are known at Pen y Crocbren (Dylife), near the headwaters of the Severn, Gibbet Hill (Penarth, Llanfair Caereinion), Glanmiheli (Kerry), and at Cae Gaer (Llangurig) near the headwaters of the Wye. Recent research has also brought to light a military supply depot at Llansantffraid-ym-Mechain, near the confluence of the Cain and Vyrnwy, and temporary forts representing a campaign base at Aber Tanat (Carreghofa), near the confluence of the Vyrnwy and Tanat.

Following the subjugation of centres of tribal authority, the native population in the county will have been dispersed into small rural communities with few if any major centres. Small civilian settlements known as vici sprang up next to the garrisons at Forden and Caersws, but these are likely to have housed merchants and tradesmen drawn from other parts of the empire, forming small enclaves of citizens leading a more Romanized way of life.

Excavations within the civilian settlement attached to the fort at Caersws have brought to light stone and timber buildings, including a bathhouse, belonging to a flourishing industrial and commercial centre, supplying goods and services to the garrison. Bake-houses and a tavern or gaming-house were set up; smithies were built for forging iron weapons; workshops produced bronze jewellery; pottery kilns were established for the production of floor tiles and pottery, probably for supply to the military. A wide range of merchandise was imported from throughout the Roman empire — fine tableware, glass jugs and drinking vessels, bronze cooking utensils, circular rotary querns for grinding corn, wine, cooking oil and pigments. Keys and padlocks have also been found; such was the accumulation of wealth that doors evidently needed to be locked and bolted to prevent theft.

Excavations at Caersws suggest that this was only a short-lived boom, entirely dependent upon the patronage of the military. There appears to be a rapid decline of activity in the civilian settlement by about AD 120, after little more than a single generation. Troop movements to secure the northern frontier of the province appear to have led to a drastic reduction in the size of the garrison and hence to the decline of a commercial centre sustained by only a vulnerable economic infrastructure. The forts at Forden Gaer and Caersws appear to have been maintained until perhaps the third or fourth century, but possibly on little more than a caretaker basis.

Wales, like the northern part of the province, but unlike southern Britain, appears to have remained a military zone, policed and administered by the army throughout much of the Roman period. This, combined with the existence of a relatively scattered native population, appears to have severely lessened the social and economic consequences of Roman imperialism in this western fringe of the empire. Roman military or civilian administration and taxation will have replaced the pre-conquest tribal organisation and fealties, but the basic farming economy is likely to have remained little changed. As in the Iron Age, the main focus of rural settlement is likely to have been centred on scattered farmsteads. Excavations at a small number of ditched enclosures, as at Collfryn (Llansantffraid Deuddwr), Arddleen, and New Pieces Camp on the Breiddin Hills, have shown that at least a proportion of the native sites first established in the Iron Age continued in occupation after the conquest. Some ditched enclosures of a more rectilinear form, of which there are concentrations in the vicinity of the Roman forts at Forden Gaer and Caersws, suggest that new farmsteads were also established. Other, possibly unenclosed settlements are known near Llandrinio and Newtown. There is insufficient evidence to gauge the distribution and density of settlement within the county at this time, but the pattern of small enclosures shown on the Iron Age map is the best guide we have at the moment, on the assumption that a proportion of these sites will either have been established or continued in occupation into the Roman period.

Evidence of renewed forest clearance in the period up to AD 250 in upland areas towards the west of the county seem likely to have resulted from increasing demands for timber production, as well as for the production of grassland for the herding of animals to support an ever expanding population. Much of the native woodland had disappeared, and by AD 300 it is likely that most of the richer agricultural land in the valleys was already partitioned into fields and much of the uplands had become open heathland similar to the present day, with only isolated stands of birch, hazel, oak and alder.

Some consumer products made their way to native sites, but the general lifestyle of most of the native population is likely to have undergone little material change. An exceptional find from the Smithfield at Welshpool, however, hints at the survival or re-emergence of a more wealthy and influential elite group within contemporary civilian society. The find, probably dating to the second century, includes an assortment of luxury goods which would seem beyond the purse of a simple native farmer — bronze, glass and pottery vessels, an iron fire-dog and a pair of lamp standards.

Evidence of industrial activity is sparse, although there have been suggestions of Roman copper mining at Llanymynech Hill and near Newtown, and of lead mining at Pen Dylife (Staylittle). Possible Roman smelting sites have been suggested near Trefeglwys and Llanfyllin.

Gold coin in mint condition, found during archaeological excavations at Caersws Roman fort in 1966. The coin, known as an aureus, was minted in Rome in AD 75. It shows the head of the Emperor Vespasian, and helps to date early history of the fort.
Photo: Charles Daniels

A small number of isolated Roman coins have been found, and there are about five coin-hoards from the county, including one of second-century date from Trefeglwys and one of early fourth-century date from Guilsfield. Bartering and exchange are likely to have been retained for most day-to-day transactions by the native population, to judge from the scarcity of coinage on some native sites.

Human burials of Roman date are known from the vicinity of Caersws, suggesting that cemeteries were established near forts and their associated civilian settlements. Apart from Roman burials in the limestone caves at Llanymynech and a possible temple site near Forden, little else is known of the burial or religious practices of the native population in the county during Roman times. It is probable that Celtic deities continued to be worshipped, although a Venus figurine from Caersws and a pebble crudely engraved with a figure of Mars or Mercury from Newtown indicate that Roman gods were also observed within some elements of society. Christianity is likely to have become one of the new eastern religions introduced during the later Roman period, but as yet no evidence of this has been found within the county at this period.

W. J. Britnell

Roman tile kiln in the northern annexe of the Roman fort at Caersws, viewed during the course of the excavation in 1990. The tiles produced by the kiln were probably used for buildings inside the fort and in the bath-house south of the fort.

Photo: CPAT

33

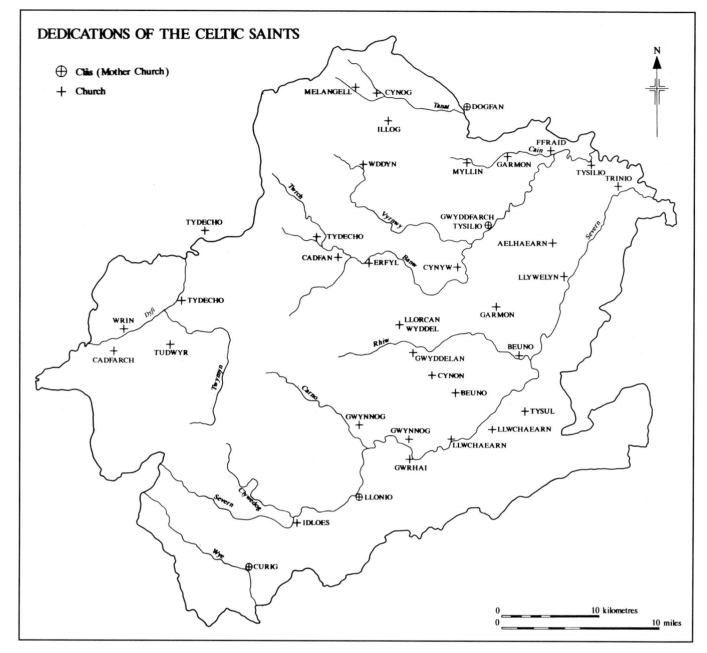

DEDICATIONS OF THE CELTIC SAINTS

⊕ Clas (Mother Church)
+ Church

The Celtic Saints

During the period that followed the collapse of Roman rule in Britain, when western Europe was over-run by the barbarians, Christianity was already well established in western Britain. The later Christian tradition could be a survivor from Roman times or re-introduced to the area by missionaries from Gaul. The late fifth century and the sixth century introduced considerable Christian activity in western Britain whilst the eastern parts of England were falling into the hands of the pagan Saxons and Angles. Holy missionaries who wandered from place to place upheld and spread the Christian faith,

maintaining links with men of similar connections in Brittany, Cornwall, Ireland and Strathclyde.

Many of these holy men were born of the princely classes, and whilst some of them were convinced of the merits of hermitage, others established holy communities in which they gathered around themselves groups of pupils. They all lived a hard life shorn of all luxuries, according to the principles of monasticism. The name given to this sort of community was a clas. A typical clas would have consisted of a wooden church, dwelling huts and

34

workshops; the entire community would have been encircled by a wooden palisade. These settlements served as missionary centres for the surrounding daughter churches that looked to the clas as the mother church. These daughter churches were generally named after the missionaries by whom they were founded. Such was the organisation of the primitive church, long before the establishment of the parish system.

From the various 'Lives of the Saints', that were written some time after the deaths of their subjects, it is possible to gain some idea of the lives of these early missionaries. In Powys there were notable figures who gathered around themselves many pupils. One of the best known was Tysilio, son of Brochwel Ysgithrog, prince of Powys. It was he who established the clas at Meifod near the court of his father at Mathrafal, near also to the cell of his tutor, the hermit Gwyddfach. Meifod grew to be an exceptionally important centre with its influence spreading over a wide area in northern Powys; to this day its importance is reflected in the large circular churchyard, once the site of the clás and its subsidiary buildings.

Another important missionary was Beuno, who counted the brothers Llwchaearn and Aelhaearn together with Cynyw amongst his pupils. Many other missionaries were linked with Cadfan, who came to Powys from Brittany via Cornwall. He is said to have landed in the estuary of the Dyfi before proceeding inland to the heart of Powys. Amongst his pupils he numbered Tydecho, Trinio, Erfyl and Llonio. The last of these established a clas in the upper Severn valley at Llandinam which remained active into the thirteenth century, serving as the mother church for many churches in Arwystli.

In the north of the county, in the Tanat valley, the brothers Dogfan and Cynog both established churches, with Dogfan's church in Llanrhaeadr-ym-Mochnant becoming an influential clas in the area. On the opposite side of the county at Llangurig was yet another clas that influenced the establishment of numerous churches in Maelienydd in northern Radnor. Also associated with Powys was Garmon, but there is some confusion as to whether he is the same person as St Germanus of Auxerre.

The Celtic church held women in equal esteem to men and, of the female missionaries in Powys, none is more famous than Melangell who established her cell at Pennant Melangell. The tale of her protecting the hare from the hunter's hounds is well known throughout Wales.

It is possible that many of the present day churches in the area once bore dedications to the better known missionaries but their names disappeared during Norman times when the newcomers deliberately abolished some of the ancient dedications, replacing them with main stream Catholic dedications to Mary or Peter.

E. R. Morris

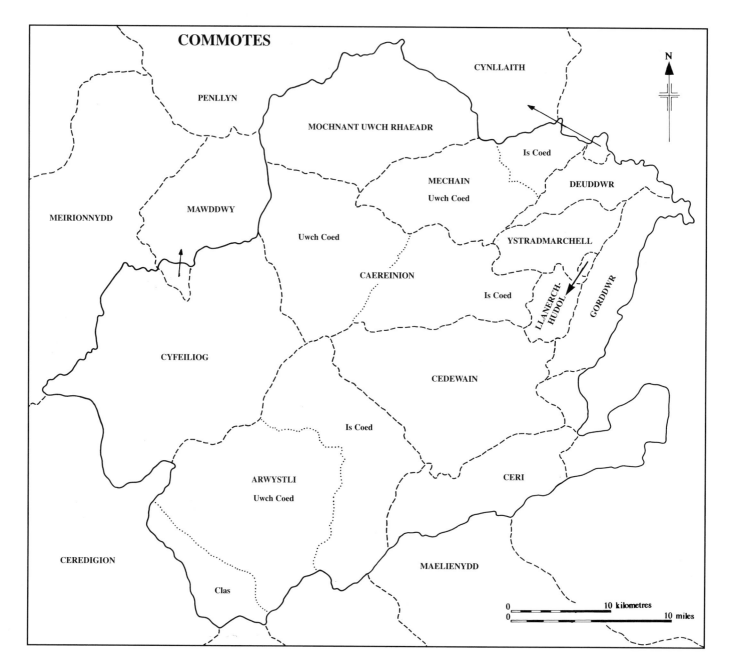

COMMOTES

The map shows the following commotes:

PENLLYN

CYNLLAITH

MOCHNANT UWCH RHAEADR

Is Coed

MECHAIN
Uwch Coed

DEUDDWR

MEIRIONNYDD

MAWDDWY

YSTRADMARCHELL

Uwch Coed

LLANERCH-HUDOL

GORDDWR

CAEREINION

Is Coed

CYFEILIOG

CEDEWAIN

Is Coed

ARWYSTLI
Uwch Coed

CERI

CEREDIGION

MAELIENYDD

Clas

10 kilometres

10 miles

Commotes

Wales was formerly divided into "gwledydd" (lands) - such as Gwynedd, Powys or Morgannwg - each with its own king. In each of these gwledydd there were sub-divisions, the larger ones being "cantrefi" and the smaller ones being "cymydau" (commotes). These territories were administered via the llys (court) by officers such as the "rhaglaw"(Lord's deputy), the "maer" (steward) and the "rhingyll" (sergeant). The "maerdref" constituted the demesne of the king or prince.

The major court of Powys is generally thought to have been Mathrafal, to which the headquarters of the kingdom moved after the court was evicted from Pengwern, whose exact location remains the subject of debate. Powys, then extending from the vicinity of Chester in the north to the river Wye in the south, came under the control of Gwynedd in the ninth century.

Following the death of Madog ap Maredudd, prince of Powys, in 1160, Powys was divided along the River Rhaeadr, with Powys Fadog to the north and Powys Wenwynwyn to the south. This somewhat artificial division persisted when Montgomeryshire and Denbighshire were formed in the Act of Union of 1536, with Mochnant uwch Rhaeadr belonging to the former, and Mochnant is Rhaeadr to the latter.

The commote of Mechain to the south of Mochnant uwch Rhaeadr had its centre at Llys Fechain near Llanfechain. Its chief church was that of Meifod, long associated with the princes of Powys. It was its situation along the banks of the Severn and the Vyrnwy that gave the commote of Deuddwr (two waters) its name. Guilsfield was the headquarters of the commote of Ystrad Marchell, though the famous Cistercian abbey of that name was actually in the neighbouring tiny commote of Llanerchydol.

Gorddwr (flood water), so named because it was the area in which the Severn flooded frequently, comprised the area around Bausley and Criggion, some parts of which are now in Shropshire. It is thought likely that prior to the creation of the lordship of Montgomery that this commote, later known in its anglicized form of Gorther, might have extended as far as Churchstoke.

It is not known who Cadaw was, but he gave his name to the hundred of Cedewain, whose borders were largely determined by the rivers Severn and Rhiw. In the 13th Century, during the territorial dispute between Llywelyn ap Gruffudd, prince of Wales and Gruffydd ap Gwenwynwyn, lord of Powys, thirteen townships between the Rhiw and the Helygi (Luggy) in the vicinity of Berriew, were taken from Llanerchydol and added to Cedewain.

Arwystli too takes its name from an individual and this major commote was subdivided into three parts. The headquarters of Arwystli is-Coed was at Penprys near Caersws, whilst Arwystli-uwch-Coed had its centre at Talgarth near Trefeglwys. The third division was Clas in the vicinity of Llangurig. Arwystli was once considered to be part of Gwynedd. Cyfeiliog, yet again adapted from a personal name, also had its disputed lands, with Llywelyn ap Gruffudd claiming the lands between the Dyfi and the Dulais, roughly equalling the parish of Llanwrin. Further up the valley of the Dyfi, the commote of Mawddwy was lost to Merioneth as a result of the Acts of Union, though the detached township of Caereinion Fechan remained in Montgomeryshire.

Having lost Mawddwy, however, Montgomeryshire gained the commote of Ceri (Kerry) in 1536, this area having traditionally been part of the lordship of Rhwng Gwy a Hafren, not Powys Wenwynwyn.

E. R. MORRIS

The Pedigree of the Rulers of Powys c365 - 1450

This shows the descent of the feudal barons from the ancient kings and princes of Powys. It should be said, however, that men on this line of descent were not always the de facto rulers.

Gwrtheyrn (Vortigern) b. c.365

Cateyrn ap Gwrtheyrn b. c.400 d. c.455

Cadell Ddyrnllug b. c.430

Cyngen Glodrydd b. c.460

Brochwel Yscithrog b. c.490

Cynan Garwyn b. c.520

Selyf Sarffgadau b. c.550 d. c.616

Mael Myngan b. c.580

Beli ab Eiludd ap Cynan Garwyn

Gwylog

Elise [of Eliseg's pillar] b. c.680

Brochwel b. c.705

Cadell b. 720 d. 808

OR

Cynan Garwyn b. c.520

Eiludd

Beli

Cyngen died in Rome 855

Nest = Merfyn Frych, prince of Gwyneed d. 844

Rhodri Mawr = Angharad ferch Meurig of Ceredigion d. 878

Gwriad d. 877

Anarawd d. 916

Cadell

Idwal Foel d. 942

Hywel Dda = Elen of Dyfed d. 950

ancestor of Llywelyn the Great

Owain d. 988

Maredudd d. 999

Llywelyn ap Seisyllt d. 1023 = Angharad b. c. 980 = Cynfyn ap Gwestan

Bleddyn d. 1075

Maredudd d. 1132

Gruffudd

Cadwgan

Iorwerth

Madog = Susanna (dau of Gruffudd ap Cynan of Gwynedd)

Gwenllian (ancestor of Henry VII)

Gruffudd Maelor I = Angharad, daughter d. 1191 of Owain Gwynedd

Owain Cyfeiliog = Gwenllian dau of d. 1197 Owain Gwynedd

Gwenwynwyn = Margaret dau Robt Corbett d. 1216

Gruffudd d. 1286/7 = Hawys le Strange

Owain Arwystli (de la Pole) d. 1293

Gruffudd d. 1309

Hawys = John de Cherleton d. 1353

John de C II d. 1360 = Maude dau of Roger Mortimer

John de C III 1334- 74 = Joane dau of Earl of Stafford

John de C IV 1362-1400

Edward de C = d. 1422

Madog d. 1236

Gruffudd Maelor II, Lord of Dinas Bran d. 1269

Gruffudd Fychan I, Baron Gwyn, d. 1289

Madog Crupl d. 1304

Gruffudd o'r Rhuddallt (Gruffudd Llwyd)

Gruffudd Fychan II

Owain Glyndwr

Joan = Sir John Grey 1399-1423

Joice = John Tiptoft 1402-46

There is a good deal of variation in the earlier genealogies but, in general, Peter Bartram's 'Welsh Classical Dictionary' has been followed

Welsh Princes to Norman Barons

Following the withdrawal of Roman forces there is a dearth of records which has led to the period being known as the Dark Ages. Most information was carried down by oral tradition for several generations and the documents now extant have been copied several times. Some of the genealogies were constructed much later by bards more to massage the egos of their patrons, by imputing illustrious ancestors, than as a strict historical record. There is thus a good deal of conjecture on many aspects. Vortigern (Gwrtheyrn in Welsh) became the ruler of all or most of what is now England and Wales and is believed to be the ancestor of the Princes of the historical Powys which should not be confused with the present unit of local government. He ruled in the early fifth century. He was assailed by Picts and Scots and is held to blame for bringing in Angles, Saxons and Jutes from what is now Germany to assist him. They settled and began to take over expanding during the second half of the fifth century. Around 500 AD they were heavily defeated at a place, not now identifiable, called Mount Badon.

However, the successes around 500 resulted in relative stability for the first half of the sixth century but the Anglo-Saxon expansion started again about 550 and the Prince of Powys was forced from his base at Uriconium to Pengwern, traditionally said to be on the site of old St Chad's church in Shrewsbury, in 584. At this time the Celts of Wales, Cumbria and Strathclyde were joined and often under one ruler but after the battle of Chester in 604 when they were defeated and the monks of the abbey of Bangor Iscoed were slaughtered by Aethelfrith of Northumbria, these kingdoms gradually lost contact despite successes by Cadwallon in the 630s. Cadwallon, in alliance with Penda of Mercia, killed Edwin of Northumbria and devastated the land in 633.

The history of Wales before the conquest by Edward I was dominated by internal strife which perhaps did even more to cause the loss of independence than the depredations of the English and Anglo-Normans. Powys was particularly vulnerable to this being sandwiched between the English and the powerful Princes of Gwynedd who claimed the overlordship of Wales. Powys thus shifted allegiance from one side to another according to their judgement as to which side was the likely winner at the time.

In the eighth century Mercia grew stronger and pushed westwards, King Offa taking Shrewsbury, probably in 765 from Gwylog and forcing the Princes of Powys into what is now Montgomeryshire. Eliseg, son of Gwylog and to whom there is a pillar near Llangollen, was the Prince who is said to have established his court at Mathrafal. Towards the end of the eighth century Offa built his dyke to mark the boundary between Mercia and Powys. Offa then ceased his attacks but they were resumed during the early part of the ninth century by his successors, until Mercia was too concerned with defending itself against the growing power of Wessex.

During the ninth century Powys came into the hands of Rhodri Mawr through his mother Nest and Rhodri, through marriage, got control of much of South Wales as well. He, and one of his sons, were killed fighting Wessex in 878. Another son, Anarawd became King of Gwynedd and Powys but acknowledging the overlordship of Wessex. Most of Wales including Powys became united again under Rhodri's grandson Hywel, but Hywel paid tribute to England thus accepting overlordship. On his death the kingdom was again divided but united temporarily at the end of the tenth century by his grandson Maredudd. From 1057 to 1063 Gruffudd ap Llewelyn ruled all Wales.

A further menace to the whole of Britain in the ninth and tenth centuries were the incursions and, later, settlement of the pagan Scandinavians. Powys, though distant from the coast, was not immune from them, but in combination with the English won a significant victory over them at Buttington in 894.

Further reverses for Powys came at the hands of Earl Harold who killed Gruffudd in 1063 before he himself was defeated and killed at Hastings by William of Normandy. Harold put a local chief, Rhiwallon, half brother to Gruffudd, on the throne of Powys as his vassal. He was killed in battle in 1070. After the Norman conquest, William established Roger de Montgomery as a marcher lord on the eastern fringes of the area thus introducing the name by which the county is now known in English. The Welsh name for the county, Trefaldwyn, also comes from a Norman baron, Baldwin de Boulers.

Marcher lords gained control of much of Wales during the reign of William I but these territorial losses were largely reversed during the reign of his successor William II.

At the beginning of the twelfth century there was a very confused period with various sons of Maredudd ap Bleddyn conspiring with or against Henry I and between themselves. In 1108 Madoc slew his brother Iorwerth at Caereinion, according to the Brut, and Henry I gave Powys to Cadwgan which illustrates the extent to which the English king already had control over the area. There was further warfare within the family a few years later. In 1118 Maredudd and the sons of Cadwgan, his brother, fought against Henry but made peace with him and paid tribute.

In 1148, Madog ap Maredudd gave Cyfeiliog to his nephew Owain ap Gruffudd which began the process of the division of Powys into Upper and Lower Powys known as Powys Wenwynwyn, after Owain's son, and Powys Fadog. The boundaries of Powys Wenwynwyn approximate to the boundaries of the County of Montgomeryshire set up following the Acts of Union.

Gwenwynwyn was imprisoned by King John in 1207 but restored two years later. He later made a pact with Llywelyn I but in 1216 renounced it, making another with King John and Llywelyn drove him out.

He died the following year. His son Gruffudd submitted again to Llywelyn following the sacking of Castell Coch (Powis Castle) in 1233.

However, the death of Llywelyn I in 1240 led to Gruffudd once more being a vassal of the English king. Llywelyn was succeeded by his son Dafydd, whose mother was Joan, daughter of King John and in 1244 Gruffudd submitted to him. In 1257 Llywelyn II drove Gruffudd out but he was later restored. In 1274, Llywelyn again defeated Gruffudd and forced him to submit but two years later he was restored by the English although Llywelyn still held Dolforwyn Castle which, however, fell to the English in 1277 for lack of water. In 1282 Gruffudd appears to have been with Roger Mortimer when Llywelyn was waylaid and killed at Cilmeri.

In 1293, his son and successor Owain attended Edward I's parliament in Shrewsbury and yielded his land as Prince receiving it back as a feudal baron.

Owain died shortly after during the same year and his infant son, Gruffudd, died in 1309 before attaining his majority. His sister Hawys, just 18, became heiress and the King gave her in marriage later that year to John de Cherleton. For several generations marriages in the family were to Anglo-Norman aristocrats and the Welsh blood was diluted progressively.

Powys Wenwynwyn thus became a Norman baronry until the formation of Montgomeryshire following the Acts of Union.

D. W. L. ROWLANDS

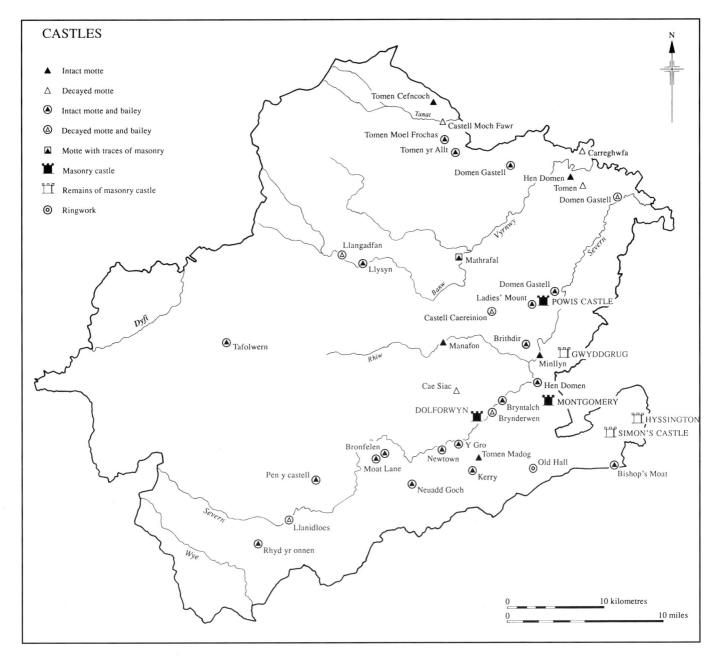

The Castles of Montgomeryshire

Roger de Montgomery became Earl of Shrewsbury in 1071 and built a castle near Montgomery. This, the first of our castles, was at Hen Domen. Like his main castle at Shrewsbury it was a motte and bailey, the most common early Norman castle type, consisting of a large flat-topped mound raised from the spoil of its surrounding ditch, and alongside it an enclosure defended by a bank and ditch. Strong timber palisades ran around the flat top of the mound or motte and along the crest of the bank around the enclosure or bailey. A timber hall or tower on the motte accommodated the lord or his castellan, and

other timber buildings for the garrison and its animals occupied the bailey. Earth and timber castles of this type were quick and cheap to build and several are illustrated on the Bayeux Tapestry. Excavations at Hen Domen have revealed massive fragments of the timber bridge from the bailey to the top of the motte, while buildings indicated by slots and post-holes in the bailey included a small apsidal church.

There are 41 castles in the county and most lie to the east. Along the Severn valley and the narrow border

41

strip to its south are 22 castles. From Hen Domen Earl Roger and his sons advanced up the Severn, and Domesday Book records that he held Arwystli, where the motte and bailey at Moat Lane is probably his castle. That part of Cedewain south of the Severn must also have fallen, and Gro Tump and Cefn Bryntalch seem worthy of the Earl.

The remaining nineteen castles are more scattered and were mainly Welsh imitations, many lacking the strength and strategic siting of the Severn Valley sites. In some cases records show them to be Welsh. Domen Gastell, Welshpool is probably the castle built there by Cadwgan ap Bleddyn in 1111, and seized from Gwenwynwyn by Hubert, Archbishop of Canterbury and Justiciar, in 1196. Faint vestiges suggesting a motte in the churchyard at Castle Caereinion may mark the castle built by Madoc ap Maredudd lost to Owain Gwynedd in 1156, though with English help he soon regained it. Another recorded Welsh motte is Owain Cyfeiliog's Tafolwern, also taken by the Prince of Gwynedd in 1162. Records also show that motte and bailey castles in Montgomeryshire survived much later than their counterparts in England. Mathrafal was destroyed in 1212, while the men of Gwynedd attacked Tafolwern in 1244 and Tomen yr Allt in 1257. Even after the new stone castle of Montgomery was built in the 1220s Hen Domen continued as an outpost until at least about 1300.

Stone castles, which sprang up widely during the 13th century, are not well represented in our county. There were only six and it seems that the native princes of Powys Wenwynwyn rarely commanded the necessary wealth and skills required. Our six stone castles support this view. All were within six miles of Montgomery, the English focal point; four were English castles, one was built by Llywelyn ap Gruffudd of Gwynedd, and only one was the only work of a local prince. They either replaced a motte and bailey on a newly chosen site or were raised on the old sites with stone in place of timber.

The four English masonry castles were Montgomery, Hyssington, and Simon's Castle within Montgomery Lordship, and Gwyddgrug in the Gorddwr Welshry of the Corbet lordship of Caus. Montgomery Castle which replaced Hen Domen, was under construction from 1223 to 1227, along with Henry III's adjacent new borough. Though the borough was sacked by Llywelyn Fawr in 1231, and by Llywelyn ap Gruffudd in 1257, the castle, on its rocky platform, held out on both occasions. Simon's Castle and Hyssington were both built on earlier motte and bailey castles but nothing is known of their history. One of them may have been the Castle of 'Snet' mentioned in 1231 and 1233. Vague traces of a rectangular tower are visible on Hyssington motte, but dense vegetation hides any similar traces which might survive within the crumbled vestiges of a crude ring-wall around the top of Simon's Castle. The Corbet castle of Gwyddgrug is also built over a motte which utilised the impressive boss of natural rock at Nantcriba, Forden. Here a small rectangular or polygonal castle with projecting half-round towers was built, traces of which are visible in dense vegetation. Gwyddgrug was first recorded in 1260 and in 1263 it was seized and destroyed by Gruffudd ap Gwenwynwyn.

The masonry castle of Dolforwyn was begun on a new site by Llywelyn ap Gruffudd of Gwynedd in defiance of Edward I in 1273. A simple rectangular walled enclosure incorporating a square keep and a round tower, it never attained the status Llywelyn hoped for it as the bastion of an intended Welsh borough in opposition to Montgomery, and a permanent safeguard against the pro-English leanings of Powys Wenwynwyn. In 1277 it fell to the English, and was granted to Roger Mortimer who gave Cedewain a new borough at Newtown rather than beside Dolforwyn.

Little survives of the only stone castle of the local Prince. This was on the site of Powis Castle, probably replacing Ladies' Mount or Domen Gastell. This first Powis Castle consisted of a simple rectangular walled enclosure with a rectangular tower and square eastern gate house. Vestiges of this early work are discernible in the cellars and at lower levels of the more substantial surviving castle, which was greatly augmented by John de Cherleton (1300-53), and much altered and restored in modern times.

It remains only to mention the sole medieval ringwork in the county at Rhysnant, Llandrinio. Ringworks were small but strongly ditched and embanked circular enclosures, sometimes built instead of mottes. Resembling a ringwork, Old Hall camp, Kerry is clearly unfinished, and is the probable site of a proposed stone castle begun by Henry III and Hubert de Burgh during their ill-fated Ceri campaign of 1228. In face of strong Welsh opposition the uncompleted castle was demolished and abandoned to the marauding natives, who named it 'Hubert's Folly'.

With the Edwardian conquest, while more strongly Welsh areas to the north and west saw the building of massive new fortresses like Caernarfon and Harlech, the castles in our area lost significance. Here no new castle was needed in a region which had, since the early 12th century, generally preferred co-operation with England, only joining the Welsh cause when the Princes of Gwynedd were strong enough to command allegiance. Only Powis Castle and Montgomery Castle continued in use beyond the Middle Ages, the latter until its demolition in 1649, the former to our own time, though much modified in the 16th Century and later.

(Note: A secondary feature of the map is to indicate the present condition of each castle as an aid to teachers or others who might arrange field trips. Mutilated or vestigial sites may prove incomprehensible to those unfamiliar with better preserved examples.)

C. J. SPURGEON

Montgomery Castle. Exterior view of Inner Ward from the north.

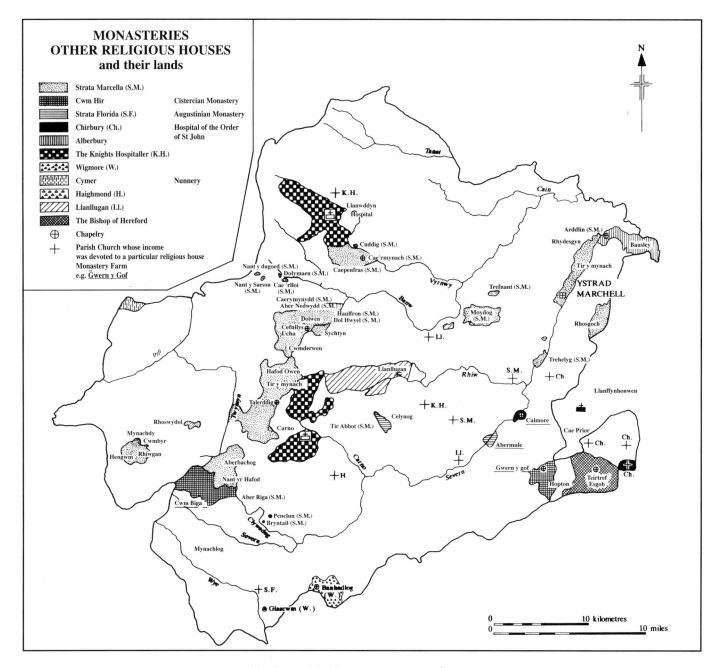

MONASTERIES OTHER RELIGIOUS HOUSES and their lands

- Strata Marcella (S.M.)
- Cwm Hir — Cistercian Monastery
- Strata Florida (S.F.) — Augustinian Monastery
- Chirbury (Ch.) — Hospital of the Order of St John
- Alberbury
- The Knights Hospitaller (K.H.)
- Wigmore (W.)
- Cymer — Nunnery
- Haighmond (H.)
- Llanllugan (Ll.)
- The Bishop of Hereford
- ⊕ Chapelry
- ✝ Parish Church whose income was devoted to a particular religious house
- Monastery Farm e.g. Gwern y Gof

The Monasteries

One of the outstanding features of the medieval Catholic Church was the existence of the monastic order. Throughout Western Europe groups of men organised themselves under the hard discipline of life in a monastery the better to serve religion. These monastic communities, introduced for the first time into Wales by the Normans, differed fundamentally from the preaching saints of the early Celtic Church in that their members dwelt in the seclusion of the monastery, following the religious life in accordance with the rule of the Order to which they belonged. The debt European civilisation, of which Wales was

an integral part, owes to the monasteries is great, for their influence and activities were widespread and varied: religion, learning, art, farming, medicine and charity.

Two great Orders were the Benedictines and the Cistercians both of whom had many houses in Wales. In Powys Wenwynwyn (the medieval equivalent of our county) there was no Benedictine monastery but the Cistercians who had built their first house at Whitland in 1140 established here the abbey called Strata Marcella, near Welshpool, in 1170. In turn,

44

Valle Crucis in Powys Fadog was founded as an offshoot of Strata Marcella in 1174.

Strata Marcella was founded by monks of Whitland invited to Powys by the poet prince Owain Cyfeiliog who died in the monastery in 1197. He gave them a site near the Severn in the district of Argungrog made famous in the 'Dream of Rhonabwy', one of the tales of the Maginobion.

Owain Cyfeiliog's son Gwenwynwyn was a great patron of the monks and by numerous charters granted them extensive lands in the upland regions of his kingdom. These lands shown on the map were valued by the Cistercians who were great sheep farmers. In some of these remote hill regions the Abbey set up small chapels - at Dolwen, Talerddig and Cae'rmynach. Ystrad Marchell had a chequered history and suffered several crises after the eclipse of Welsh independence in 1282. Eventually the Welsh monks were turned out and the Abbey placed under the control of Buildwas Abbey in Shropshire. Its end came when Henry VIII dissolved all the monasteries in 1536. Its extensive lands and sheep walks were sold and eventually many of them passed into the ownership of the local gentry.

Apart from the two small houses of the Knights Hospitallers and the Llanllugan nunnery, Ystrad Marchell was the only house situated in Powys Wenwynwyn. But much land and wealth was owned in this Welsh Kingdom by houses situated outside its border. The map shows the distribution of lands owned by the Welsh Cistercian houses of Cymer (Meirionnydd), Cwm Hir (Maelienydd), Ystrad Fflur (Ceredigion), as well as those of the Augustinian houses of Chirbury, Haughmond and Wigmore and the Reformed Benedictines of Alberbury, all in Salop.

Monasteries frequently obtained possession of the tithes and other revenues of a parish and then became responsible for the spiritual welfare of the inhabitants. Such parish churches are shown on the map and the monasteries to which they were appropriated are named.

The Knights Hospitallers of the Order of S John of Jerusalem had their headquarters (as far as north Wales and the borders are concerned) at Halston near Whittington. The two ysbytai in Powys Wenwynwyn at Llanwddyn and at Carno were both subject to Halston. A few remains can be seen of the Ysbyty at Llanwddyn on the hill Mynydd St Ioan and recently what are believed to be the foundations of their house at Carno were revealed by excavation. Wales had three nunneries and one of these was Llanllugan whose history is rather obscure. It had lands and several churches were appropriated to it. At the dissolution the last prioress was Rose Lewis. Place names reminiscent of the monasteries abound - Tirymynach (Guilsfield and Llanbrynmair), Cae'rmynach (Llwydiarth), Monksfield (Long Mountain), Abbey Well (Guilsfield), Court (Abermule), Tir Abbot and Wtra Abbot (Carno). There are, however, few tangible remains of these religious houses - nothing can be traced of the chapels at Gwern-y-gof, Talerddig and Cae'rmynach nor of the nunnery at Llanllugan. The site of Strata Marcella - on a field by the Severn - has only a pile of broken stonework. At Llanidloes Church can be seen the magnificent arcade and roof of Cwm Hir. The wooden chimney piece of Gwernfyda (Llanllugan) may have come from the dissolved nunnery nearby.

E. R. MORRIS

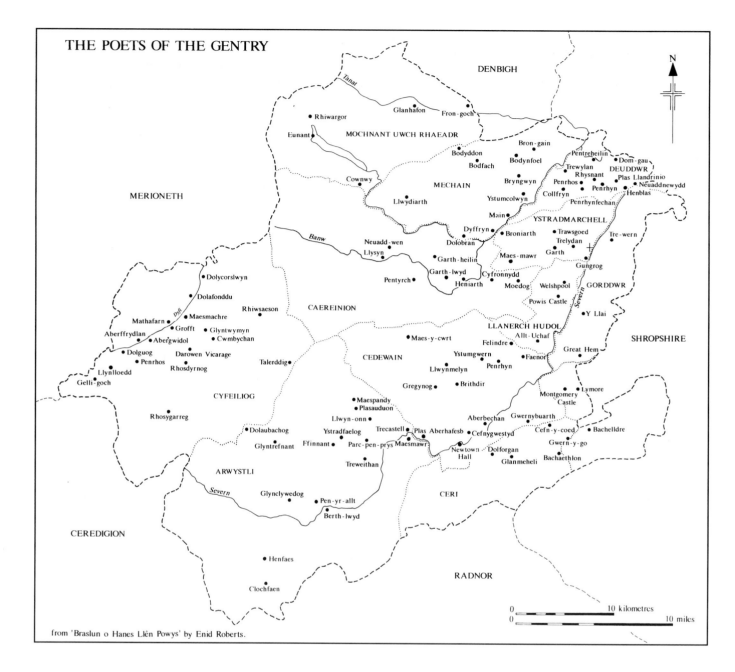

The Welsh Poets of Montgomeryshire

Following the death of Llywelyn ap Gruffudd in 1282 the Welsh princes vanished and with them vanished their traditional support for many aspects of Welsh culture, particularly the patronage of poets who had eulogized them over many centuries. After 1282 it was the gentry of Wales who were to emerge as the chief supporters of the bardic tradition through the patronage of the poets. The days of the court poets were gone and each poet now had to cultivate the support of a number of patrons among the gentry, travelling from house to house singing their praises. This process developed gradually during the later middle ages, but the increased wealth evident in many parts of Wales following the Acts of Union led to a notable flowering of poetic patronage in the sixteenth century that continued in some cases until the mid seventeenth century.

In Montgomeryshire, the gentry families who continued to patronize the poets were chiefly those families who claimed descent from Madog ap Maredudd, and also those descendants of Gruffudd ap Beli, lord of Guilsfield, Broniarth and Deuddwr around 1300. Some of the gentry themselves were competent poets; in their midst were Gruffudd Llwyd ap Dafydd ap Einion Llyglin of Llangadfan, Dafydd Llwyd ap Llywelyn ap Gruffudd of Mathafarn, Ieuan ap Bedo Gwyn of Llyssun, Dafydd ap Dafydd Llwyd of Dolobran and Lewis Owen of Betws Cedewain.

The longest tradition of singing the praises of gentry families in the county was that of the family of Mathafarn in the Dyfi valley; poetry was composed to this family from the fourteenth to the seventeenth centuries. The families of Gregynog, Llwydiarth, Newtown Hall and Rhiwsaeson were eulogized from the fifteenth century to the seventeenth. Throughout the sixteenth and seventeenth centuries, poetry was composed in praise of the families of the following houses; Vaynor, Plasauduon, Dolcorslwyn, Trewythan, Penrhos, Penrhyn Fechan, Brongain, Bodynfoel, Berthlwyd, Gungrog, Aberbechan, Llynlloedd, Ystymcolwyn and Ystradfaelog. Most of the poets who visited these houses were not natives of Montgomeryshire, and some of the greatest Welsh poets of this age, such as Guto'r Glyn, Lewis Glyn Cothi, Tudur Aled, William Llŷn and Tudur Penllyn were made welcome by the gentry of the area. The county itself did produce some notable poets however, such as Owain Gwynedd (fl. 1564-1601) who visited some thirty gentry homes, and Siôn Cain in the seventeenth century who visited some forty homes in the county.

All the poetry composed by these poets was in strict Welsh metre, normally in the form of the Cywydd. Praise is the general theme of this poetry, either direct praise to a living patron, or fine memorial verses to a patron recently deceased. Sometimes poetry was written to request a gift of some kind from a wealthy patron; on other occasions the art of the poet might be employed in an attempt to bring about a reconciliation between feuding branches of a great family. The virtues of the gentry eulogized in these poems are a fascinating mirror of the values of a bygone age, when there was virtually no provision for the welfare of the poor, and charity was naturally expected from those most fortunate in their material circumstances.

The most noted of fifteenth century prophetic poets was a native of Montgomeryshire, Dafydd Llwyd of Mathafarn. There was a widespread belief at the time that some great Welsh leader, similar to Arthur, would rise one day to save the nation - the Mab Darogan - the prophetic son. In the mid fifteenth century, there appeared to be a number of potential candidates for the title, regardless of whether they were of the party of Lancaster or York in the Wars of the Roses; the paramount factor was that a Welshman should wear the crown. All these hopes and prophesies were ultimately invested in the figure of Henry Tudor, a descendant of the family of Penmynydd in Anglesey, despite his very tenuous claim to the crown.

Another important aspect of the work of the poets of the gentry was to record and recite the often lengthy genealogies of their patrons. It was their genealogies more than anything else that made them what they were, proving their rights to an exalted social position, riches and land. Lewys Dwnn in particular was, as Welsh Herald at arms, responsible for the recording of genealogies of the Welsh gentry families.

Amongst the most famous of the poets of the gentry, the following eulogized Montgomeryshire families.

Guto'r Glyn: Vaynor, Llwyn Onn, Newtown Hall and the Abbot of Strata Marcella .
Lewis Glyn Cothi: Broniarth (Guilsfield), Rhiwsaeson, Mathafarn, Penrhos (Penegoes), Montgomery Castle, Glyntrefnant, Bacheldre and Newtown Hall.
Tudur Aled: Broniarth (Guilsfield), and the Abbot of Strata Marcella.
William Llŷn: Trawscoed and Maesmawr (Guilsfield), Nantysgolion (Llanbrynmair) and Dolobran.
Tudur Penllyn: Trawscoed and Maesmawr (Guilsfield), Llwydiarth, Leighton Hall.

ENID P. ROBERTS

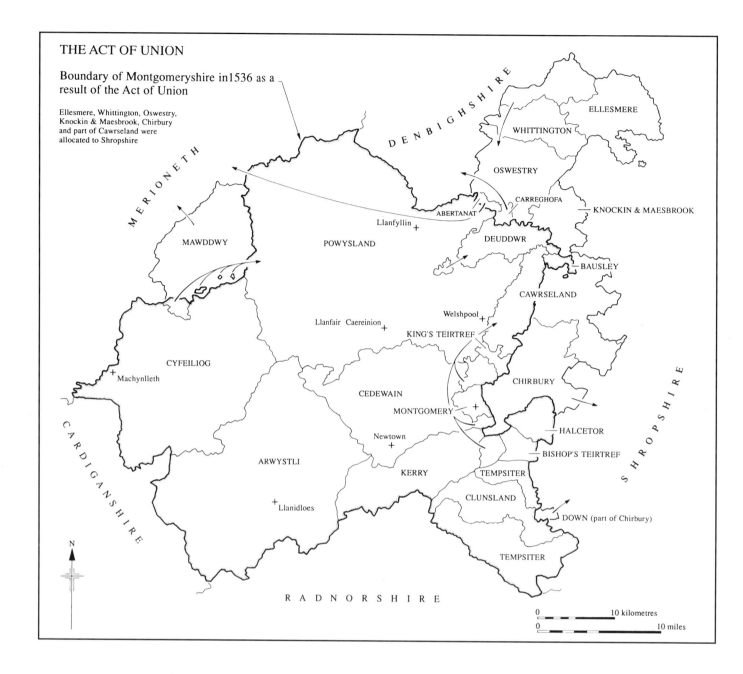

THE ACT OF UNION

Boundary of Montgomeryshire in 1536 as a result of the Act of Union

Ellesmere, Whittington, Oswestry, Knockin & Maesbrook, Chirbury and part of Cawrseland were allocated to Shropshire

DENBIGHSHIRE

MERIONETH

ELLESMERE

WHITTINGTON

OSWESTRY

CARREGHOFA

ABERTANAT

KNOCKIN & MAESBROOK

Llanfyllin

MAWDDWY

POWYSLAND

DEUDDWR

BAUSLEY

CAWRSELAND

Welshpool

Llanfair Caereinion

KING'S TEIRTREF

CYFEILIOG

Machynlleth

CHIRBURY

SHROPSHIRE

CEDEWAIN

MONTGOMERY

Newtown

HALCETOR

BISHOP'S TEIRTREF

ARWYSTLI

KERRY

TEMPSITER

CLUNSLAND

Llanidloes

DOWN (part of Chirbury)

CARDIGANSHIRE

TEMPSITER

N

RADNORSHIRE

0 ____ 10 kilometres
0 ____ 10 miles

The Creation of the County of Montgomery

By Act of Parliament (27 Henry 8 c.26) entitled 'An Act for Laws and Justice to be Ministered in Wales in Like Form as it is in this Realm', the county of Montgomery was created. Section 7 of the Act recites that '. . . the Lordships, Townships, Parishes, Commotes and Cantreds of Montgomery, Kedewen, Kerry, Cawrsland, Arustely, Keviliock, Doythur, Poweland, Clunesland, Balesely, Tempcester and Alcester, in the said country of Wales, and every of them, ... shall stand be for ever, from the Feast of All Saints, [1 November 1536] guildable, and shall be reputed, accepted, named and taken as Parts and

Members of the said County or Shire of Montgomery'.

The Act specified that Montgomery was to be the county town and that county courts were to be held alternately at Montgomery and Machynlleth. The county courts were held monthly and presided over by the sheriff.

Prior to the passing of the above Act, the Crown had acquired various marcher lordships and indeed clause 3 of the Act recites '. . . many of the said

Lordships Marchers be now in the Hands and Possession of our Sovereing Lord the king and the smallest Number of them in the Possession of other Lords'. At the time of the Act the Crown had possession of the lordships of Montgomery, Halcetor, King's Teirtref, Kerry, Hopton and Cedewain which had descended to the Crown from the Mortimer family by marriage (Anne Mortimer being the grandmother of King Edward IV) and Arwystli and Cyfeiliog which had been obtained by purchase in about 1531 from the Dudley family.

The map indicates the extent of the county of Montgomery as constituted by this Act. It differs from the extent which was finally established in that the hundred of Clun was later removed from the county of Montgomery and allotted to the county of Salop instead.

The Act also specified that the lordship of Chirbury was to be allocated to the county of Salop, thereby defining fairly closely the Eastern boundary of the new county of Montgomery, but what constituted Causland may be open to some doubt. Also, the Act did not mention the lordships of Hopton and Bishop's Teirtref although it may be implied from their disposition that they were intended at the outset to be a part of the new county of Montgomery.

It is therefore not surprising, in view of some anomalies and areas of doubt, that in the following year, Parliament had to pass 'An Act giving the King's Highness Authority to Allot the Townships of Wales at any time within three years next ensuing'. It is evident that three years was insufficient time to complete the work of allocating the townships as provided for in the Act of 1536, and so by a further Act of Parliament passed in 1539 a further three years was allowed for the task to be completed.

As far as the county of Montgomery was concerned it would appear that during the six year period 1536-1542, there were no obvious adjustments made to its boundaries. The time may have been spent determining and adjusting the boundaries of the new hundreds within the county.

The Montgomeryshire Court of Great Sessions was established in 1542 by 'An Act for Certain Ordinances in the King's Dominion and Principality of Wales'. Section 87 of that Act did provide for the transfer of the township of Abertanat, a detached portion of the county of Merioneth to the county of Salop.

The hundred of Clun was transferred to the county of Salop on 25 March 1546 by virtue of the Arundel Jointure Act of 1546 (37 Henry VIII c.24). This was a private Act and the transfer of Clun to Shropshire is the last clause of the Act suggesting it was an afterthought. Thereafter, the extent of the county remained fixed until 1 April 1974 when it ceased to exist and, subject to some boundary changes, formed part of the new county of Powys.

M. L. CHAPMAN

BOROUGHS, MARKETS AND FAIRS

■ Boroughs

O Other Markets and Fairs

N

■ LLANFYLLIN

LLANDRINIO O

LLANFAIR CAEREINION O

WELSHPOOL ■

O TREFNANT

■ MACHYNLLETH

MONTGOMERY ■

CAERSWS ■

■ NEWTOWN

O KERRY

■ LLANIDLOES

0   10 kilometres

0   10 miles

Establishment of Boroughs, Markets and Fairs

Historic Montgomeryshire had seven ancient chartered borough towns (Caersws, Llanfyllin, Llanidloes, Machynlleth, Montgomery, Newtown and Welshpool), although the charters for Caersws and Machynlleth are lost. Indeed, it is as recently as October 1988 that the long lost charter confirming the borough status of Llanidloes came to light, after having been pawned in the city of Gloucester during the Commonwealth period. The Commonwealth period was a time when a great many municipal and estate muniments were lost.

The map shows the locations of places which were given borough status, markets and fairs. A large majority of the more important grants were enrolled in the Charter and Patent Rolls, which are now kept at the Public Record Office, London. Supplementary details concerning various grants are also contained in law suits, especially during the late sixteenth and early seventeenth centuries when disputes arose over the rights and customs of various lordships.

The establishment of new fairs, markets and

boroughs by charter had ceased prior to the Act of Union in 1536 although there were subsequent charters to confirm and widen the rights and privileges already granted.

The granting of rights and liberties by the lords of the various lordships was motivated, not out of munificence, but out of economic expediency. The lord could receive a substantial sum for making a grant, depending on the type of grant made. For example, Richard Plantagenet, Duke of York, the lord of Cedewain lordship, received 600 marks (£400) for a charter dated 31 August 1447, by which he acquitted the inhabitants of Cedewain from various fines, amercements and a rent known in Welsh as 'cylch gŵyl'. The reason for this grant was probably motivated by a need to raise money to help finance his campaigns in the Wars of the Roses.

The rights and liberties which could be granted were extremely diverse of which the granting of borough status was the most important. Each borough charter granted rights and liberties modelled on those for the city of Hereford and included the caveat that they were not to be damaging to existing adjacent markets and fairs.

Available details of grants of borough status are given at Appendix A. Details of the charters of Caersws and Machynlleth have not been found, but there is a body of supportive and suggestive evidence which confirms they were chartered borough towns.

In the case of Machynlleth, the most persuasive evidence is that it held a borough court. A dispute was heard before the mayor of Machynlleth in the borough court, in 1621, when Rees ap Howell brought a suit against Rhudderch ap Thomas and Elizabeth his wife for a debt of £3. The recital in the record of this dispute, which went to appeal at the Court of Great Sessions, states that 'there had been a borough court at Machynlleth with the memory of man not knowing the contrary'. This is further supported by evidence given in a dispute concerning the tolls of the town which was heard in the Court of Exchequer, London, in 1603, at which Owen John ap Owen Goch, aged 80 years, stated that 'for all the time of his Remembrance the said Town of Machynlleth was a Town Corporated with maior and burgesses and the maior thereof has been usually elected yearly by the voice of the burgesses greater number thereof that were dwelling within the said town'. This was further corroborated by other witnesses. Machynlleth was also listed in the records of the Court of Great Sessions as a borough town and was bound to make a return into that court and to provide jurors to serve on the Jury for the boroughs and liberties.

Similarly the documentation for Caersws is sparse and reliance has to the placed on the records of George Owen of Henllys, co. Pembroke, who recorded in about 1600 that the 'auncient charter of Caersowse was made by John Lorde Tiptoft, Lord Powis'. That Caersws had a charter is supported by information contained in a dispute heard in the Court of Exchequer, London, which was commenced in 1615, over the appointment of the Recorder for the town, indicating that it too had a borough court. An order issued out of the Court on Friday 17 November 1625 states:

'Whereas Sir Roger Owen, kt. [lord of the manor of Arwystli in which Caersws occurs] hath exhibited an english bill into this Courte against Thomas Morrys and William Morrys his sonne touchinge the nomynatinge of a Recorder within the Towne of Caersouze in the Countie of Mountgomery unto which bill the saide Thomas Morrys this terme appeared and hath made affadavit that he cannot make direct aunswere to the saide bill without the sight of a Charter which remayneth in the Countie of Mountgomery.....'

Caersws appears to have lapsed as a corporation during the time of the reign of King Charles I, for it no longer made any returns into the Montgomeryshire Court of Great Sessions. It consequently lost all its rights and privileges.

Newtown also suffered the same fate after the Restoration and it was recorded in a new atlas by Richard Blome published in 1673 that Newtown was a town 'which formerly had a Corporation, but lately taken awaye'.

Caersws and Newtown never recovered their former status.

All the borough towns were given rights to hold markets (weekly events) and fairs (yearly events). There are two further grants by charter for holding of markets, vis.: Trefnant and Llandrinio.

The right to hold markets and fairs at Trefnant was granted by the Crown to Gruffudd ap Gwenwynwyn on 26 April 1278; the grant being made for the markets and fairs to be held there instead of at Welshpool which were thought to be damaging to the King's markets and fairs at Montgomery. However, on the advice of Roger Mortimer and others, it was understood that the markets and fairs at Welshpool had not been damaging to those held at Montgomery and so the King, by his charter dated 11 June 1282, removed the markets and fairs from Trefnant and regranted them to Welshpool.

The market and fairs at Llandrinio were granted by Gruffudd ap Gwenwynwyn and this grant was subject to an inquiry by the Crown under a process known as *Ad Quod Damnum* to determine if they were damaging to the King or anyone else. The Commission to inquire into the matter was issued to Roger Mortimer and others who returned that they were not damaging to existing and adjacent markets and fairs.

A market was also held at Llanfair Caereinion on Saturdays, to the great consternation of the bailiffs, burgesses and aldermen of the borough of Welshpool who believed that it would be damaging to their market. On 13 January 1719, they passed a resolution to take means to suppress this unlawful market. Nevertheless, the market continued until recently, despite the efforts of the corporation of Welshpool to get rid of it.

Only one charter has been found which confines itself to doing no more than granting a fair. This was a grant from the King to Thomas Bek, Bishop of St. Davids, dated 20 May 1290, for him to hold a fair, at Kerry, on the Vigil and Feast of St. Michael the Archangel and the three days following (28 September - 2 October).

Other one day fairs were held within the county for which documentary evidence has not been found, if any did exist at all.

Montgomery Town Hall, built 1748, the lower floor was originally an open arcaded market area. It still accommodates a weekly market.

The most striking feature concerning the borough towns is the relatively uniform distance between those in the Severn Valley, which is about 7.5 miles as the crow flies, except in the case of Caersws for which the distance between it and Llanidloes was about 6.5 miles and Newtown about 4.5 miles. The medieval lawyer, Bracton, recorded that a market or fair could not damage an adjacent market or fair provided that it was at a distance of six and two thirds miles away. The logic to such an odd distance is that it was assumed a man could walk twenty miles in one day of which one third of this distance would be taken up in walking to the market or fair, a third walking about the market or fair and the final third walking home. The close proximity of Caersws to Llanidloes and Newtown meant it could not sustain competition from those two places and consequently decayed. Caersws also suffered the major disadvantage of not possessing a parish church; the nearest being Llanwnnog.

Why Llandrinio never developed as a market town is not clear. It was reasonably remote from the borough towns of Welshpool and Oswestry (about 7.5 miles away) and also Llanfyllin (9.3 miles away). It may be that its site, on low lying ground subject to frequent flooding from the River Severn militated against it.

M. L. CHAPMAN

Appendix A
DETAILS OF BOROUGH CHARTERS

Borough	Name of grantor	Date of Original grant
Caersws	John Tiptoft, Lord of Powis	Not known
Llanfyllin	Llewelyn ap Gruffudd ap Gwenwynwyn, Lord of Mechain Uwchcoed and Mochnant Uwchcoed	Undated but must have been granted between Dec. 1293 and June 1295
Llanidloes	John de Charlton with the consent of his wife, Hawys	3 October 1344
Machynlleth	Not known	Not known
Montgomery	King Henry III	13 February 1227
Newtown	Richard Plantagenet, Duke of York (possible earlier grant by the Mortimers)	Between 1425 and 1460 18 July 1334
Welshpool	Gruffudd ap Gwenwynwyn, Lord of Cyfeiliog	Undated but must have been granted between 1241 and 1245

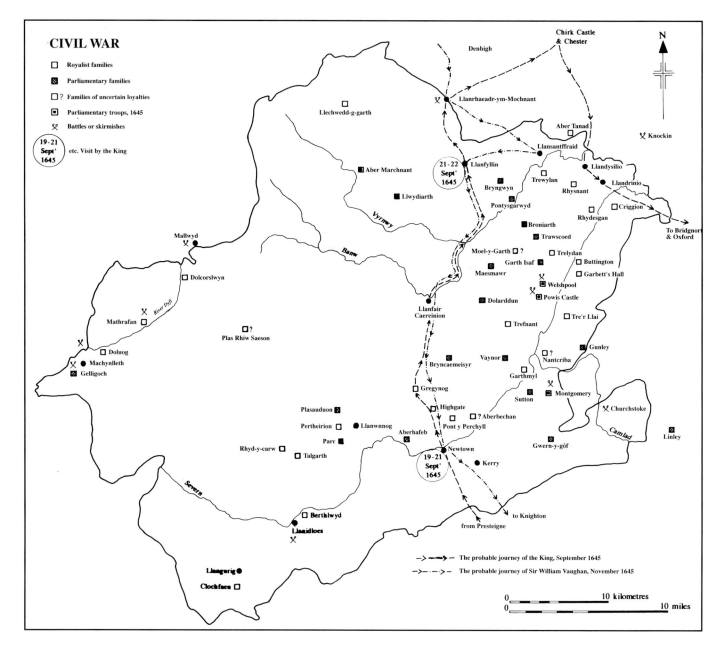

The Civil War

Montgomeryshire played a significant role in the Civil Wars of the mid-seventeenth century for two main reasons. Firstly, the county was an important recruiting area for the Royalist armies, being particularly convenient to Shrewsbury which was one of the main training centres for the King's forces. Secondly, the county was strategically significant, in that it controlled important routes into Wales as well as the main road from south Wales to Chester and the north of England.

It was these factors that led the prominent Parliamentarian leader, Sir Thomas Myddleton to

move into the area in 1644, and from this move resulted the numerous battles and skirmishes that were witnessed in the county after that date during the first Civil War. Prior to 1644, the county's gentry were overwhelmingly Royalist in their sympathies. On 5 August 1644, Sir Thomas Myddleton led a successful attack upon Welshpool and a month later at Newtown, he intercepted and seized a gunpowder train bound for the north of England. On 6 September that year, Montgomery Castle was surrendered to Myddleton, but almost immediately Royalist forces from Shropshire, Cheshire and north Wales laid siege to the castle. The siege was lifted as a result of the Parliamentary victory in the Battle of Montgomery, the biggest battle in Wales in the First Civil War, on 18 September, when opposing forces totalling some 7000 men fought, with the loss of over 1500 Royalist troops. Shortly afterwards, on 2 October, Powis Castle was taken, and the result of these combined actions was to give Parliamentary forces control over the upper Severn valley for the remainder of the conflict.

This did not prevent the outbreak of occasional local skirmishes, however. On 2 November 1644, Parliamentary troops were pelted with stones and turves near Mallwyd, having been collecting taxes in the Machynlleth area; they had also despoiled Dolguog. Towards the end of the month, there were further skirmishes near Machynlleth between forces from Merioneth loyal to the King and a party of Parliamentary troops marching north from Pembrokeshire. Mathafarn was attacked and burnt during this bout of hostilities. In March 1645, the Royalist Colonel Charles Gerard, retreating southwards after his failure to take Chester, won a victory at Knockin over Parliamentary forces from Powis Castle. In September that year, Charles I passed through the county from the south, calling at Newtown Hall, Gregynog and the Hall in Llanfyllin, and he passed back through Montgomeryshire again, following his defeat at Rowton Heath near Chester.

During his journey southwards, he was harried by forces under the command of Edward Vaughan of Llwydiarth. In November 1645, there were further skirmishes between Llanfyllin and Llanrhaeadr, as Vaughan attacked Royalist troops retreating from a defeat at the Green, near Denbigh. There was also a clash in the graveyard at Churchstoke in March 1646 as Parliamentary troops attacked Royalists retreating southwards after the surrender of Chirk Castle.

The county was also drawn into the second Civil War, with the most prominent gentry in the area proclaiming their allegiance to Parliament on 20 May 1648. Following an unsuccessful attempt by Lord Byron to take Shrewsbury for the Crown, he moved into mid-Wales, with the aim of taking Powis Castle and Montgomery Castle. However, he was defeated in another battle near Montgomery in August 1648. There was also a clash near Llanidloes when the Parliamentarian General Horton defeated a Royalist force from Herefordshire moving up to north Wales to strengthen forces loyal to the Crown. In the summer of 1649, fearful that Royalist forces might recapture Montgomery Castle, it was ordered that the fortifications there be demolished, though a further order that Powis Castle too should be dismantled was never acted upon.

E. R. MORRIS

Montgomery Castle, looking towards the Long Mountain, overlooking the battlefield.

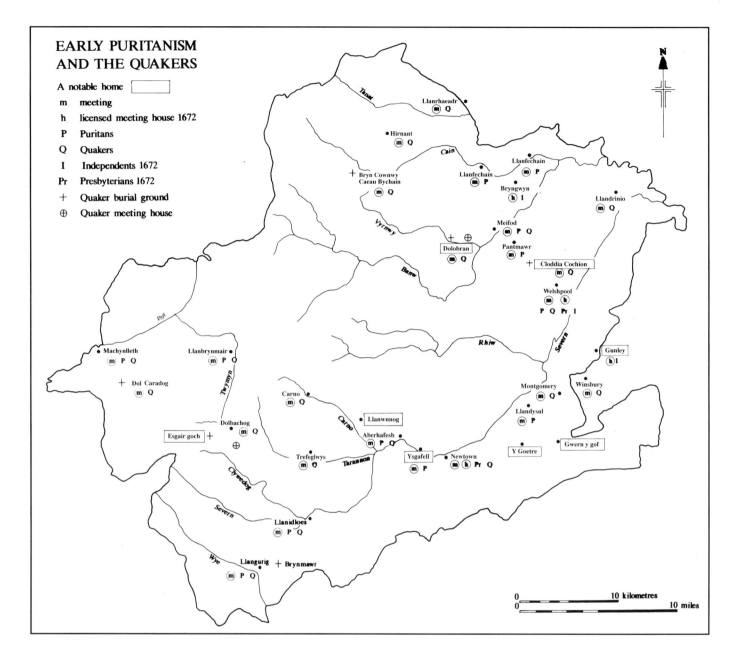

EARLY PURITANISM
AND THE QUAKERS

A notable home ☐
m   meeting
h   licensed meeting house 1672
P   Puritans
Q   Quakers
I   Independents 1672
Pr   Presbyterians 1672
+   Quaker burial ground
⊕   Quaker meeting house

The Puritans and the Quakers

The Puritan movement which arose in England during the reign of Elizabeth I did not establish itself in Wales until the time of the Civil War. Montgomeryshire was not really affected by it until the county was subjected by Parliament in the Civil War, for the gentry were predominantly Anglican and Royalist. During the time of the Civil War and the succeeding Commonwealth 1649-60 some of the lesser gentry became staunch supporters of the Puritan movement particularly Hugh Price of Gwern y gof, Richard Price of Gunley and Lewis Price of Llanwnnog. At this time too the great itinerant preacher Vavasor Powell was active, when he formed Puritan congregations especially in the east and north east parts of the county. Walter Cradock was also active in the Llanidloes and Llangurig districts.

The Act for the Propagation of the Gospel in Wales 1650 was the Commonwealth's attempt to puritanize a Royalist Wales. Unsuitable Anglican parsons were ejected and Puritan clerics took their places under the scrutiny of the Commissioners and Approvers set up by this act. All the men above mentioned took a prominent part in enforcing this measure which also set up schools in the county.

These early Puritans were mainly of two kinds - Presbyterian or Independents - the latter being the more radical in their views; some later became Baptists. They were numerous in the Meifod and Llanfyllin districts where Powell was particularly active.

The Restoration in 1660 brought about a complete reversal in the fortunes of the Puritans and they endured a bitter persecution under the Penal Code from 1660 until 1689. Heavy fines and imprisonment were inflicted on those convicted of holding illegal religious meetings (conventicles) in their homes. The map shows the sites of some of these conventicles. Some, such as Henry Williams of Ysgafell, the noted Baptist (of Cae'r Fendith fame) were especially harshly treated.

In 1672 Charles II attempted to alleviate their condition by allowing them to worship by granting licences - this was the short lived Indulgence. The map shows some of the places which were granted licences for religious meetings under this measure. In 1689 toleration was at last granted by Parliament and the Puritans or Dissenters, as they were now called, were allowed to build their own chapels or meeting houses. One of the oldest of these is Pendref (Llanfyllin); in other instances they continued to meet in licensed houses e.g. Pantmawr (Guilsfield).

During the Commonwealth period the Quakers or Society of Friends made their appearance in the county and many Puritans joined this group which grew rapidly in certain districts such as Meifod, Llanwddyn and Llanidloes. Their most important leader in the county was Richard Davies (1635-1708) of Cloddiau Cochion (Guilsfield) a remarkable figure. Socially their most important converts were the brothers Charles and Thomas Lloyd, squires of Dolobran (Meifod). The Quakers suffered more severely than any other group during the years 1660-89 and many, especially from Llanwddyn and Meifod, emigrated to the Quaker colony of Pennsylvania established by Penn in 1682. After the Toleration Act 1689 the Quakers, although allowed freedom of conscience, were still punished for their refusal to pay tithes. They erected meeting houses at Dolobran 1701 (which is still intact), Caeaubychain (Llanwddyn) and at Esgairgoch (Staylittle) in 1725. Their most important leader in the first half of the 18th century was John Goodwin, Esgairgoch (1681-1763). The movement declined rapidly in the next hundred years and the last Montgomeryshire Quaker meeting ended at Llanidloes in 1848. Yearly meetings were often held in the county. Today, although there is a Friends Meeting House in Newtown, all that remains to remind one of the old Quaker centres are the meeting house at Dolobran, the old Quaker farmsteads and the lonely graveyards.

E. R. MORRIS

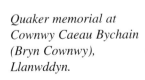

Quaker memorial at Cownwy Caeau Bychain (Bryn Cownwy), Llanwddyn.

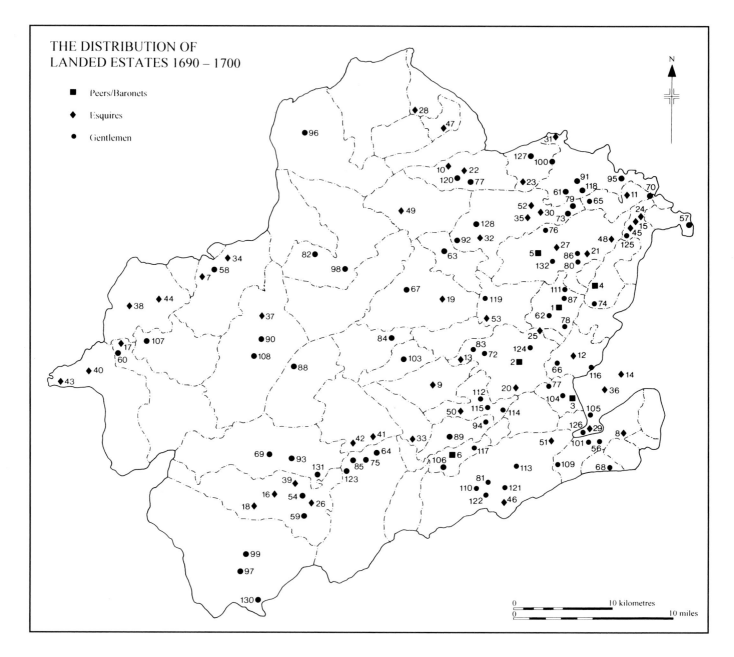

THE DISTRIBUTION OF
LANDED ESTATES 1690 – 1700

■ Peers/Baronets

◆ Esquires

● Gentlemen

Gentry

For five hundred years the mansions of the gentry were the prominent features in the social, economic and political landscape of Montgomeryshire. Early cartographers, such as Christopher Saxton or William Kip, picked out these mansions with many-gabled houses, tiny symbols which belied their immense influence, and the greatest houses, such as Llwydiarth, Powis Castle, Berthlwyd and Mathafarn, were named points of reference in Montgomeryshire's hill terrain. The map of North Wales, published by John Evans, the Llanymynech cartographer, in 1795, was as much an itinerary of the region's mansions as a useful guide to growing numbers of tourists. During the Second World War, the Ordnance Survey remained deferential, depicting a landscape that was still adorned with lush green parks, surrounding mansions which, in truth, were now anachronistic intrusions in a world of freehold farms. There is ample justification for including a map of the gentry seats in any county's historical atlas.

But who are we to include among Montgomeryshire's gentry? Lewys Dwnn of Betws Cedewain, 'the debyt Herawt at Arms for the three provinces of Kymru', recorded the pedigrees of just over 100 Montgomeryshire families in the late-sixteenth century. In turn, Richard Blome, in his *Britannia* of 1673, listed fifty-five named gentry, while John Adams, in his *Index Villaris* of 1680 identified seventy-seven gentry mansions. In all likelihood, Blome and Adams were too discriminative; in the 1690s the government's commissions for the levying of the land tax in Montgomeryshire routinely included 130 gentry. Some two centuries later, Thomas Nicholas, in his *Annals and Antiquities of the Counties and County Families of Wales* (1872) described Montgomeryshire's thirty-eight worthy families, while Walford's *County Families* of 1888 listed seventy-two named gentry. In the clearly subjective art of listing gentry Walford was probably nearer the mark, for the government's 'New Domesday' of 1872 had shown that this county had some sixty resident landowners with in excess of 500 acres or £500 in rented land. In an attempt to depict the gentry at some mid-way point in their history, the land-tax commissions of the 1690s provide the basis for this section's map and appendix.

Their uninterrupted ownership of about two-thirds of Montgomeryshire's agricultural land over the course of half a millennium gave the county's gentry a semblance of physical permanence. This was deceptive, for as some families and their estates rose to prominence others just as surely faded from the scene. Of Lewys Dwnn's 100 or more pedigreed families, half at least had ceased to be gentry of county status by the early eighteenth century. Of those 132 families of gentry who enjoyed the status of commissioners of the land tax in 1700, 109 had vanished from this county by 1810. Likewise, forty of Walford's *County Families* were new men whose perspective of gentility stopped short at 1800. Membership of the landed élite was ever subject to a process of regeneration. Patterns of inheritance and marriage had always spelt the doom of some families while providing an uplifting bonus for others. When Brochwell Griffiths of Broniarth died in 1741, a lament was etched in marble in Guilsfield church to the gentleman 'by whose death that ancient family name became extinct', but his death served to double the extent of the estates of his up-and-coming nephew and heir, Edward Lloyd of Domgae. Inheritances of this sort had been of long currency, but from the middle of the eighteenth century there was a strong tendency for English landowners to prey upon well-endowed Welsh heiresses. It was

thus not entirely surprising that Mary Cornelia Edwards (1828-1846), heiress of the extensive Garth and Greenfields estates in west Montgomeryshire, should find her very eligible hand snapped up by the son and heir of the third Marquess of Londonderry. Such marriages created the great, trans-county aggregations of landed property with their rarely seen, absentee landlords, which typified the Welsh rural scene of the late nineteenth century.

A further opportunity for the continued renewal of the gentry was provided by debt, sale and purchase. Every century seemingly held its examples of sensational debt-related sales: the passing of the Leighton estate of the Lloyds in 1612-23; the collapse of the Newtown Hall estate of the ill-fated Pryce baronets in 1786, or the final sale of the rump of the once-great Llwyn estate of the Humffreys family in 1850-52. But the leave-taking of one family was often an introduction for a dynasty founded by men of new wealth. Leighton passed to Edward Waties, a judge in the Court of the Council in the Marches at Ludlow; much of the Newtown Hall estate passed to David Pugh, the formidably wealthy London tea merchant, and Llwyn passed to John Dugdale, a Liverpool merchant. Among the less spectacular arrivistes (but no less significant to the renewal of the gentry class) were those lesser or village gentry who hauled themselves into the county élite over the course of two or three generations. Arthur Davies Owen marked his arrival in county society by building his Greek classical mansion at Glansevern in 1802-7. His success had been drafted in part by the prudence and far-sighted marriages of his father and grandfather (a very humble Llangurig gent.), and it was sealed by his own determined activities as an attorney, agent, entrepreneur and banker.

The coming and going of landed families over the course of five centuries underlies the gentry class's otherwise confident solidarity throughout this period. That confidence derived, first and foremost, from the gentry's ownership of a disproportionately large share of Montgomeryshire's prime economic asset, its agricultural land. Until the mid-eighteenth century, the gentry were active farmers in their own right. Sir John Pryce of Newtown Hall was doubtless pleased to be informed in March 1641, 'for your husbandry, God be praised it is in a good forwardness', and his correspondence with his steward Richard Amyas speaks of this baronet's intimate interest in his estate, farm, crops, hay, hedges and oxen. Like most landowners, much of his energy was devoted to such issues as his lease agreements, rent arrears, repairs of buildings, the preservation of his woodlands and the disciplining of wayward tenants. The gentry also prided themselves on their continuing role as the facilitators of economic development. In the history of industry and commerce in Montgomeryshire it is impossible to avoid mention of Charles Lloyd of Dolobran in iron-forging; William, second marquess of Powis in lead-mining and smelting; John Mytton of Penylan in early banking, and the Revd George Arthur Evors in the Newtown woollen industry. The gentry were the trustees and creditors of the turnpike trusts; landowners such as William Mostyn Owen of Bryngwyn and William Pugh of Brynllywarch were the prime movers behind the Montgomery Canal, and railway minded landowners included David Pugh of Llannerch Hudol, John Naylor of Leighton, Arthur James Johnes of Garthmyl, Anne Warburton Owen of Glansevern and John Davies Corrie of Dysserth/Diserth, prime movers for the Oswestry-Welshpool-Newtown railway in 1855-61, or Arthur Charles Humphreys Owen, chairman of the successor company, Cambrian Railways, between 1900 and 1905. (When once confronted with the notorious unpunctuality of his company's trains, he made the timeless apologia for railways: 'Be to our faults a little blind and to our virtues very kind'.)

For all but the greatest landowners in Montgomeryshire, social and cultural recreation was prescriptive and modest: the embellishment of his mansion, laying a new garden or park, treasuring his library, hare-coursing with a couple of friends, and occasional outings to Welshpool or Montgomery to undertake his business or duties as a justice of the peace consumed the gentleman's leisure hours. And for the wives of the gentry the routines of domestic economy were relieved by music-making, piety and charity. Admittedly, some landowners were drunks and fornicators, with a record of violent behaviour and a string of bastards; others were learned and devout. Thus the family of Martin Williams of Bryngwyn provided the village of Bwlchycibau with its National School in 1855 and its pretty Anglican church in 1862-3. Until the mid-seventeenth century, the gentry were the custodians of the national heritage of Wales, particularly as the patrons of the bards and wandering minstrels. Even so, from about 1750 most of the gentry were discarding the Welsh tongue, and in the century that followed they were effectively left out of the great religious and cultural developments in Wales.

The growth of large, absentee estates and the gradual cultural and social withdrawal by the Welsh landed élite were to play a part in their eventual demise. The nineteenth was, of course, a commercial and industrial century, in which the spell of landownership was finally broken, not least in the progress towards a universal franchise and a growing fiscal antagonism towards the landowners. Before 1880 the landowners' political supremacy was untouchable. Montgomeryshire's fractious and often violent elections were really only feuds within the ruling class, which split into factions of Herbert versus Vaughan, Powis versus Wynnstay or Whig versus Tory, and they were certainly not a challenge to their rule. In truth, the abdication of political supremacy came only slowly. If nearly a century of Wynnstay dominance of the county seat in parliament came to an end in the election of 1880, subsequent Liberal MPs included A.C. Humphreys-Owen of Glansevern and David Davies of Llandinam, both substantial landowners, albeit of relatively recent provenance. Likewise, when Montgomeryshire's first county council was elected in 1889, the landowner-councillors included Lord Powis, Lord Sudeley, David Evans of Glascoed, G.H.H. Hayhurst-France of Ystumcolwyn, R.J. Harrison of Caerhowell, J.H. Heyward of Crosswood, R.E. Jones of Cefn Bryntalch, D.H. Mytton of Garth and C.J. Naylor of Leighton.

Before the First World War, well below ten per cent of farmholdings in Montgomeryshire were owned by their occupiers, and the county was one of the more landlord-dominated in Wales. After 1911, when the earl of Powis sold extensive tracts of his upland estates, or 1914, when Lord Joicey sold the great Gregynog estate, the pace of sale quickened, and after the war it was particularly brisk, with perhaps more land changing hands at auction than at any other time in Welsh history. By the Second World War the ownership share of the owner-occupiers stood at about half the county's land. A number of landed families survive on their estates to this day, and they are held in the traditional respect in their communities. Even so, Montgomeryshire's, like much of rural Wales, is now a society dominated by its freehold farmers and, to a lesser extent, by its town and rural middle class.

MELVIN HUMPHREYS

Gentry in the 1690s, according to land tax returns

Peers
1 William, Marquess of Powis
2 Pryce, Viscount Hereford
3 Henry, Lord Herbert of Chirbury
4 Roger, Earl of Castlemaine

Baronets
5 Sir Charles Lloyd of Moelygarth
6 Sir Vaughan Pryce of Newtown Hall

Esquires
7 William Lewis Anwyl of Cemais Bychan
8 Henry Biggs of Broadway
9 John Blayney of Gregynog
10 Sydney Bynner of Bodyddon
11 Walter Clopton of Llandrinio
12 Arthur Devereux of Nantcriba
13 George Devereux of Cefngwernfa
14 John Edwards of Rorrington
15 Philip Eyton of Crugion
16 Evan Glynne of Glyn (Clywedog)
17 Francis Herbert of Dolguog
18 Richard Ingram of Glynhafren
19 Evan Jones of Llanloddian
20 Humphrey Jones of Garthmyl
21 Thomas Juckes of Trelydan
22 John Kyffin of Bodfach
23 John Kynaston of Bryngwyn
24 Richard Lee of Crugion
25 Edmund Lloyd of Trefnant
26 Edward Lloyd of Berthlwyd
27 Pierce Lloyd of Trawscoed
28 Robert Lloyd of Glanhafon
29 Thomas Mason of Rockley
30 John Matthews of Trefnannau
31 David Maurice of Penybont
32 Nathaniel Maurice of Trefedryd
33 Matthew Morgan of Aberhafesb
34 Richard Mostyn of Dolycorsllwyn
35 Richard Mytton of Pontysgawrhyd
36 Henry Newton of Heighley
37 Athelustan Owen of Rhiwsaeson
38 Richard Owen of Aberffrydlan
39 Richard Owen of Garth
40 Rowland Owen of Llynlloedd
41 Vincent Pierce of Llwynybrain
42 Matthew Price of Parc Penprys
43 Walter Price of Glanmerin
44 John Pugh of Mathafarn
45 Thomas Rocke of Crugion
46 Richard Stedman of Drefor
47 John Thomas of Llechwedd-y-garth
48 Arthur Vaughan of Trederwen
49 Edward Vaughan of Llwydiarth
50 Arthur Weaver of Highgate
51 Daniel Whittingham of Hem
52 Lumley Williames of Ystumcolwyn
53 Gabriel Wynne of Dolarddun

Gentlemen
54 Edward Bowen of Penyrallt
55 Solomon Bowen of ?
56 John Bright of Pentre (Churchstoke)
57 Edward Barrett of Pentre (Alberbury)
58 John Carreg of Cemais
59 Price Clunne of Glandulas
60 Morgan David of Bacheiddon
61 Hugh Davies of Collfryn
62 Hugh Davies of Dysserth/Diserth
63 Richard Davies of Cynhinfa
64 Robert Davies of Maesmawr
65 Hugh Derwas of Penrhos
66 Vaughan Devereux of Munlyn
67 Morgan Edwards of Melin-y-grug
68 Thomas Edwards of Pentre (Mainstone)
69 Edward Evans of Rhydycarw
70 William Evans of New Hall
71 John Felton of Caerhowell
72 Thomas Foulkes of Penrhyn
73 Henry Fox of Rhydesgyn
74 Thomas Garbett of Garbett's Hall (Cletterwood)
75 Richard Glynne of Maesmawr
76 Brochwell Griffiths of Broniarth
77 John Griffiths of Bachie
78 John Griffiths of Glanhafren
79 Thomas Griffiths of Rhydesgyn
80 Thomas Gwynne of Trelydan
81 John Herbert of Cwmyddalfa
82 George Higgins of Penylan
83 Thomas Hodson of Bryncaemeisir
84 Richard Hughes of Llanllugan
85 Evan Jones of Trewythen
86 Edward Jones of Trelydan
87 Gilbert Jones of Welshpool
88 John Jones of Glanhanog
89 Rees Jones of Gwestyd
90 Thomas Jones of Clegyrddwr
91 Robert Kynaston of Trewylan
92 Charles Lloyd of Dolobran
93 Edward Lloyd of Talgarth

94 Humphrey Lloyd of Aberbechan
95 John Lloyd of Domgae
96 John Lloyd of Eunant
97 Rees Lloyd of Clochfaen
98 Rees Lloyd of Cowny
99 Samuel Lloyd of Bwlchygarreg
100 William Lloyd of Ffinnant
101 Matthew Matthews of Wernddu
102 Richard Matthews of Brynbwa
103 David Meredith of Llanwyddelan
104 Edward Morris of Montgomery
105 John Myddelton of Churchstoke
106 Humphrey Owen of Castell-y-dail
107 Richard Owen of Darowen
108 Rondle Owen of Gellidywyll
109 William Pierce of Pentrenant
110 Theophilus Porter of Kerry
111 Edward Powell of Gungrog
112 Edmund Price of Tircoch
113 James Price of Penygelli

114 John Price of Dolforwyn
115 Richard Price of Betws Cedewain
116 Richard Price of Gunley
117 Richard Price of Penarth
118 Richard Price of Trewylan
119 Thomas Price of Cyfronnydd
120 Thomas Price of The Hall, Llanfyllin
121 Adam Pryce of Glanmiheli
122 John Pugh of Cilrhwyth
123 John Read of Llandinam
124 Griffith Robinson of Brithdir
125 Thomas Severne of Crugion
126 John Thomas of Brompton
127 Roger Trevor of Bodynfoel
128 John Vaughan of Glascoed
129 Richard Whittingham of Ffarme
130 Lewis Williams of Llwynyrhedydd
131 Richard Wilson of Bwlchyllyn
132 Brochwell Wynne of Garth

Powis Castle in 1776

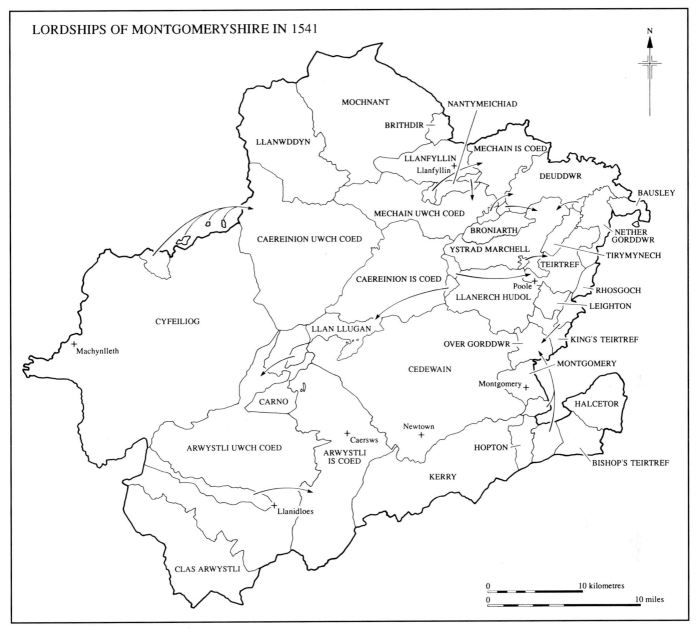

LORDSHIPS OF MONTGOMERYSHIRE IN 1541

N

Lordships and Manors

The union of Wales with England, which commenced with the Act of 1536, resulted in the creation of the county of Montgomery. Prior to this time, the area which constituted the new county of Montgomery, was controlled by several lords by virtue of them holding or possessing lordships. The extent of the various lordships in Montgomeryshire is shown on the above map and their number and extent have remained largely unaltered from the late Tudor period. At the time of 1536 Act, the Crown was in possession of a significant area in that it held the lordships of Arwystli, Cyfeiliog, Cedewain, Kerry, King's Teirtref, Halcetor, Hopton and Montgomery.

This left the Barony of Powis (which comprised the lordships of Mochnant, Llanwddyn, Caereinion Uwchcoed and Iscoed, Llanfyllin, Mechain Uwchcoed and Iscoed, Ystrad Marchell, Plas Dinas, Broniarth, Deuddwr, Nantymeichiad, Tirymynech and Llannerch Hudol) together with the lordships of Nether Gorddwr, Over Gorddwr, Teirtref, Tempsiter, Leighton, Rhos-goch, Bausley, Carno and Bishops Teirtref which were held by several Marcher lords.

In general terms, each lordship was administered by its lord as a single unit. Essentially, the lord provided protection to the tenants in return for their

63

services and rents. The precise nature of these mutual obligations was defined and regulated by the custom of the lordship, as evolved over the years in its own court. For example, in a charter dated the 31 August 1447, concerning the lordship of Cedewain, it is recorded that it was the custom for the perpetrator of a murder and his family to pay £90 compensation to the family of the victim, of which £30 was payable to the lord of the manor. This particular custom indicates the application of the laws of Hywel Dda in Cedewain lordship. With a need for money, the land within the lordship was, over a long period of time, alienated away, by means of several forms of land tenure, including copyhold. With the Law of Property Acts, 1922-25, many medieval forms of land tenure were abolished.

The lord was omnipotent and he was the fountain of any grants to the inhabitants within his lordship. Each lord had absolute power in the administration and regulation of justice. The union of Wales with England resulted in the sovereignty of the various lords being ceded to the English Crown. What residual rights were left to the lord following the union was by no means clear, resulting in much litigation over the following two hundred years.

In 1542, with the establishment of the Courts of Great Sessions in each county, the lords were forbidden to try cases of felony in their manorial courts, the Courts Leet. The Courts Leet continued to hear cases of misdemeanour and civil actions, but the Administration of Justice Act 1977, finally saw the end of the jurisdiction of the lord in legal proceedings, although the Act did allow it to transact other business. Nevertheless, the Courts Leet had largely ceased to function by the mid-nineteenth century for a variety of reasons; most of its business had already disappeared and it was not financially viable.

Some of the most common presentments at the Court Leet related to disputes over common land, such as encroachment, failure to maintain its state in good order and strangers wrongly depasturing their animals there. With the majority of commons being enclosed as a result of the various Enclosure Acts during the period of the mid eighteenth to the mid nineteenth centuries, such disputes largely disappeared. As for the financial viability of the court the customary dues, amercements and fines had remained fixed from the late medieval period, with no increases in their amounts to take account of inflation. A typical due was that of a heriot. This was payable on the death of a tenant and originally comprised the delivery to the lord of the deceased tenant's best animal commuted to a cash payment by the time of the Act of Union in 1536.

Manors still continue today but their importance as administrative units has completely disappeared. What residual rights remain continue to be further regulated by statute. The Commons Registration Act 1965 resulted in all remaining common land being defined together with a register of all commoners and their rights.

One of the most important residual rights is that of minerals and sometimes this resulted in disputes of the boundary of lordships, especially in areas of mining. Such a dispute existed between the boundary of the lordship of Clas Arwystli and the Crown lordship of Mefenydd, Co. Cardigan. Indeed, this particular dispute affected the county boundary. It was finally resolved by an agreement dated 8 January 1860.

M. L. CHAPMAN

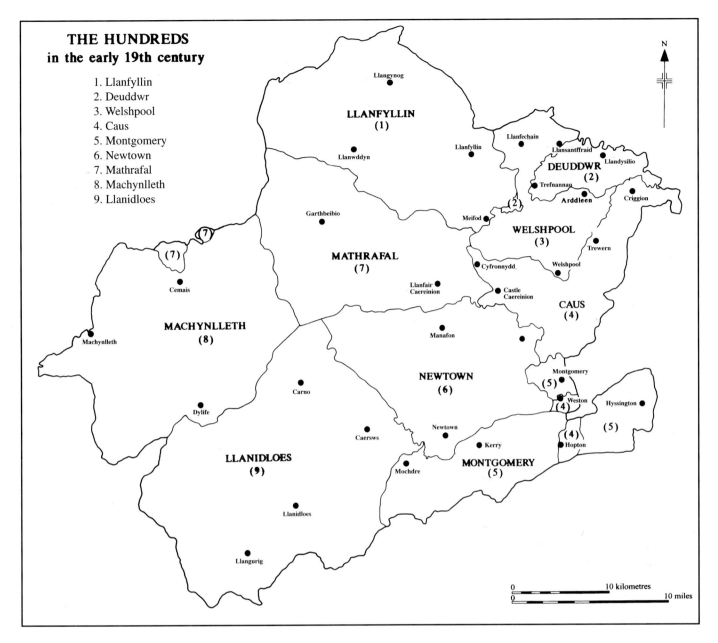

1. Llanfyllin
2. Deuddwr
3. Welshpool
4. Caus
5. Montgomery
6. Newtown
7. Mathrafal
8. Machynlleth
9. Llanidloes

The Hundreds

From the creation of the county in 1536 until the great local government reforms in the last twenty years of the 19th century control of the county's affairs, by and large, was vested in the magistracy (the Justices of the Peace) recruited from the landowning class. These met in the Quarter Sessions where they not only tried offenders but also administered the county in much the same way as a modern elected council does.

The act of 1542 divided the new county into districts known as Hundreds - this followed the pattern which had long prevailed in the counties of England. The Hundred was an old division dating from Saxon times.During the Middle Ages its functions were considerable both judicially and in administration. However, by the 16th century it had been subordinated to the JPs of the shire and its importance slowly declined.

In every Hundred there was a High Constable (usually two) and a Bailiff - chosen yearly from substantial inhabitants and these, together with a Grand Jury chosen usually from the 40 shilling freeholders in the Hundreds, made presentments at Quarter Sessions.

The presentments included neglect of highways and bridges by the inhabitants, unlicensed ale houses, misdemeanours of many kinds and in the 17th century such offences as recusancy, illegal conventicles, breaking of the Sabbath etc. The Hundred officials likewise performed the same service at the Assizes of the Court of Great Sessions, held twice yearly in the county.

The Hundred was also used as the unit when the national censuses were taken in the 19th century. Parliamentary voters were listed under their respective Hundreds and polling figures issued for each Hundred. In this century the Hundred steadily lost importance and especially after 1834 (when Poor Law Unions were set up), until they were abolished to make way for the elected Rural District Councils in 1894.

There were nine Hundreds in Montgomeryshire and some of these were subdivided into upper and lower districts. Their boundaries changed slightly during the period of their existence 1542-1894. In most cases the boundaries were those of the old lordships, cantrefi and cymydau e.g. the Hundred of Machynlleth, for instance, corresponded to the old cwmwd of Cyfeiliog. (It is interesting to note that the former Machynlleth Rural District had similar boundaries.) The Hundreds of Llanidloes, Mathrafal, Newtown and Deuddwr showed a similar state of affairs but in the north and east of the county there was considerable deviation from the pre-county divisions: the Hundred of Llanfyllin consisted of Mochnant uwch Rhaeadr and part of Mechain, whilst others such as Caus and Pool were even more novel.

Today, little remains to remind one of these once important divisions of local government. In Radnorshire there is a place called Hundred House. Two present day civil parishes both in the former Rural District of Llanfyllin are still distinguished by being termed Llansantffraid Pool and Llansantffraid Deuddwr because they were in the days of the Hundreds in those two respective divisions.

E. R. MORRIS

The market hall at Llanidloes would also have served as the court of the hundred of Arwystli.

Dependent Chapels

Churches

Monastic Churches

PENNANT
LLANGYNOG
LLANRHAEADR
Tanat
HIRNANT
LLANSANTFFRAID
LLANYMYNECH
Llanfechain
LLANWDDYN
Llanfyllin
Llandysilio
Llanfihangel
LLANDRINIO
MEIFOD
Vyrnwy
Garthbeibio
Guilsfield
Severn
Llangadfan
Banw
Llanerfyl
Llangynyw
Welshpool
LLANFAIR CAEREINION
Castle Caereinion
LLANWRIN
Dyfi
CEMAIS
LLANLLUGAN
MANAFON
Rhiw
MACHYNLLETH
LLANBRYNMAIR
Llanwyddelan
BERRIEW
PENEGOES
DAROWEN
TREGYNON
CARNO
MONTGOMERY
Betws Cedewain
Llanwnnog
LLANLLWCHAEARN
LLANDYSUL
CHURCHSTOKE
Aberhafesb
Llanmerewig
TREFEGLWYS
NEWTOWN
PENSTROWED
KERRY
LLANDINAM
Severn
Llanidloes
Wye
LLANGURIG

0   10 kilometres
0   10 miles

The Church in Wales

The Norman invasion in 1066 had a decisive effect on the life of the church in Wales. Within the next two hundred years Wales was brought out of isolation and integrated into a European community, which found its ecclesiastical organization in the observance, practice and governance of papal Christendom.

When Gilbert was chosen by the mutual agreement of the King of England and the Archbishop of Canterbury to occupy the newly created territorial see of St. Asaph in 1143 Powys formed its basis. If the kingdom of Powys determined the extent and

shape of the new diocese then its division into archdeaconries, rural deaneries and parishes, followed those of the traditional civil divisions of *cantrefi* and commotes. In the twelfth and thirteenth centuries the parochial geography of the country was determined with many of the parishes assuming the names of local saints. Some parishes contained both the elements of civil and ecclesiastical origins — Llanfair Caereinion, Llansantffraid-ym-Mechain, are examples. Mochnant, Mechain, Caereinion, Cedewain and Cyfeiliog gave their title to parishes and rural deaneries. Arwystli was retained by the diocese of Bangor. In 1176 archdeacon Gerald successfully claimed Ceri for the diocese of St David's. Daniel, son of bishop Sulien of St David's is referred to in 1127 as archdeacon of Powys. The creation of parishes and rural deaneries in the thirteenth century is seen in the records of taxation (1254 and 1291) levied on the church by the Papacy to finance projected crusades. In spite of being compelled by external forces to absorb itself into the ecclesiastical framework of England and the Papacy the church in Wales did not lose its identity. Together with the acceptance of new ideas old traditions were reshaped and a new vision of the origins and mission of the Welsh church emerged. Part of the inspiration for this was the historical fiction of Geoffrey of Monmouth, (d.

Pennant Melangell Church.

1154), bishop of St Asaph, who counted the conversion of the Britons by Joseph of Arimathea. The Welsh retained their faith in spite of persecution by Roman and Saxon pagans. They were a people chosen by God with a history, language and literature of their own and cherished a prophetic message of future triumph. Of particular importance to them were their native saints and associated relics enshrined in the landscape of settlements, holy places and wells, as places of veneration and pilgrimage.

The Welsh Church in the Middle Ages had its own distinctiveness. Its language and literature continued to flourish. Cynddelw Brydydd Mawr (fl. 1155-1195), sang in praise of Meifod church and addressed an *awdl* to Tysilio. Lewis Glyn Cothi (c. 1420-1489) appealed to the saints of Wales to rule 'a second time so that the present hope of Wales might rest in the saints of this island.' Religious drama players from Montgomeryshire were active in the second half of the fifteenth or early sixteenth centuries.

Early inscribed stones to the dead are found in the county. The earliest late fifth or early sixth century is at Llanerfyl with a Latin inscription to a young girl of Roman origin. Meifod has a fine richly carved stone cross c. tenth century and Llandrinio a sculptured cross slab of the same date. No doubt the churches of Powys like those of Gwynedd in the thirteenth century 'came to shine with white-washed churches like stars in the firmament'. Many churches were destroyed by the English conquerors in 1282 - 1283 and in the rebellion of Owain Glyndwr, 1400-1415. The fifteenth and sixteenth centuries witnessed the great age of church building with new lady chapels and towers. The use of timber is a notable feature in bell turrets. A number of fine church roofs survive from this period (Kerry, Cemais, Llanfechain, Montgomery, Llanidloes, Mochdre, Guilsfield etc.). The glory of these rebuildings were the rood screens and lofts. The county had over thirty of the finest produced by the Newtown school of carvers. Gruffudd Llwyd composed a *cywydd* in praise of the Rood at Welshpool. Most, including that of Welshpool, have perished, though fragments remain at Newtown, Llanwnnog, Montgomery, Pennant Melangell and Llanwrin. The drawings of the Reverend John Parker (1798-1860), incumbent of Llanmerewig, are an invaluable record. A fourteenth century figure of Christ from the Mochdre Rood has been preserved but the magnificent frescos depicting scenes of the Passion at Llanwddyn were lost in the middle of the nineteenth century.

Welsh pride was displayed at the accession of Henry Tudor to the throne of England in 1485. For the Welsh church and nation the prophecies were fulfilled; Llywelyn was avenged, 'Cadwalader's blood lineally descending.' Links with the Tudor dynasty were strengthened by the Act of Union in 1536. The gentry class in Wales found greater opportunities in the professions and in the service of the Crown either in the locality or the capital. Ecclesiastical preferment was widened.

The houses of religion were dissolved, 1536 -1539. The glory of Strata Marcella Abbey was ruthlessly sold off by Nicholas Purcell of Forden, agent to Lord Powis. Some parish churches were enriched by the spoliation: the stallwork at Montgomery from Chirbury and the roof at Llanidloes from Cwmhir. Richard Conway the former head of Denbigh friary became vicar of Llandinam. The 'stripping of the altars', the suppression of shrines and pilgrimages, the white washing of wall paintings, the destruction of the images of the saints in woodwork and stained glass, the introduction in 1549 of the Book of Common Prayer enforced by the Act of Uniformity banished the old faith.

The rectorial tithes of some parishes which had been appropriated by the religious houses were re-distributed elsewhere than to the benefit of the church. For example, Henry VIII endowed the cathedral church of Christ Church Oxford with the tithes of Meifod, Guilsfield and Welshpool. Lay impropriators received the rectorial tithes from the parishes of Llanfair Caereinion, Llanllugan, Berriew and Betws. In 1678 by Act of Parliament Bishop Barrow re-directed the rectorial tithes of Llanwddyn and Llanrhaeadr-ym-Mochnant to the dean and chapter of St Asaph Cathedral for its repair. In 1685 two-thirds of the Llandinam revenue was allocated towards the repair of the Cathedral at Bangor.

The new learning had a tremendous impact on the religion, language and literature of Wales and was the greatest gift to the Welsh nation. In 1563 Parliament passed the Act for translating the Bible and the Prayer Book into Welsh. Bishop Richard Davies collaborated with William Salesbury and the Prayer Book and New Testament appeared in Welsh in 1567. In 1588 William Morgan, when vicar of Llanrhaeadr-ym-Mochnant published his Welsh translation of the Bible. He was encouraged in this great endeavour by his appointment to the parishes of Llanfyllin, Pennant Melangell and Welshpool. Amongst those who shared his labours was David Powel, historian and humanist, who held the livings of Llanfyllin, Meifod and Llansantffraid ym Mechain. His contribution to Welsh learning was the *Historie of Cambria now called Wales* (1584). In 1620, Bishop Parry of St Asaph with the assistance of the greatest of all Welsh renaissance scholars, Dr John Davies of Mallwyd, brought out a revised edition of Bishop Morgan's Bible. Davies provided the ground work for the Welsh language with his Welsh grammar in 1621, a Catechism in 1631, his Latin-Welsh Dictionary, his *Llyfr Plygain* and Catechism in 1633. A new revised edition of the Prayer Book followed in 1621 and in 1630 the first popular edition of the Welsh Bible *Y Beibl bach*.

This was not a happy period in the history of Wales. The Act of Uniformity of 1662, which required allegiance to the bishops through episcopal ordination, led to the expulsion of ministers who had been intruded into parishes during the Commonwealth period. The Clarendon Code — the Coventicle Act of 1664, forbidding all non-Anglican meetings for worship — the Five Mile Act of 1665, restricting the movements of ministers — was seen as a 'Royalist Act of Vengeance for all sufferings since 1642'. Under these Acts the vicars of Llanidloes and Trefeglwys reported a Quaker's conventicle to the magistrates. The Act of Uniformity sowed the seeds of future divisions and from this time on Anglicans and Dissenters pursued their separate ways.

The overwhelming majority of the population of Montgomeryshire were loyal to the established church and devoted to the use of the Welsh language in their church services. There was a revival in the church which is reflected in the number of endowments made for the provision of bread and clothing to the poor and for the instruction of the church catechism to the young together with the provision of elementary education and assistance towards apprenticeships in a trade. The moral influence of this revival is seen in the emphasis on this instruction and the display of the ten commandments in the walls of churches.

Good spiritual leadership was provided by the bishops of the diocese of St Asaph. George Griffiths (1660-1666) of Llandrinio played a leading part in the revision of the Welsh Prayer Book of 1664. The episcopacy of William Lloyd (1680-1692) was marked by his dialogue with Dissenters in public conferences held at Llanfyllin and Oswestry.

Persecution was eased by the Toleration Act of 1689 which permitted Dissenters to worship freely in meeting houses. This in the long run weakened the 'monopoly' position and authority of the Anglican Church in Wales. Enlightened Anglicans and Dissenters were beginning to co-operate together to teach the poor to read the Bible.

Church records throw light on the important developments which took place in the religious community in Wales in the eighteenth century. Pastoral care in the parishes was regular. The church fostered and encouraged the educational movements which provided a continuous supply of Bibles and taught children and adults to read them. Most of the clergy were resident or provided curates. Some of them were scholarly and active in the literary renaissance.

Ordinations were held annually and confirmations performed on a deanery basis with the triennial visitation. Bishop Shipley had over 12,000 candidates presented to him for Confirmation in the diocese in six years. Thomas Richards, rector of Llanfyllin and rural dean of Pool in 1748, described the clergy as 'unexceptionable and a reputable set of clergy, some of ye curates here have continued in that humble station many years.' If the incumbent was non-resident he provided a curate. On the whole the fabric of the churches and their furnishings were in a good condition. The numbers of Welsh Bibles 'bespoke' for the deanery of Llanfyllin was 499. Catechism was a regular feature and Easter communicants a high percentage of the parishioners. Richards noted the language of the services and brought what was wanting to the notice of the bishops — Berriew, 'some of the Parishioners make great complaints that they have not sometimes Welsh duty' - Newtown, 'All English Duty' - Betws, 'The vicar promises to do more Duty in Welsh it being agreeable to the Majority of his parishioners'. But these criticisms were the exception.

In 1791 the rural deans in Montgomeryshire on the whole reported that the state of the churches was good as was the pastoral care of the people by incumbents, curates and schoolmasters. Not all was satisfactory. At Llanwrin, 'the Rector inducted in August 1789 read the 39 Articles and preached and went off'. The curate at Llanllugan evoked the verdict that 'no possible good can be done with him being much addicted to drinking, and has lodged and boarded in an ale house for some years.' At Llanwyddelan — 'the Rector non-resident: a Methodist church built in the parish.' 'Sectaries' were reported at Machynlleth, Llanwrin and Cemais. The success of the Methodist revival was due to the fact that it overcame the isolation imposed by the parish boundaries and was confident enough to go its own way. The story of Ann Griffiths (1776-1805) illustrated this. Born at Llanfihangel-yng-Ngwynfa she was brought up in the church 'and became familiar there with the prayers and praises' of the Welsh versions of the Bible and the Book of Common Prayer. She was influenced by the Independents at Llanfyllin and found her spiritual home with the Methodists at Bala under the leadership of Thomas Charles.

Thomas Gouge (1605-1681) was a non-conformist divine and philanthropist. In 1674 a 'trust' was set up 'to teach the poor Welsh children to read and write English, cast Accompts and repeat the Catechism.' Devotional books were translated into Welsh and in 1677, an octavo edition of the Welsh Bible, edited by Stephen Hughes, was published. The Welsh Trust included churchmen and dissenters and set the pattern for the voluntary societies, for the education of the poor in the eighteenth century. In Montgomeryshire schools were set up in Welshpool, Meifod, Crugion/Criggion and Guilsfield. Books and Bibles were distributed in Welshpool, Montgomery, Llanfair, Castle Caereinion, Llangynyw, Llanfechain, Llansantffraid and Llanbrynmair.

The Society for Promoting Christian Knowledge was founded in London in 1699. It continued the work of Thomas Gouge in distributing devotional books and pamphlets in Welsh and English. Clergy societies were set up in Wales including Montgomeryshire. It was decided to set up Welsh schools 'that being the language which the parents best understood.' During the period 1699 to 1740 twelve Charity Schools were established in this county at Ceri, Llanfihangel, Llanfyllin, Llangynog, Welshpool, Llanwrin, Llwydiarth, Mathafarn, Llanbrynmair, Llanerfyl and Meifod. In 1690 Bishop William Lloyd promoted a Welsh folio edition of 10,000 copies known as *Beibl*

Buttington Church.

Yr Esgob Llwyd. From 1777 to 1789 the SPCK published about 100,000 people's Bibles in the Welsh language. The work of the SPCK was continued by *The Circulating Welsh Charity Schools* 1738-1761 under the organization and guidance of Griffith Jones, rector of Llanddowror, Carmarthenshire. The object was to teach the children to read the Welsh Bible and to learn the church Catechism, to sing psalms, to pray at home and attend public worship on the sabbath. The schools moved from place to place. They were usually held in the winter and moved on after about three months. For success they needed the co-operation of the parish clergy. Eighty seven schools were held in twenty places in Montgomeryshire, Aberhafesb, Trefeglwys, Llanbrynmair, Llanfair Caereinion, Cemais, Carno, Darowen, Llanllugan, Llangurig, Ceri, Llandinam, Llanwddyn, Llanidloes, Llangadfan, Llangynog, Llanwrin, Llanwennog, Pennant, Penegoes and Llanwyddelan. Thus the ground was well prepared for a religious and national revival. As Dr Melvin Humphreys has remarked 'many of the county's clergymen were moved to produce or translate worthy texts for their unenlightened flocks.'

Among *Yr Hen Bersoniaid Llengar*, 'the old literary clerics' were Walter Davies (Gwallter Mechain), John Jenkins (Ifor Ceri), Thomas Richards, vicar of Darowen, David Evans, rector of Llanerfyl. They were interested in Welsh language, literature and traditional melodies. The Montgomeryshire *carolau plygain* recited from the Bible the mystery of Christ's birth in a stable. They were responsible for the revival of the eisteddfod at the beginning of the nineteenth century.

The nineteenth century was a period of tremendous change in Wales when all aspects of church life were transformed. In 1811 the Calvinistic Methodists left the Anglican church in Wales and by the time of the Religious Census

in 1851 the nonconformists were in the ascendancy having nearly 80% of those who attended a place of worship. The church was on the defensive for the entire century.

It was A. J. Johnes (1809-1871), of Garthmyl, an Anglican and a high court judge, who in a prize winning essay of 1831, pointed out *The Causes which in Wales have produced Dissent from the Established Church*. This was a wholesale attack on church abuse. A detailed analysis of the ills of the church: the unequal distribution of wealth, the misappropriation of patronage and in some cases the indifference to the Welsh language.

An attempt was made to reform the abuses in the Anglican church by setting up the Ecclesiastical Commissioners in 1835. One of their first proposals was to unite the dioceses of Bangor and St Asaph and appropriate part of their revenue for the new diocese of Manchester. This was anathema to Lord Powis (1785-1848) who successfully defeated the measure in Parliament. In this he had the support of Johnes. Other measures introduced by the Ecclesiastical Commissoners were positive and lasting.

In Montgomeryshire new parishes were established and financed by a redistribution of revenues. Money was provided by the Commissioners for the building of parsonage houses and the National Society made regular grants for the provision and maintenance of schools. A feature of nineteenth century Montgomeryshire was the complete overhaul of 'parochial plant' — churches were either restored or rebuilt, houses provided in every parish for the parson and the school master and schools built and enlarged. For this purpose Bishop T. Vowler Short (1846-1870) devoted both his energy and fortune, with support from the landed gentry.

A sign of the polarization of Welsh society was the reaction to the publication of *The Inquiry of the Commissioners into the State of Education in Wales* in 1847. It made rash and injudicious statements about the prevalence of immorality, blaming nonconformity. The Eisteddfod was said to be a hindrance to the development of true learning and the Welsh language was 'a vast draw-back to Wales and a manifest barrier to its moral progress.' The Report was stigmatized as *Brâd Y Llyfrau Gleision — The Treachery of the Blue Books*.

1847 was a turning point. The church was under attack. It was regarded by nonconformity as an 'alien church', *Eglwys Loegr*, 'the Church of England in Wales', a minority body. Justice would only be done when the church was disestablished and disendowed.

In this attack national issues became identified with spiritual issues. Welsh radicalism claimed that special legislation should apply to Wales. The church in the Welsh countryside was seen to be in a privileged position, propped up by English landlords. Much that was wanted was achieved. The removal of the disabilities of Nonconformity — church rates, burial according to nonconformist rites in churchyards, marriage in chapels, the transference of the liability for tithe to the landlord. Other demands met were Sunday closing, grants to the Welsh University Colleges, Welsh Intermediate Education and the local Government Act of 1888 which put an end to the domination of local administration by the aristocracy and the squirearchy.

After a long struggle the Welsh church was disestablished and disendowed by Act of Parliament in 1914. This came into force on 18 April 1920 because of the Great War. The Anglican church in Wales ceased to be part of the Province of Canterbury and became a new Province of Wales with its own government and finance. Out of the secularized property of the disendowment measure Montgomeryshire County Council eventually received £198, 290 12s 11d - the Welsh Church Acts fund.

In 1891 Dean John Owen of St Asaph asked W. E. Gladstone his opinion of the effect of disestablishment on the Church in Wales. He replied, 'Death, Mr. Dean, but after death Resurrection.'

Disestablishment and disendowment brought independence. The Constitution of the Church in Wales with the twin organs of the Governing Body, the legislature, and the Representative Body, the executive and the embodiment of the continuation of the Anglican tradition with flexibility for cultural change. A close relationship between dioceses in Wales was established in the Provincial Structure.

After the Second World War the Representative Body developed the policy of reconstruction, the word used for the essential development of available but shrinking resources. This led to the grouping of parishes and the sale of surplus parsonage houses. The term reconstruction implied retrenchment and this was haphazardly achieved. Other changes seen against a decline in numbers of Easter communicants, baptisms, confirmations and regular church attenders may be described in terms of renewal and reassessment and the gradual shaping of a new model and area of ministry.

The Church in Wales has pursued a policy of ecumenism, the coming together of Churches. A Covenant for Union was signed in January 1975 with the Church in Wales, the Methodists and the United Reform Church: 'We recognise that ordained ministries of all our churches as true ministries of the word and sacraments, through which God's love is proclaimed, his grace mediated, and his Fatherly care exercised.' The care of parish churches, the national heritage, continues and there has been since 1944 a policy for the preservation of church records.

T. W. PRITCHARD

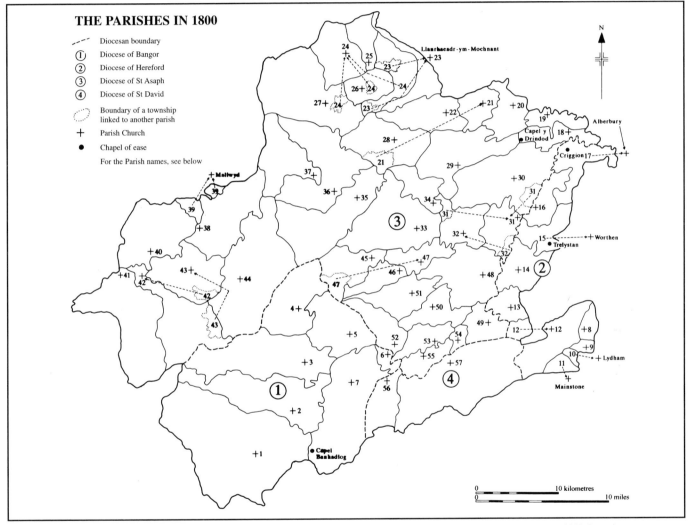

THE PARISHES IN 1800

- - - Diocesan boundary
① Diocese of Bangor
② Diocese of Hereford
③ Diocese of St Asaph
④ Diocese of St David

⋯⋯ Boundary of a township linked to another parish

+ Parish Church

● Chapel of ease

For the Parish names, see below

I Diocese of Bangor
1 Llangurig
2 Llanidloes
3 Trefeglwys (Saint Michael)
4 Carno (Saint John)
5 Llanwnnog
6 Penstrowed (Saint Gwrhai)
7 Llandinam (Saint Llonio)
II Diocese of Hereford
8 Hyssington (Saint Etheldreda)
9 Snead (Holy Trinity)
10 Lydham (part)
11 Maidstone (Saint John y Bedyddiwr) (part)
12 Churchstoke (Saint Nicholas)
13 Montgomery (Saint Nicholas)

14 Forden (Saint Michael)
15 Worthen (All Saints) (part)
16 Talybont (All Saints)
17 Llanfihangel (Alberbury) (part)

III Diocese of St Asaph
18 Llandrinio
19 Llandysilio
20 Llansantffraid
21 Llanfechain (Saint Garmon)
22 Llanfyllin
23 Llanrhaeadr-ym-Mochnant (Saint Dogfan) (part)
24 Pennant Melangell
25 Llangynog
26 Hirnant (Saint Illog)
27 Llanwddyn (Saint John)

28 Llanfihangel yng Ngwynfa
29 Meifod (Saint Tysilio and St Mary)
30 Guilsfield (Saint Aelhaearn)
31 Welshpool (Saint Mary)
32 Castle Caereinion (Saint Garmon)
33 Llanfair Caereinion
34 Llangynyw
35 Llanerfyl
36 Llangadfan
37 Garthbeibio (Saint Tydecho)
38 Cemais (Saint Tydecho)
39 Mallwyd (Saint Tydecho) (part)
40 Llanwrin
41 Machynlleth (Saint Peter)
42 Penegoes (Saint Cadfarch)
43 Darowen (Saint Tudur)

44 Llanbrynmair
45 Llanllugan (Llorcan Wyddel)
46 Llanwyddelan
47 Manafon (Saint Michael)
48 Berriew (Saint Beuno)
49 Llandysul
50 Betws Cedewain (Saint Beuno)
51 Tregynon (Saint Cynon)
52 Aberhafesb (Saint Gwynog)
53 Llanllwchaearn
54 Llam-yr-ewig (Saint Llwchaearn)
55 Newtown (Saint Mary)

IV Diocese of St Davids
56 Mochdre (All Saints)
57 Llanfihangel yng Ngheri (Kerry)

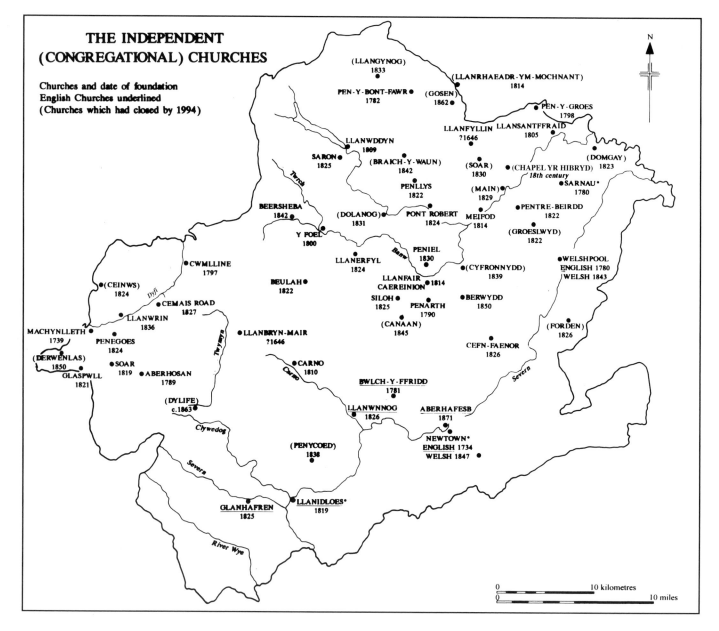

THE INDEPENDENT
(CONGREGATIONAL) CHURCHES

Churches and date of foundation
English Churches underlined
(Churches which had closed by 1994)

N

(LLANGYNOG)
1833

PEN-Y-BONT-FAWR ●   (GOSEN)   (LLANRHAEADR-YM-MOCHNANT)
1782   1862 ●   1814

PEN-Y-GROES
1798

LLANFYLLIN   LLANSANTFFRAID
?1646   1805

LLANWDDYN
1809

SARON ●   (BRAICH-Y-WAUN)   (SOAR)   (CHAPEL YR HIBRYD)   (DOMGAY)
1825   1842   1830   18th century   1823

PENLLYS   SARNAU ●
1822   (MAIN) ●   1780
                      1829

BEERSHEBA   (DOLANOG) ●   PONT ROBERT   MEIFOD   PENTRE-BEIRDD
1842 ●   1831   1824   1814   1822

Y FOEL   (GROESLWYD)
1800   PENIEL   1822
                       1830

CWMLLINE   LLANERFYL   ●WELSHPOOL
1797   1824   ENGLISH 1780
                       (CYFRONNYDD)   WELSH 1843
(CEINWS)   BEULAH ●   LLANFAIR   1839
1824   1822   CAEREINION ● 1814
CEMAIS ROAD   SILOH ●   ●BERWYDD
1827   1825   1850
LLANWRIN   PENARTH
1836   1790   (FORDEN)
MACHYNLLETH   PENEGOES   LLANBRYN-MAIR (CANAAN)   1826
1739   1824   ?1646   1845
(DERWENLAS)   ● SOAR   CEFN-FAENOR
1850   1819 ● ABERHOSAN   1826
GLASPWLL   1789
1821   ● CARNO
                             1810
               (DYLIFE)   BWLCH-Y-FFRIDD
               c.1863   1781

                    LLANWNNOG   ABERHAFESB
                    1826   1871

                    (PENYCOED)   NEWTOWN●
                    1838   ENGLISH 1734
                                 WELSH 1847

GLANHAFREN ● LLANIDLOES●
1825   1819

Tanat   Banw   Carno   Cerniog   Dyfi   Twrch   Severn   Clywedog   River Wye

0   10 kilometres
0   10 miles

The Independents

The Toleration Act of 1689 brought to an end the persecution suffered by the Nonconformists since 1662, but there were only three main centres at which they met in Montgomeryshire at that time. They were:

i)   Newtown and Llanllwchaearn
ii) Llanfyllin and Pantmawr
iii) Llanbrynmair and Trefeglwys

There is some evidence to suggest that other groups with similar beliefs met at Welshpool, Tregynon, Llangurig and Machynlleth, and they were known for many years as Pobl Vavasor Powell - the people of Vavasor Powell. Some semblance of unity was maintained between the various congregations until

about 1700, but thereafter certain theological differences became apparent. According to the details gathered by Dr. John Evans of Wrexham between 1717 and 1729 the 120 strong congregation at Newtown had adopted Presbyterianism, but those at Llanfyllin (110) and Llanbrynmair (90) retained Independent beliefs.

Between 1715 and 1780, the Independent causes weakened throughout the county. This was particularly true of Llanfyllin during the ministry of Dr John Johns and his successors. Fierce debates on the finer points of theology tore churches apart, whilst Pendref chapel at Llanfyllin was destroyed by rioters in 1715. Ironically, however, it was the Methodist revival that brought new life to many of the Independent causes in the county. The witness of Lewis Rees at Llanbrynmair was upheld by Richard Tibbott, whilst at Llanfyllin John Griffiths and John Lewis led the revival, establishing the Easter meetings at which the great hymn-writer Ann Griffiths experienced her conversion. The removal of the Independent Academy from Abergavenny to Oswestry in 1782 gave a great boost to the Independent causes locally, and this influence was maintained with the later moves of the Academy to Wrexham (1792-1816), to Llanfyllin (1816-21) and to Newtown (1821-38). The presence of the Academy was seminal in the establishment of new congregations in the east of the county. In the west Capel Y Graig came under the ministry of the church historian David Morgan between 1814 and 1836, and a number of new chapels were founded in the area during those years.

By December 1833, the rector of Llanfyllin reported that the Independent chapel at Pendref had the largest following of any of the town's places of worship. At Llanbrynmair too, where Yr Hen Gapel had been built in 1739, the Independent cause prospered. John Roberts (senior) arrived there in 1795 to assist Richard Tibbott, and during the next fifty years he and his sons Samuel Roberts (S.R.) and John Roberts (J.R.) were to be outstanding figures in many aspects of the religious and social history of Wales. Samuel Roberts especially was one of the outstanding Welshmen of his age, an advocate of international peace, religious freedom, Free Trade and a strong supporter of the Penny Post. He was also one of the chief supporters of the creation of a Union of Independent churches to promote co-operation between the Welsh Independent causes.

J. LLOYD THOMAS*

Pendref Independent Chapel, Llanfyllin.

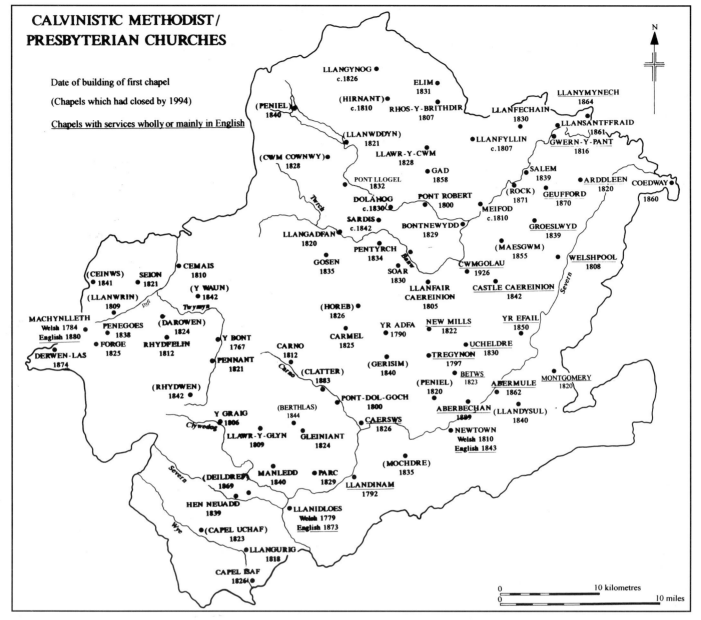

**CALVINISTIC METHODIST /
PRESBYTERIAN CHURCHES**

Date of building of first chapel

(Chapels which had closed by 1994)

Chapels with services wholly or mainly in English

N

LLANGYNOG ●
c.1826

ELIM
1831

(HIRNANT) ●
c.1810

RHOS-Y-BRITHDIR
1807

LLANYMYNECH
1864

LLANFECHAIN
1830

LLANSANTFFRAID
(1861)

(PENIEL) ●
1840

(LLANWDDYN)
1821

LLANFYLLIN
c.1807

GWERN-Y-PANT
1816

(CWM COWNWY) ●
1828

LLAWR-Y-CWM
1828

SALEM
1839

ARDDLEEN
1820

COEDWAY
1860

GAD
1858

(ROCK)
1871

GEUFFORD
1870

PONT LLOGEL
1832

DOLÀHOG
c.1830

PONT ROBERT
1800

MEIFOD
c.1810

GROESLWYD
1839

SARDIS ●
c.1842

BONTNEWYDD
1829

LLANGADFAN
1820

PENTYRCH
1834

(MAESGWM)
1855

WELSHPOOL
1808

GOSEN
1835

SOAR
1830

CWMGOLAU
1926

CEMAIS
1810

SEION
1821

(CEINWS) ●
1841

(Y WAUN) ●
1842

LLANFAIR
CAEREINION
1805

CASTLE CAEREINION
1842

(LLANWRIN)
1809

(HOREB) ●
1826

YR EFAIL
1850

MACHYNLLETH
Welsh 1784
English 1880

PENEGOES ●
1838

(DAROWEN) ●
1824

YR ADFA ●
1790

NEW MILLS
1822

CARMEL
1825

FORGE
1825

RHYDFELIN
1812

Y BONT
1767

UCHELDRE
1830

DERWEN-LAS
1874

PENNANT
1821

CARNO
1812

(CLATTER)
1883

(GERISIM)
1840

TREGYNON
1797

BETWS
1823

ABERMULE
1862

MONTGOMERY
1820

(RHYDWEN) ●
1842

(PENIEL)
1820

PONT-DOL-GOCH
1800

(LLANDYSUL)
1840

Y GRAIG ●
1806

(BERTHLAS)
1844

ABERBECHAN
1899

CAERSWS
1826

LLAWR-Y-GLYN
1809

GLEINIANT
1824

NEWTOWN
Welsh 1810
English 1843

(DEILDREF)
1869

MANLEDD
1840

PARC
1829

(MOCHDRE)
1835

HEN NEUADD
1839

LLANDINAM
1792

(CAPEL UCHAF) ●
1823

LLANIDLOES
Welsh 1779
English 1873

LLANGURIG
1818

CAPEL ISAF
1826

0   10 kilometres

0   10 miles

Calvinistic Methodists

The great pioneer of Welsh Calvinistic Methodism was Howell Harris of Trefeca, and he had a considerable influence on the emergence of the movement in Montgomeryshire. He first visited the county early in 1738, and returned on a number of subsequent occasions. The result of these visits was the establishment of numerous societies (seiadau), being groups of people who met to discuss religious topics and to share their spiritual experiences. At a General Assembly held in Carmarthenshire on 1 March 1743, a certain Morgan Hughes was given responsibility for the societies at Tyddyn (Llandinam), Mochdre, Bwlch Cae Haidd (Aberhafesb), Llanwyddelan, Llanllugan, Llanfair

Caereinion, Llanbrynmair, Llanidloes and Trefeglwys. He was to be assisted by Benjamin Cadman of Llandinam, Lewis Evan of Llanllugan and Thomas Bowen of Tyddyn, Llandinam. At the same time Richard Tibbott of Llanbrynmair was recalled to Pembrokeshire to assist in his native county.

It was also decided that representatives of the societies of Montgomeryshire and Radnorshire should hold monthly meetings to be chaired by the great hymn-writer of Welsh Methodism, William Williams of Pantycelyn. A number of these monthly meetings were held at Tyddyn, Llandinam, where the

76

Bowen family provided a vital early centre for the development of Methodism in the county. Further societies came into being; reports made at General Assemblies later in the 1740s noted groups meeting at Carno, Darowen, Llangynog and Betws Cedewain. Serving these groups were a number of hard-working missionaries and lay-preachers such as Evan Jenkins and Rheinallt Cleaton at Llanidloes, Thomas Meredith at Mochdre, Andrew and Richard Whitaker at Llanwyddelan, Evan Thomas and Benjamin Rowland at Llandinam and Edward Oliver and David Jehu at Llanfair Caereinion.

During the eighteenth century Calvinistic Methodism took a hold on numerous areas in the county, and the influence of the three great revivalists, Howell Harris, Daniel Rowland and William Williams was considerable. In 1750, however, a serious rift occurred between Harris and Rowland which impeded the progress of the Revival for some time. Most of the Montgomeryshire societies sided with Howell Harris, holding their own assemblies at a number of locations in the county in the early 1750s. Richard Tibbott worked hard to try to bring about some compromise, but in 1752 Harris moved to Trefeca where he established his "Family" of followers. Many Methodists moved from Montgomeryshire to Trefeca, and Hannah Bowen of Tyddyn, Llandinam, was for some time the "Mother" of this "Family".

The Methodist Revival eventually recovered from this potentially destructive period, and during the latter years of the eighteenth century the various societies began to build meeting houses. Hitherto they had met chiefly in each others' homes and in barns, but in 1767 their first chapel was built in Bont, Llanbrynmair. It was followed by chapels at Llanidloes (1779), Machynlleth (c.1784), Adfa (1790), Llandinam (1792) and Tregynon (1797). Sunday Schools were another important force that accompanied the Revival, and there were a number of industrious teachers in numerous parts of the county such as John Pierce and Humphrey Gwalchmai at Llanidloes, Ishmael Jones at Llandinam, Evan Griffiths at Meifod and John Hughes at Pontrobert.

In 1811 the Methodists formally left the Established Church. This resulted in the building of a number of new chapels, for the Methodists no longer attended the parish church for Communion. The Sunday School movement also gathered strength in the early nineteenth century and the establishment of new Sunday Schools often led eventually to the building of a small chapel and the growth of new causes. This largely accounts for the great number of small chapels with tiny congregations that the Methodists have in the county. Between 1805 and 1818 fifteen chapels were built in Montgomeryshire, and a further forty had been built by 1840. By today, some of the more remote chapels have been closed, and others that were formerly Welsh causes now hold their worship in English. Nevertheless, the majority still worship in Welsh, in the language of Ann Griffiths and John Hughes, Pontrobert, two of the foremost hymn-writers of Welsh nonconformity.

GOMER M. ROBERTS*

The interior of Adfa Calvinistic Methodist Chapel.

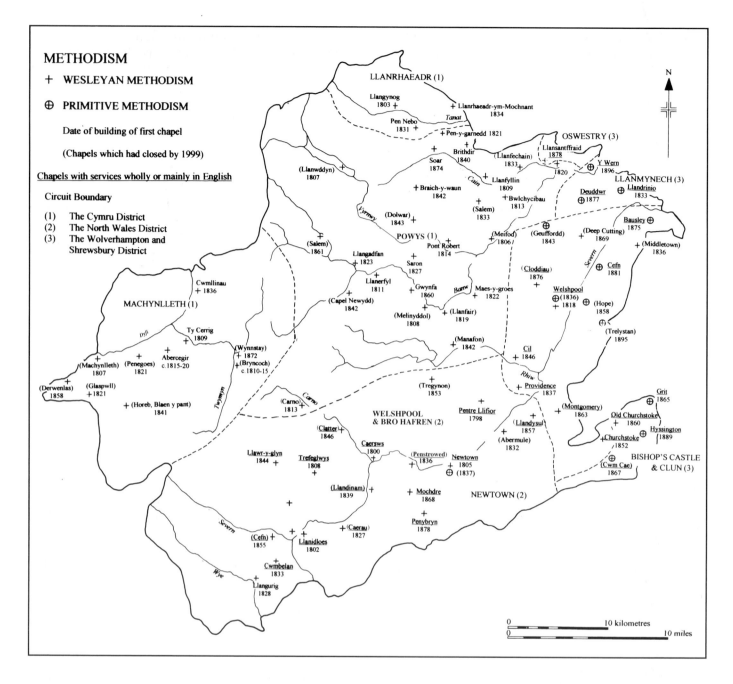

Wesleyan and Primitive Methodism

John Wesley passed through western Montgomeryshire on a number of occasions on his frequent travels between north and south Wales, and he also travelled from Shrewsbury to Cardiganshire on at least three occasions. He preached to large congregations in Llanidloes Market in February 1748, April 1749 and July 1764, and on his last visit to the county in 1769, he visited Welshpool, Newtown and, once again, Llanidloes. Other itinerant preachers also passed through the county at various times during this period. From 1770 onwards a number of preachers from Brecon did much to further the cause of Wesleyan Methodism in the county, establishing the first permanent cause at Pentre Llifior between Berriew and Betws Cedewain in 1778, followed by Newtown towards the end of the century. In 1798 a chapel was built at Pentre Llifior at a cost of £218!

One of Wesley's best known itinerant preachers was the hymn-writer and pamphleteer Thomas Olivers, born at Tregynon in 1725. Much of his life was spent preaching outside Wales and his contemporaries do seem to have seen him as the rougher cutting edge of the Methodist revival. One unsympathetic critic described him as Wesley's 'bully in chief' and Wesley himself called him both 'dear Tommy' and 'a rough stick of wood.' He died in 1799, and lies buried in Wesley's chapel in the City Road, London.

The English causes in the county were well-established before Welsh-language Wesleyan preachers came to Montgomeryshire from 1800 onwards. Initially, small groups of converts met in their houses to worship, whilst other congregations met in places such as the old Smithy at Llangurig or an old woollen factory at Llanrhaeadr. As time went by the congregations were able to build chapels as centres for their worship, though some smaller groups, long since defunct, continued to meet in houses. The Welsh Wesleyan Press was situated in the county at Llanfair Caereinion (1824-27) and Llanidloes (1827-59).

One of the most important divisions that took place in the history of Methodism was the formation at Stafford in 1810 of Primitive Methodism. A radical evangelical movement, some of its missionaries had reached the east of the county by 1823 and by 1840 they had established small chapels at Llandrinio and Welshpool. They made no progress elsewhere in the county however, and in 1932 the two branches joined ranks to form the Methodist Church.

Most of the present chapels in the county have only a small membership. They are organized in circuits, as are all Methodist chapels, which in turn belong to a particular District.

A. M. JONES

Pentre Llifior Chapel, Berriew.

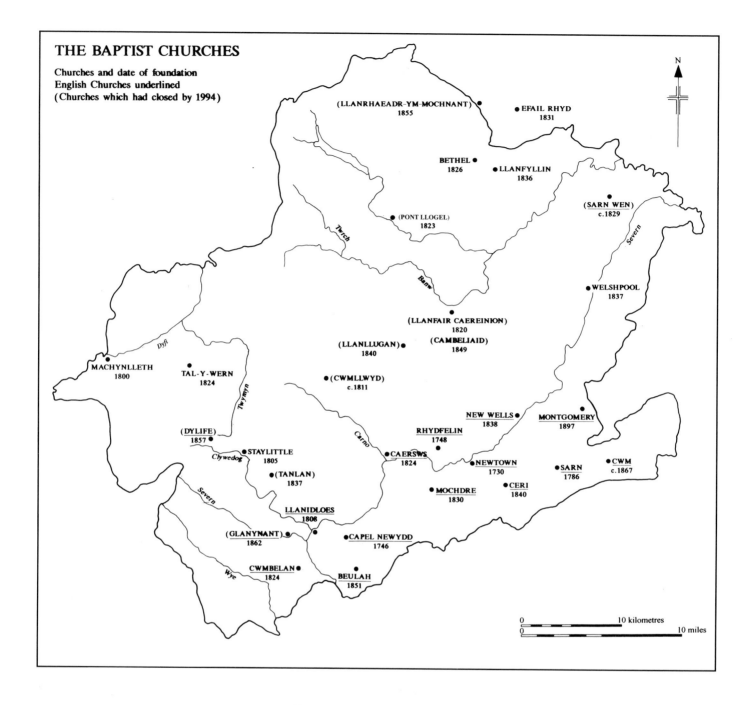

THE BAPTIST CHURCHES

Churches and date of foundation
English Churches underlined
(Churches which had closed by 1994)

N

(LLANRHAEADR-YM-MOCHNANT)
1855

● EFAIL RHYD
1831

BETHEL ●
1826

● LLANFYLLIN
1836

(SARN WEN)
c.1829

(PONT LLOGEL)
1823

● WELSHPOOL
1837

(LLANFAIR CAEREINION)
1820

(LLANLLUGAN) ●
1840

(CAMBELIAID)
1849

MACHYNLLETH
1800

TAL-Y-WERN
1824

● (CWMLLWYD)
c.1811

NEW WELLS ●
1838

MONTGOMERY
1897

(DYLIFE)
1857 ●

● STAYLITTLE
1805

RHYDFELIN
1748

● CAERSWS
1824

● NEWTOWN
1730

● SARN
1786

● CWM
c.1867

● (TANLAN)
1837

● CERI
1840

● MOCHDRE
1830

LLANIDLOES
1808

(GLANYNANT) ●
1862

● CAPEL NEWYDD
1746

CWMBELAN ●
1824

BEULAH
1851

Dyfi

Twrch

Banw

Severn

Carno

Twymyn

Clywedog

Severn

Wye

0   10 kilometres
0   10 miles

The Baptists

One of the key dates in the history of Protestant Nonconformity in England and Wales is 1689. With the accession of William III and his wife Mary to the throne, following an era of post-Restoration repression a new period of relative freedom, if not exactly of prosperity, dawned on the Protestant Dissenting communities of the land. Nowhere was this welcomed more than among the Baptists of Montgomeryshire whose sufferings after 1660 had been acute. Vavasor Powell, their leader, had spent much of the final decade of his life imprisoned in Shrewsbury, the Fleet and Caronne House, Lambeth, where he had died, in great pain, aged 53 in 1678.

The reputation which was gained by his deputy and successor, Henry Williams of Ysgafell near Newtown, for enduring hardship was no less remarkable than Vavasor's. Unwilling to conform to the legal restrictions of the Clarendon Code imposed upon Nonconformists following 1660, he too spent nine years imprisoned during which time his home was repeatedly ransacked and eventually burned down, his wife and children were abused and his father died after an attack by opponents. Following his release from prison he was set upon more than once while preaching and was fortunate, it is said, to escape with his life. The story of 'the field of blessing', the one field left untouched by his plunderers which bore fruit a hundred-fold thus helping to recompense him for revenue losses from fines, became part of Nonconformist mythology in the area for years to come. Henry Williams died, aged 60, in 1685.

Baptist witness had been introduced into Montgomeryshire during the Puritan ascendancy of the 1640s and 50s, though its nature was less dogmatically defined than that which characterised the movement in neighbouring counties. Despite Vavasor Powell's undergoing of the rite of believer's baptism in 1655, his emphasis was upon gathering congregations of Protestant Dissenters, paedo-Baptists as well as credo-Baptists, rather than forming specifically Baptist churches. His own church, the main gathering of which was centred upon Llanbrynmair, practised both forms of the rite. Nor had the unambiguously Baptist causes in mid-Wales - Hugh Evans' Radnorshire Arminians around Dolau, John Lewis' Calvinist community at Glasgwm in the same county, the Brecknockshire open-communion church led by Thomas Evans of Llanafan, to say nothing of the most northerly of John Lewis' closed-communion congregations, those Hay-on-Wye and Olchon, - penetrated sufficiently far north to have made any effect upon the population of Montgomeryshire. The general paucity of the Baptist presence in the county throughout the 18th century stems from this fact.

Following the generations of Vavasor Powell and Henry Williams, the Baptist cause in the area weakened considerably. Apart from the continued existence of the small congregation at Garth and Capel Newydd in the parish of Llandinam, which was finally received into the south-eastern association as the Nantgwyn church in 1797, it was not until the end of the eighteenth century that a new Baptist church was established. With help from David Evans, minister of Dolau in Radnorshire, a sixteen member fellowship was incorporated at Rhydfelin near Newtown in 1792 from which developed by 1810 a separate congregation in Newtown itself. For the next 20 years, until his untimely death aged 49 in 1831, its pastor was John Jones 'of Newtown' who enjoyed much success as a preacher, evangelist and church planter. Through his zeal and hard work daughter congregations were formed at such places as Sarn, Ceri, Mochdre, New Wells, Llanfair Caereinion and Caersws. Without doubt he was one of the two major figures responsible for the renewal of Baptist life in Montgomeryshire during the early nineteenth century.

The other important name is that of Thomas Thomas, pastor at Nantgwyn, who settled there from Carmarthenshire via the Bristol Baptist College in 1802. Like John Jones he too planted churches, at Staylittle, Llanidloes and Cwmbelan, and by the end of his career - he died an octogenarian in 1852 - he had had the satisfaction of seeing the Baptist cause becoming firmly rooted in the county's soil. The first half of the 19th century was an age of rapid, and in some places startling, expansion for Orthodox Dissent throughout Wales. Amongst those to benefit from this advance were the Montgomeryshire Baptists and such of their leaders as John Jones, his successor Benjamin Price, 'Cymro Bach', and Thomas Thomas.

By the mid nineteenth century there were as many as twenty-five separate and burgeoning Baptist fellowships in Montgomeryshire. Apart from those mentioned above others had grown from missionary efforts from both without and within the county. Since 1776 there had been a concerted campaign to spread the Baptist message from its Welsh heartland in the South, in Gwent and Dyfed especially, to North Wales. The missioners had, since around 1796, been invited to preach regularly at Machynlleth on their way into Gwynedd. Those who responded to their preaching by seeking baptism were initially incorporated into church membership at Aberystwyth but in 1800 a separate fellowship was formed in Machynlleth itself. The Aberystwyth minister, John James, took pastoral responsibility for the new cause and used it as a base to extend the movement's influence further afield. As a result the church at Cwmllwyd was planted around 1811 as was that at Tal-y-wern some ten years later. The Cwmllwyd fellowship in turn took its missionary responsibility sufficiently seriously to establish further churches, one at Pont Llogel in 1823 and another at Llanllugan in 1840. So too did the

Staylittle fellowship establish daughter congregations, at Tanlan in 1837 and in the mining area of Dylife twenty years later. At the opposite end of the county the churches of Bethel and Llanfyllin were formed, in 1826 and 1836 respectively, through the efforts of the long established Baptist cause at Glyn Ceiriog in Denbighshire. Other churches such as Beulah, Llanrhaeadr-ym-Mochnant, Cwm and Montgomery were formed in the latter part of the century.

The period of confidence, buoyancy and advance in Montgomeryshire Baptist life was that of the first four decades of the nineteenth century. The consolidation, which occurred thereafter has yielded, during the present century, to a marked weakening of the movement's presence in the county as elsewhere. Between rural depopulation and the process of secularization, the churches in Wales have been forced to meet new and often painful challenges. However, the truth of the Christian faith stands and it retains its hold on a not insignificant number of the people of Montgomeryshire to the present day.

D. DENSIL MORGAN

Newtown Baptist Chapel.

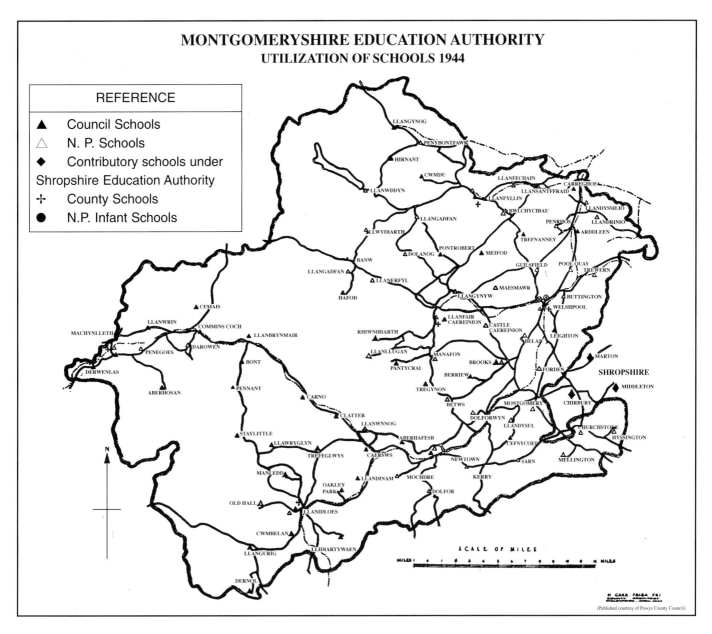

MONTGOMERYSHIRE EDUCATION AUTHORITY
UTILIZATION OF SCHOOLS 1944

REFERENCE

▲ Council Schools
△ N. P. Schools
◆ Contributory schools under
Shropshire Education Authority
✛ County Schools
● N.P. Infant Schools

(Published courtesy of Powys County Council)

Education

Any general survey of education in Montgomeryshire can by definition only give a bird's eye view of the complicated sometimes intricate, pattern of changes that occurred. Of necessity many developments have been summarily recorded or the barest outline indicated for in its entirety it is a rich, sometimes confusing but always vibrant story – a worthy testimony to the efforts of many men and women who by their dedicated efforts enabled the children of their remote, extensive rural county to have a measure of deserved opportunity.

Prior to the Government assuming responsibility for education in 1870 the provision in Wales as a whole

and indeed in Montgomeryshire had been scant and represented rather ephemeral and fleeting attempts to alleviate the situation. Few distinct organized movements can be discerned. The first came in mid seventeenth century under the Puritan regime with the short-lived experiment by which the Puritans strove to establish free schools. A sixth of the tithes of Wales was devoted to their maintenance, in common with all the other Welsh counties. Montgomeryshire saw schools established at Welshpool, Montgomery and Llanidloes in 1650 and in Llansantffraid a year later; then in 1652 at Llanfyllin, Llanfair Caereinion, Newtown and Machynlleth. With a paucity of evidence on their working it was probable they emulated the other Grammar Schools of the period, following on the Classics and the English Bible.

Later in the seventeenth century came the second movement, the Welsh Trust, supported by both Anglicans and Nonconformists. Its short term aim was assumedly and exclusively religious; in order to facilitate this their books were published in Welsh – the language of the people so that the proselytizing force could be given maximum momentum. In the longer term the Trust also sought to establish schools. Within the county these were set up at Welshpool (41 pupils), Meifod (32 pupils), Criggion (20 pupils) and Guilsfield (12 pupils).

The third initiative came with the work of the Society for the Promotion of Christian Knowledge; here again there were strong parallels with that of the Welsh Trust but it was confined to members of the Church of England. Whereas in England its curriculum also embraced useful trades, in Wales it was confined to reading and catechizing. Between 1699 and 1740 twelve charity schools were set up in the county: at Kerry, Llanfihangel, Llanfyllin (two schools), Mathafarn, Llanbrynmair, Llanerfyl and Meifod. However the attempt to impose a pattern of provision devised for urban areas failed to meet the requirements of rural Wales. By 1720 most of the schools had foundered. The few Charity Schools set up by Nonconformists in the county, including one at Montgomery, were unsuccessful apart from the school at Llanbrynmair set up in 1711 under the terms of the will of the Reverend Doctor Daniel Williams of Wrexham. It survived and eventually became the British school.

Fourthly, although having a large adult education element, the Circulating School Movement, established by the Reverend Griffith Jones, Vicar of Llanddowror, was of considerable significance in the country. In Montgomeryshire schools were established in Llanfair Caereinion and Llanidloes but more especially in the villages in the remote parts. The schools were normally conducted in Welsh, the only way to reach the mass of the population. In Montgomeryshire the approach of taking the schools to the people rather than expecting them to travel to particular fixed centres suited admirably such an extensive sparsely-populated county. After Griffith Jones's death the work was continued under the leadership of Bridget Bevan, daughter of John Vaughan of Derllys near Carmarthen; with her death

in 1779 the schools declined and foundered as a result of losing her guidance and the gradual emergence of the schools of the National Society.

An illustration of the approach adopted in establishing the schools in Montgomeryshire under Bridget Bevan is found in the records relating to the parish of Llangynog. They record that Richard Vaughan was the schoolmaster appointed by the Trustees in 1817 and that the school had been established in the following parishes 1817 at Llangadfan; 1819 at Garthbeibio; 1821 at Llanwddyn; 1823 at Pennant; 1825 at Llangynog; 1827 at Llanwddyn (second time); 1829 at Hirnant; 1831 at Pennant (second time); 1833 at Llangadfan (second time); 1836 at Llangynog (second time); 1837 again at Llangynog. Yet the Commissioners of Enquiry in their Report of 1847 criticized some of the inadequacies of their schools during this period.

Although possibly marginal to the mainstream of educational development in the county, the outstanding contribution of nonconformity made by the Sunday School movement led by the Reverend Thomas Charles of Bala to popular education needs to be recognized. The Sunday School movement had an early impetus in Montgomeryshire. The first Sunday School in Wales was recorded near Llanidloes in 1770, sixteen years before the schools were to become general in Wales. In addition an afternoon school was held in Tregynon in 1783 and at Llanwyddelan in 1789 and also at Pontrobert at that time. In 1805 a meeting of the Association for the Sunday School movement was held at Llanfair Caereinion at which the Reverend Thomas Charles himself spoke. His eloquent address was received with enthusiasm and it heralded a new beginning for the movement in the county. The movement although outside the mainstream development had a very significant influence on attitudes towards education throughout the eighteenth and nineteenth centuries in Montgomeryshire; it also had a formative effect on views prevailing towards the Education Act of 1870 and its subsequent implementation and policy in the county.

Religion and education were not only linked through the Sunday Schools. The other agencies which provided much of the elementary education during the nineteenth century were religious bodies, originated in England, the National Society founded by the Church of England and the British Society sponsored by the Nonconformists. The National

Society proved to be far more successful in establishing schools. By around 1850 there were 375 National Schools, yet fewer than fifty British schools. The National Society for promoting the Education of the poor in the principles of the Established Church was founded in 1811 to establish schools on the monitorial principle. In effect it was a direct continuation of the charity schools organization of the previous century since the Society was sponsored by the S.P.C.K. Its ambitious aim was to establish a school in every parish in England and Wales; this hinged on only one master being required to convey information to monitors who in turn instructed the younger pupils. Their aim was to educate the poor, inculcating the virtues of humility, honesty and hard work together with the acceptance of one's station in life thus contributing towards social harmony. Inevitably the education provided was minimal.

The early period of expansion between 1811 and 1817 saw 33 schools built or affiliated, mainly in North Wales. Montgomeryshire figured prominently in their development. The first National School to be established in the county was at Montgomery in 1812. Others followed, Welshpool in 1821, Meifod in 1825, Llandrinio in 1827, Machynlleth in 1829 and Llanidloes in 1845. In contrast the British Schools movement made much slower progress; by 1843 there were only two such schools in the whole of North Wales. Some others including Llanidloes survived for a short duration.

Thus despite the efforts of both societies by 1846 there were severe inadequacies in the existing provision which were highlighted in a report published by the National Society in 1845. Subsequent efforts, notably by William Williams, M.P. for Coventry, emphasizing the need for improvement resulted in the setting up of a Commission of Enquiry on educational provision in Wales. The uproar which ensued following the publication of the report, 'Brad y Llyfrau Gleision' has been fully documented elsewhere. Its indictment of the alleged moral depravity, ignorance and barbarism of the Welsh nation entered the folk memory and created lasting bitterness. They helped sharpen the edge of radicalism and nonconformist opinion.

The report on Montgomeryshire was particularly scathing: 'No county in North Wales has been so much neglected in respect of education. The schools are not different in number but they remain for the most part in the transition state and bear more resemblance to the Private Adventure Schools, being in a great measure self-supported and held in churches, chapels or cottages, but rarely in a school built for that purpose. The parishes of Newtown, Llanllwchaearn, Llanidloes and the scattered inhabitants of the minor parishes at the foot of the Berwyn mountains have experienced the worst consequences from the want of education.'

The Commissioners identified two main causes for the unsatisfactory state of education in the existing schools in the county, the inadequate and unsuitable buildings and poor training and lack of quality of the great majority of teachers. Of the 120 schools situated in the county at the time of the inspection only 35 were conducted in school rooms, the lowest percentage provision in North Wales. Thus the 85 other schools utilized a range of premises such as chapels, churches, cottages, shops and even kitchens and bedrooms. Numerous examples in the Report illustrated this. At Llanllugan the church school was held in the church itself which was reported to be cold and damp. At Llanerfyl the schoolmaster of the free school which had 20 pupils although he had conducted the school for 18 years had never been trained to teach. In addition he was also tenant and farmed the estate of 41 acres on his own account and this seemed to occupy a large portion of his time. The inspector had to make several visits to his school before he could be found at home; he apparently made regular visits to the fair. He stated 'I learn 'em to read, spell and write too; nothing more is required here'.

At Llanfair Caereinion the Inspectors deplored the absence of any provision. However, there was a significant reason for this situation. The ministers and deacons of chapels in the area Horeb, Siloh and the Calvinistic chapel, Llanfair Caereinion submitted 'A memorial upon the State and Prospects of Education in the parish.' They had undertaken their own comprehensive survey and tabulated the information ascertained – the population, linguistic background and in particular the tremendous support accorded the Sunday Schools.

They argued that the parish of Llanfair Caereinon was proverbially a place of dissent. Further that the contribution of 21 Sunday Schools within and on the borders of the parish needed to be recognized. They instanced also the fourteen chapels built at a cost of

£3,600. Finally they condemned the injustice of also having to pay tithes to the established church. However an active committee had been set up to establish a British school in Llanfair Caereinion and the school opened in 1848. Two years previously applications to landowners met with little success. Similar submissions were also made on behalf of Castle Caereinion and Manafon.

At Newtown the Inspector noted "It appears that previously to the year 1845 no district was more neglected in respect of education than the parishes of Newtown and Llanllwchaiarn. The effects were partly seen in the turbulent and seditious state of the neighbourhood in the year 1839". Again it deplored 'the circulation of even at the present day low and unprincipled publications of a profane and seditious tendency also operatives have access to the writings of Paine and Volney, to Owen's tracts and to newspapers and periodicals of the same pernicious tendency'.

Such were the inadequacies and shortcomings of the schools that the commissioners discovered. By the 1860s there were growing demands on the government for a national system of education. However some nonconformists still adamantly opposed any state-sponsored assistance which they saw as a means of securing Church dominance in education. Yet in the intervening period some progress had been made: between 1848 and 1870 twenty church schools had been established under the voluntary system and four British schools in the county.

Eventually the Forster Education Act of 1870 was passed which gave increased aid to the National and British societies and time for them 'to fill in the gaps' in provision. The gaps which remained would be filled by locally elected school boards. There resulted strong nonconformist opposition in Wales with its large preponderance of Church schools which continued to give denominational instruction under the Act. Yet the 1870 Education Act had a significant impact in Montgomeryshire. However its implementation was influenced directly by the strength of nonconformity in much of the county which occasioned considerable controversy as the landlords and church endeavoured to retain their erstwhile dominance and opposed establishment of School Boards. In some parishes agreement was easier; so by June 1871 measures had been taken to elect School Boards in Carno, Llandinam, Llangurig,

Llanidloes, Llanllwchaearn, Newtown and Trefeglwys. Initially Welshpool and Berriew both rejected the proposal, the Nonconformists at Berriew reluctantly conceding after pressure from the Church and squire. The Endowed Schools Amendment Bill of 1874 caused the religious debate to be continued. Eventually these difficulties were, to a considerable extent, overcome. In some areas such as Trefeglwys, the Board had to establish completely new schools. The Llawryglyn school was opened in May 1873 the first new Board School in Montgomeryshire; the new school at Staylittle was completed a month later. The third school in the district the Gleiniant School was formerly the Trefeglwys British School and transferred to the Board in October 1871. Thus by June 1873 sixteen parishes – a quarter of the parishes in the county - had adopted the provisions of the Act, and in all between 1870 and 1902 British Board Schools and twelve church schools were built in the county.

In the period 1902 to 1906 the whole administration of the elementary schools in the county was convulsed with a bitter and protracted dispute caused by the passing of the Education Act of 1902. The Act itself enabled the County Council to become the Local Education Authority; however the measure encountered bitter opposition at the proposal to support the Voluntary Schools by means of the rates. Naturally given the strong Liberal-Nonconformist tradition of the county, there were strong objections to the measure; it was regarded as an attempt at the abolition of popular control of elementary education and the permanent establishment and endowment of sectarian schools. Again the religious test imposed upon teachers in the Voluntary Schools was resented.

One of the intentions behind the Act was to safeguard the future of the Church Schools, for whereas the Board Schools had received assistance from the rates under the Education Act of 1870, the Church Schools did not. Thus, despite its merits on other counts, the Act of 1902 was bitterly opposed by the Nonconformists because it ensured that denominational education would be provided at the cost of the ratepayers. Thus for the next four years the Montgomeryshire Liberals and the Montgomeryshire County Council were deeply embroiled in the struggle. An attempt in 1903 to work out a compromise with the Church Authorities failed and eventually as part of a Liberal-Nonconformist campaign mounted throughout Wales, the County Council refused to implement the

Act and cut off funds from the Non-Provided Schools. The Government replied with the Education (Local Authority Default) Act; Montgomeryshire became one of the leading counties in the struggle and in July 1905 the Act was applied against it. Eventually in December 1905 the Conservative Government fell and its successor, the Liberal Government of Campbell Bannerman announced that it would not implement the 'coercion' Act. Thus by January 1906 a measure of harmony was restored and the Education Authority renewed its work.

For a number of reasons the Education Authority pursued an extremely frugal policy, exercising the strictest economy in education. As a result of the Education Act of 1902 all British Schools were transferred to the Authority together with Tregynon Church School and Mellington Church School which had been purchased. In addition the Authority had built new schools at Pennal, Llangurig and also at Clatter, Llanwnnog so that by 1908 there were 61 Voluntary Schools (including Mochdre) and 39 Council Schools. Furthermore the Authority had to spend additional amounts of money bringing the Council Schools up to an acceptable standard of repair following the take-over subsequent to the Act. In addition the condition of the Voluntary Schools was enhanced as a result of pressure brought to bear by the Authority and the Board of Education so that by 1908 the Chairman of the Education Authority claimed schools of both classes had been considerably improved structurally.

However, the dominant trend in the period was the Authority's pursuit of a deliberate policy of keeping down the rates and the preoccupation of the Education Committee with running the service as economically as possible was reflected in the education service in the inter-war years. Thus between the Education Act of 1902 and the outbreak of the Second World War in 1939, only sixteen new Council Schools and three new Church Schools were built in Montgomeryshire. Concurrently the inter-war years saw a gradual decrease in the school population. Thus whereas in 1912 there were 8,764 elementary school children by March 1938 this number had fallen to 6,048 — a decrease of 30%. Subsequently although in 1913 there were 112 schools or departments — 58% of whom had 60 pupils or fewer; only 19 schools had over 100 pupils — the remainder between 60 and 100. This undoubtedly reflected the sparsely populated and extensive nature of this rural county. Thus 81% of the schools had fewer than 100 pupils. Although some

new schools had been built and improvements made at a limited number of others, the situation remained far from satisfactory; thirty Church Schools and six Council Schools had been built before 1870 and twelve, still utilized, dated from the time of the 1847 Commissioners Enquiry. Much still needed to be done.

In 1926 the Haden Report, 'the Education of the Adolescent' focused attention on the needs of the older pupil in the elementary school. However, the severe economic recession of the inter-war years prevented any effective implementation of new policies in such impoverished rural counties, thus reorganization schemes formulated in 1930 and 1936 in Montgomeryshire remained unfulfilled. The one significant change had been the extension of practical activities in Handicraft, Domestic Science and Gardening in the thirties in the elementary schools. By 1938 1,650 senior pupils still remained in the elementary schools. However, a Senior School had been opened at Machynlleth in 1937 and at Welshpool in 1939. In addition a 'Senior Top' was established at Banw School.

However, it was not until 1944 with the passing of the Butler Education Act that a dramatic transformation took place in the elementary schools of the county. T. Glyn Davies was appointed Director of Education in 1943 and energetically led the process of reorganization. Thus by July 1946 the Development Plan for Primary and Secondary Education in the County, as required by the Act, was completed.

In 1945 there were ninety-five elementary schools in the County, fifty one Provided and forty-four non-Provided schools. Seventy four of the schools had been built before the 1902 Act; thirty four of the schools had been built before 1870. According to previous standards the elementary schools accommodated 9,752 pupils but as a result of continual depopulation there were only 5,235 pupils on books. Since 1921 nine schools had been closed but the vast majority were one or two teacher schools. The transfer of all children over eleven to the secondary schools under the terms of the 1944 Education Act reduced their size even further and brought their viability into question. However, the Policy Committee resolved to adhere strongly to the principle of retaining the one or two teacher schools. Although a few schools were closed, three main principles were observed regarding the future policy on closures. Firstly that where appropriate two or three primary schools should be grouped and superseded by one new primary school with community provision; that rural children should not be transferred to town schools; that where the majority of children were Welsh-speaking they would be transferred to another Welsh school.

An ambitious building programme was begun to remedy the deficiences of the existing stock. By 1971 with the completion of Glantymwyn Primary and Community Centre replacing the four existing schools at Cemais, Commins Coch, Llanwrin and Darowen C. in W. the building programme was completed. It involved the building of seventeen new primary schools and extensive improvements and extensions at twenty six of the primary schools together with the building of three new Nursery and Infant Schools and three new Nursery wings attached to existing schools.

A significant decision taken by the Authority in 1947 recognized that certain of the primary schools should serve the needs of the whole community and that the new premises should be designed specifically as school and community centres. This innovation proved strikingly successful: the first was opened at Llanwddyn in 1950 and replicated at ten other centres in the County.

Following the publication of the Gittins Report, twelve one-teacher primary schools were closed. In 1965 the Gittins proposal advocating the creation of area primary schools with a minimum of three teachers was accepted.

Between 1967 and 1974 fifteen primary schools had been closed. Thus by the time of local government reorganization in 1974 the whole pattern of primary education in the county had been dramatically transformed. A virtual educational revolution had been carried through successfully giving larger schools with enhanced facilities which compared favourably with any other county in Wales and beyond. It said much for the vision and energy of those who drew up the Development Plan in 1946 and they, together with their successors brought an ambitious and far-sighted blueprint to effective reality. In the period since 1974 these policies have been continued and the primary schools of Montgomeryshire have responded to the new challenge and maintained their enviable record of achievement.

Montgomeryshire played a distinguished and leading role in the movement to bring intermediate education to the pupils of Wales. As with elementary education, there was a growing recognition of the overriding need for an effective system of intermediate education from the second half of the nineteenth century onwards. The sole 'grammar' school existing in the county was that at Deuddwr established by an endowment in 1690 by Andrew Newport. However by 1857 the school had declined and only about twenty pupils attended; even the Education Commissioners in 1847 criticized its inadequacies and to all intents and purposes it functioned as the elementary school for the locality. Although by 1875 its numbers were twenty four boarders and fifty four boys but apart from the head, the two staff were young and untrained. The only other Endowed Grammar School at Welshpool had ceased to function in 1837; by the early nineteenth century it had declined to an elementary school; eventually the schoolmaster absconded.

By the latter part of the nineteenth century the Liberal Nonconformists in the county, increasingly irked by the dominance of the Anglican-Conservative landowners pressed even more intently for reasonable provision to afford their children intermediate education. In 1880 when the Aberdare Committee appointed to enquire into Intermediate and Higher Education visited the County, a Liberal-Nonconformist deputation strongly pressed their case, instancing the heavy burden the middle class had to shoulder, spending some £175,000 to establish chapels with a further £10,000 a year to maintain them and citing that the eight private adventure schools for boys and six for girls were totally inadequate to meet the county's needs. Stuart Rendel, elected as Liberal M.P. for the County in 1880 and breaking the erstwhile dominance in the seat of the Wynns of Wynnstay, introduced the Intermediate Education Bill in 1889.

The response to the Intermediate Education Act in Montgomeryshire was whole-hearted and enthusiastic. Eventually, after much discussion and consultation, the Joint Education Committee (empowered under the Act) under the able chairmanship of A. C. Humphreys-Owen, a barrister and landowner of Berriew, formulated an intermediate education scheme for the county. Humphreys-Owen, who became the first chairman of Montgomeryshire County Council, advocated the principle Matthew Arnold enunciated of "taking the education to the doors of the pupils", thus siting the schools in the towns or larger villages and thereby establishing as many schools as possible consistent with efficiency. Eventually in 1893 the scheme was accepted whereby intermediate schools were to be established in the main towns of the County. The planning and implementation of the scheme were to be characterized by promptitude and foresight.

The first school was opened at Llanfair Caereinion in September 1894 and in the same month Newtown Boys Intermediate and Newtown Girls Intermediate also opened in temporary premises. Machynlleth Intermediate and Llanidloes Boys and Llanidloes Girls Intermediate followed a month later. Thus by the end of October 1894 and within a year of the County intermediate education scheme receiving parliamentary approval, four of the District Governing Bodies had opened their schools in temporary premises. Difficulties relating to the Berriew school endowment and the possibility of establishing an intermediate school there delayed matters at Welshpool; thus Welshpool Boys Intermediate and Welshpool Girls Intermediate opened on 30 April 1895. At Llanfyllin progress towards an intermediate school had been hindered by strong opposition of a local landowner and squire John Marshall Dugdale. However by 1895 Dugdale changed his mind and though under the official terms of the scheme the time had elapsed, the combined representations of Humphreys-Owen and Dugdale to the Charity Commissioners eventually enabled an amendment of the scheme to be secured so that a school was opened in temporary buildings at Llanfyllin on 12 November 1897.

In their early years the schools were plagued with daunting problems in particular the limitations imposed by temporary buildings, severe understaffing and the extensive incidence of early leaving by pupils. Fundamentally up until 1920 they were to remain small institutions which exposed them to particular weaknesses. Thus in 1906 numbers at Llanfair Caereinion slumped to a low level and Inspectors questioned the school's viability; however strong local representations prevented closure. Eventually low numbers and the financial difficulties compelled the amalgamation of Llanidloes Boys and Llanidloes Girls Intermediate in 1901. In the early period up until 1914 none of the schools exceeded 100 pupils; the majority hovered around 50. Yet the Fisher Education Act of 1918 afforded valuable financial assistance to the schools,

increasing support for those unable to pay fees. Thus by 1920 a number of schools had grown in size, particularly Machynlleth and Welshpool Girls, yet the majority just exceeded 100.

A distinctive feature of these years of the first decades of the century, after the schools had been established in permanent buildings, was the quest for an appropriate curriculum to reflect the distinctive needs of the neighbourhood served by the school. Machynlleth Intermediate concentrated with great success on developing Honours and Higher Certificate work in Classics and Languages, establishing an outstanding academic record. Welshpool Boys, whilst maintaining a sound academic record, pursued a distinctive trend with the introduction of Agriculture and an agricultural bias into the curriculum; whereas the idea was first mooted at Newtown Boys, the initiative had fallen away there. In contrast at Welshpool Boys it was developed effectively so from 1913 to 1916 the school was given a Ministry of Education grant to pursue this initiative and an impressive curriculum project was completed which won international recognition. Llanidloes Intermediate however eschewed the development of Higher School Certificate courses and concentrated instead on developing commercial courses, thus equipping pupils for their future careers. Newtown Boys Intermediate achieved a very sound academic record, particularly at Higher School Certificate level. The particular needs of the girls also received attention, particularly in the two separate Girls Schools at Newtown and Welshpool; courses focusing on the technical aspect of Intermediate education — Domestic Science and later Commercial work were skilfully developed. Llanfair Caereinion was limited severely by its small size and Higher School Certificate was not introduced until 1916.

Undoubtedly the nineteen twenties and early nineteen thirties were dominated by severe economies and retrenchment; a series of measures implemented such as increased fees, reduction in free places and decrease in staff all had a stultifying effect on the development of the schools. This brought a severe decline in school rolls: thus throughout the nineteen twenties the roll of all the schools did not exceed a hundred, Llanfair Caereinion remaining at fifty. A related problem was that of staff salaries with the introduction of the Burnham Scale provoking bitter disputes between Governors and staff at Machynlleth and Llanidloes.

The early thirties brought no respite with further curtailment of financial assistance for pupils. Despite this, certain schools, particularly Welshpool Boys and Welshpool Girls, Newtown Boys and Newtown Girls developed Higher School Certificate courses with creditable success, as did Llanfyllin despite its size and also Machynlleth in the late 1930s. Again at Senior Certificate level by the late thirties the schools with increased numbers achieved impressive results. Despite national initiatives Montgomeryshire Education Authority lacked the funds during the inter-war period to initiate a scheme for reorganization although plans were drawn up. However new Senior Schools were opened at Machynlleth in 1937 and Welshpool in 1939; a Senior "Top" was also established at Llangadfan School.

Thus at the end of the Second World War Montgomeryshire was ripe for sweeping changes and a virtual education revolution took place with many original features. In 1943 T. Glyn Davies was appointed Director of Education and he set about the task of reorganization energetically. By 1946 the Reorganization Sub-Committee had produced the Development Plan for the County and the County Surveyor had surveyed all school premises. In 1944 a junior technical school had been opened at Newtown for boys 13 to 15. The Development Plan represented a challenging and far-sighted attempt at a solution to the problems of reorganization of secondary education. The Plan proposed three more recommendations regarding the line of development in relation to secondary education. First, one technical school providing agricultural and technical education would be sufficient and more economic than several such centres; secondly the needs of the majority of children would be best met in secondary modern schools and thirdly that it was desirable that one grammar school with provision for residence should be set up. Four Bilateral (Grammar and Modern) schools would be established at Machynlleth, Llanfair Caereinion, Llanidloes and Llanfyllin. Its proposals were characterized by an imaginative range of innovative mechanisms to support effectively the concept of secondary education for all. Yet its most radical and original features found scant support from either the local population or the Ministry of Education. Thus, the proposals for a residential grammar school at Glansevern, midway between Newtown and Welshpool involving the closure of grammar schools at both towns was fiercely opposed and ultimately rejected. Similarly the idea for phased transfer of pupils at 11 and 13 with a network of secondary modern schools — an earlier version foreshadowing the much-lauded 'Leicestershire Plan' also did not find favour. Thus inevitably some of the most innovative elements of the plan did not survive the long process of public consultation and ministerial scrutiny that followed. In effect a greatly amended version of the Plan emerged and was finally implemented.

Nevertheless certain notable achievements were unarguably secured; the speed of their implementation being particularly impressive. By September 1945 the Intermediate and existing Senior Schools at Machynlleth were merged; it was claimed that this was the first experiment in bilateral education in England and Wales. This policy of establishing bilateral schools continued apace; thus by September 1947 the complete reorganization of the education of all children in the county over 11 had been achieved. The emasculated version of the plan that did emerge provided the framework for the future. Each town retained its school but now in a bi-lateral form, subsequently these became fully comprehensive with the decision in 1960 to close the Junior Technical School. It also enabled the Authority to abolish the special places examination although it was a further four years before this could be implemented in Welshpool.

Concurrently the Education Authority had embarked on an extensive building programme. By April 1949 large-scale extensions had been completed at Machynlleth. In 1953 new secondary bilateral schools were opened at Llanfair Caereinion (cost £135,000) and at Llanidloes (£132,000). A unique feature of the 20 acre site at Llanidloes was the provision of both bilateral and primary schools on one campus; at the time it was stated the scheme had no equal in any part of the country. In June 1954 the new Llanfyllin bilateral school building including an adapted extension (cost £116,237) was opened. A month previously, following the death of the headmaster of Welshpool Boys Grammar School, it had been decided to amalgmate the Boys' and Girls' Grammar School at Welshpool. Then in 1957 the new grammar-modern school at Newtown to house the Boys' and Girls' Bilateral Schools was opened, having cost £187,750. At the same time the Authority resolved to adopt the term 'High School' for the various bilaterals in the County. Finally in 1964 the Boys' and Girls' Bilateral Schools at Newtown were amalgamated into a mixed comprehensive school and a similar amalgamation took place at Welshpool of the Grammar and Secondary Schools to create another comprehensive school. The total cost of the building for the project exceeding £200,000.

Special provision had also been made by the Authority in their Post-War development for pupils with special education needs. In 1946 the Authority had taken initial steps to acquire two mansions, one at Cyfronnydd, Castle Caereinon and another at Brynllywarch, Kerry. The Cyfronnydd Residential School for Girls was officially opened in 1951 with 18 pupils; it accommodated girls ranging from 11 to 16 years. The Ministry of Education authorized the Committee to admit pupils from other parts of Wales. The Brynllywarch Residential School for Boys opened in September 1951 and in a similar scheme admitted pupils from all parts of Wales. Subsequently both schools developed successfully but in July 1974 it was decided to amalgamate the schools into a mixed residential school on the Brynllywarch site and the Cyfronnydd premises were closed.

A hundred years after A. C. Humphreys-Owen's vision of extending opportunities for the children of Montgomeryshire living in its sparsely populated area the High Schools of the 1990s strive with impressive achievement to continue to bring that dream to reality.

L. H. WILLIAMS

Gardening lessons at Darowen c.1906.

The new primary school at Llanfair Caereinion.

The new area primary school and community hall at Tregynon, project completed in 1996.

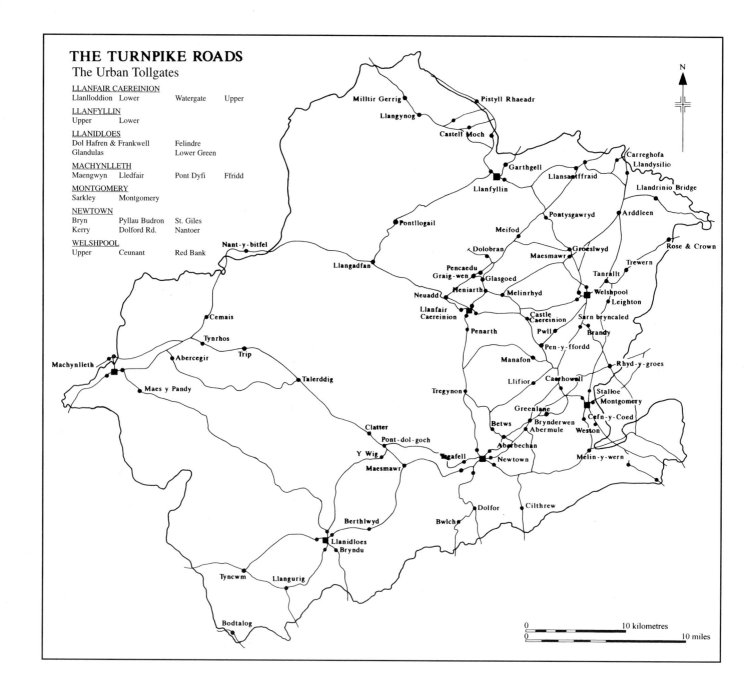

THE TURNPIKE ROADS
The Urban Tollgates

LLANFAIR CAEREINION
Llanlloddion   Lower   Watergate   Upper

LLANFYLLIN
Upper   Lower

LLANIDLOES
Dol Hafren & Frankwell   Felindre
Glandulas   Lower Green

MACHYNLLETH
Maengwyn   Lledfair   Pont Dyfi   Ffridd

MONTGOMERY
Sarkley   Montgomery

NEWTOWN
Bryn   Pyllau Budron   St. Giles
Kerry   Dolford Rd.   Nantoer

WELSHPOOL
Upper   Ceunant   Red Bank

0   10 kilometres
0   10 miles

The Turnpike Trusts

Until the mid 18th century roads were mere earthen tracks and were frequently quite impassable. Parishes were responsible for their upkeep and the townships which made up the parishes looked after their own particular sections of the road. With the increase of traffic and the need for better communications to facilitate agricultural and industrial developments this system became inadequate and it was deemed necessary to supplement it by more up to date means.

Enterprising local landowners organised themselves into companies or Turnpike Trusts which undertook the repair of roads. They obtained a return on their expenditure by levying tolls which varied in amount and were collected by keepers at the gates which were erected at intervals along the turnpiked roads.

The number of turnpike trusts increased rapidly from 1760 onwards; they were looked upon as sound investments and much local money was lent to them on the security of the tolls which were to be collected. However their income fell far short of what had been anticipated and the Trusts fell into debt. Such a public spirited figure as William Pugh of Brynllywarch, Kerry, was a great promoter of turnpiking and spent a considerable fortune on it without any remuneration at all.

The first roads to be turnpiked in Montgomeryshire were done by Shropshire Trusts - the road from Pool to Oswestry in 1756 and that from Pool to Salop in 1758. The first Montgomeryshire Turnpike Trusts were formed by Parliamentary Act 1769. This set up three Districts of roads in the county, each of which worked as a separate body and had its own group of Trustees. In 1834 a more comprehensive Act was passed which remained in force until the turnpike system ended. This rearranged the Districts and a 4th District was formed of the roads around Machynlleth. New and much higher tolls were enacted. Altogether over 400 miles were turnpiked in Montgomeryshire. By 1886 the system had come to an end and nearly all the roads of the county were free of gates and tolls.

The map shows the distribution of turnpike gates and houses for the entire period of the turnpike system. Not all gates shown on the map were in existence in any one year; some gates were taken down and re-erected elsewhere when new sections of road were made.

There was no great opposition to the tollgates in Montgomeryshire like the well known Rebecca riots which broke out in south west Wales in the 1840s, but three tollgates in the extreme south - Bodtalog, Llangurig and Glandulas - were attacked by rioters largely from Radnorshire.

Many of the tollhouses survive as dwelling houses and are usually easy to recognize, some turnpike roads have old and interesting milestones, which help to identify them.

E. R. Morris

A toll cottage for the former Llanfyllin north gate.

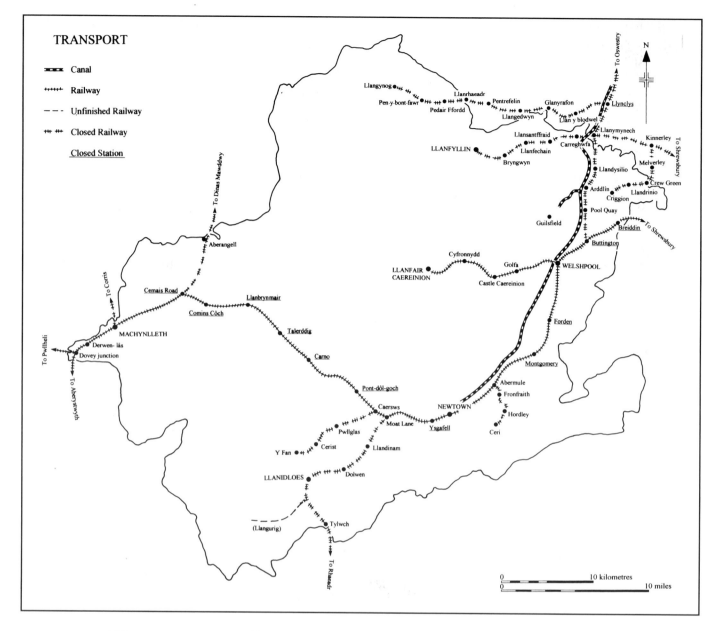

Transport from the eighteenth century

Until the industrial revolution gathered momentum during the latter part of the eighteenth century, there was little need for any form of organized transport in Montgomeryshire and as the county is virtually land-locked the mainly agrarian population had remained somewhat insular in character for many centuries. A short journey of some ten miles or so, which would be extremely modest by present day standards, would have represented a major undertaking and been attempted by only a small percentage of the population. The vast majority were content to live their entire lives within the restricted compass of a day's journey on foot. When travel did become necessary for the few, they relied upon inadequate tracks or poor roads, which were much affected by erosion and lack of maintenance.

During this period perhaps the most travelled people in Wales were the drovers who, in addition to herding the animals, were frequently called upon to transport letters or parcels on their journey to and from the markets in England.

The coming of the industrial revolution, however, brought about enormous changes in travel patterns. Initially these centred upon the development of a network of canals throughout England. This form of transport offered both economy of operation and a

Repairs to the aqueduct on the Montgomeryshire Canal at Berriew, c. 1880.

Pleasure cruisers now ply the Montgomeryshire Canal.

reduction of damage to goods whilst in transit. Progressive landowners, wool merchants and manufacturers quickly saw the advantages of the new system but construction of a Montgomeryshire branch to Newtown from the Ellesmere canal at Carreghofa was not completed until 1821.

Until this development, the use of water for transportation to Montgomeryshire had been confined to the use of the river Severn, which was navigable from the Bristol Channel as far as Pool Quay, whilst those who lived in the western part of the county with access to the coast via the river Dyfi enjoyed the advantages provided by the coastal shipping trade.

Lime, coal and bricks, together with cheaper by-products of the new English factories represent examples of materials brought into the county by canal, whilst wood and wool products, and much mineral wealth was transported in the reverse direction. Timber for building purposes was exported and Montgomeryshire oak was also in demand for shipbuilding, with at least one recorded incidence (May 1800) of a merchant sailing from distant Lanarkshire via Dublin to Derwenlas to purchase Dyfi valley oak for a new vessel.

Thus matters continued until the coming of the railways. As with the canal system the railway network was first developed and established in England. Trunk railways in Wales were confined to the north and south coast routes which linked London and Ireland (c1850). The remainder of the country apart from areas of heavy industry held little attraction for financial speculators with the result that great tracts of land, including the whole of

Montgomeryshire were bereft of the civilizing influence of the railways.

Yet there was no shortage of schemes and one of the greatest advocates of improved transport for the county - both rail and road - was the Reverend Samuel Roberts of Llanbrynmair, popularly known as 'S R'. Indeed the railways of Montgomeryshire were eventually financed, surveyed and largely built by the men of the county. Notable figures include the engineers Benjamin and Robert Piercey of Trefeglwys, the contractor David Davies of Llandinam and the brothers Abraham and David Howell, originally also from Llanbrynmair but later of Welshpool and Machynlleth respectively: as solicitors they were the 'generals' who ensured the viability and direction of the early railway schemes.

The question of finance was the principal stumbling block at the outset; scheme after scheme, usually instigated outside the county by the large English companies, failed to raise sufficient capital until it appeared that an 1852 plan for a railway from Shrewsbury to Aberystwyth, via Minsterley, Montgomery, Newtown, Llanidloes and Llangurig could succeed. Matters appeared to proceed satisfactorily until the promoters were influenced by the powerful London & North Western Railway Company to modify the route to exclude Montgomery in favour of a detour through Welshpool. Llanidloes was also avoided, thereby abandoning the difficult and costly section across Pumlumon, in order to follow an easier route westward from Newtown via Machynlleth and the Dyfi valley.

The people of Llanidloes, incensed at thus being deprived of a place in the scheme, resolved to plan, finance and construct their own railway, to be known as the Llanidloes and Newtown Railway (L&NR), to connect with the larger scheme at Newtown. Ironically the Bill for the Shrewsbury - Aberystwyth railway failed in parliament whilst the L&NR was successful. Construction of the Llanidloes line commenced in 1855 and it was opened for goods and passengers by September 1859.

The first of the Montgomeryshire lines was thus born in grand isolation, although at the time 'people laughed at it because it had no head or tail'. Such circumstances were short-lived, however, for it was soon discovered that despite lack of finance for one large scheme, the people of the county were prepared to finance short sections within their own locality and it was not long before the L&NR was joined by the Oswestry & Newtown railway (opened throughout by June 1861) and the Newtown & Machynlleth railway (opened January 1863). The Shrewsbury-Welshpool line (1862) and the Oswestry, Ellesmere & Whitchurch Railway (1864) provided further links with the national network, whilst the Aberystwyth & Welsh Coast Railway (opened as far as Borth by July 1863) provided access to Cardigan Bay. By 1865 all the foregoing systems had amalgamated to form the Cambrian Railway Company and by 1867 the line stretched along the coast from Aberystwyth to Pwllheli. South of Llanidloes, the route to Rhayader became the territory of the Mid Wales Company (1864) but by 1888 the Cambrian had gained control through to Brecon.

Goods traffic along the main lines was never particularly heavy, despite the construction of several branch lines, which facilitated the flow of minerals outward and coal, lime and agricultural requirements inward. The Van Railway, connecting with the main line at Caersws, was built to carry lead ore from the Van mines, whilst the Mawddwy Railway was used for transporting slate from the Dinas Mawddwy and Aberangell region. This line was also used for agricultural traffic, as were the branches to Kerry, the Tanat Valley and Llanfyllin. Another branch left the Shropshire & Montgomeryshire line at Kinnerley, between Shrewsbury and Llanymynech, and crossed the county boundary at Crew Green before proceeding to the quarries at Crugion/Criggion but it was always operated on a shoe-string and was never the source of much traffic.

Passenger numbers on all the Montgomeryshire lines were undramatic, save for the summer months when the company took the fullest advantage of the attractions of the beautiful Mid Wales countryside and coast, and heavily-laden trains worked into the area via Oswestry, Shrewsbury and Brecon.

Narrow-gauge lines, much favoured in north Wales for transporting slate along tortuous valleys, were not particularly evident in Montgomeryshire. The Welshpool & Llanfair Light Railway (1903) was the most prominent: it still survives as a tourist line and is run largely by volunteers.

Apart from the feeder tramways found in the Llanymynech, Kerry and Aberangell areas, mention must be made of the Corris Railway (1859-1948). Although it hugged the county border on the Merioneth side from the quarries in the Aberangell-Corris area, it crossed into Montgomeryshire just north of Machynlleth. It was originally constructed as a horse tramway and proceeded westward along the Dyfi Valley to the wharves at Derwenlas and Morben. Here the slates were transferred to sloops or flat bottomed boats. When the slates and slate slabs were bound for the continent or further afield, they were transferred again at nearby Aberdyfi to larger vessels more suitable for the longer voyages.

The advent of the standard gauge railway saw a gradual decline of the coastal shipping trade in this area from around 1865. The section of the Corris tramway west of Machynlleth was abandoned soon afterwards although the remainder of the line was up-graded and converted to steam haulage. Unlike the other narrow-gauge line in Montgomeryshire the Corris experienced heavy passenger traffic for many years and operated horse drawn wagonettes and early petrol driven buses to extend the scope of its rail services.

Following the first world war the groupings of hundreds of Britain's private railways into four large companies occurred in the 1922/23 period, when the Cambrian amalgamated with the Great Western Railway. A further major development took place when the GWR along with the other three companies was nationalized from January 1948.

The increased use of motor cars, buses and lorries from the 1920s through to the 1950s saw a gradual but continuing erosion of the railways' dominance in the field of transport. From the 1850s until the coming of Dr Beeching, the non-railway specialist who was appointed in 1961 by the government of the day to rationalize the rail network, vast tonnages of the county's goods were carried by train; mail, newspapers, milk and parcels by the thousand, in addition to the more bulky loads of coal, agricultural products, pit-props, slate and other minerals; all went successfully by rail.

The effect of the Beeching cuts was far-reaching and inflicted further isolation on many country communities. Although the main artery across the county survived, all of its smaller stations lost their services. Connecting lines from Buttington to Oswestry and Moat Lane with Llanidloes were closed during the 1960s and the branch lines, with the notable exception of the Welshpool & Llanfair all disappeared. The daily restaurant car service to Paddington was withdrawn in 1967 and the whole line suffered a chronic lack of investment during the 1970s. Happily, matters have improved during the past twenty years for, although a through service to London was reinstated only to be withdrawn again in May 1991, we now witness the opening of the final decade of the twentieth century with the introduction on the Cambrian for the first time, of modern and comfortable trains capable of speeds of up to 90 mph.

The present century has also seen a gradual improvement in the standards of the county's roads, particularly those on the east-west axis although no sections of dual-carriageway exist even at hazardous or busy locations.

As for the future it is obvious that air travel will offer many advantages, particularly for businessmen, but this mode will prove expensive to establish and maintain for the limited use expected by the travellers of mid Wales. Also, there are clear indications that air travel can be as prone to congestion as some forms of surface transport. Perhaps Montgomeryshire's greatest need is for the efficient integration of high quality rail, road and air systems, representing the best that the area can realistically be expected to support.

GWYN BRIWNANT JONES

An Aberystwyth-bound train passes through David Davies's cutting at Talerddig in April 1990.

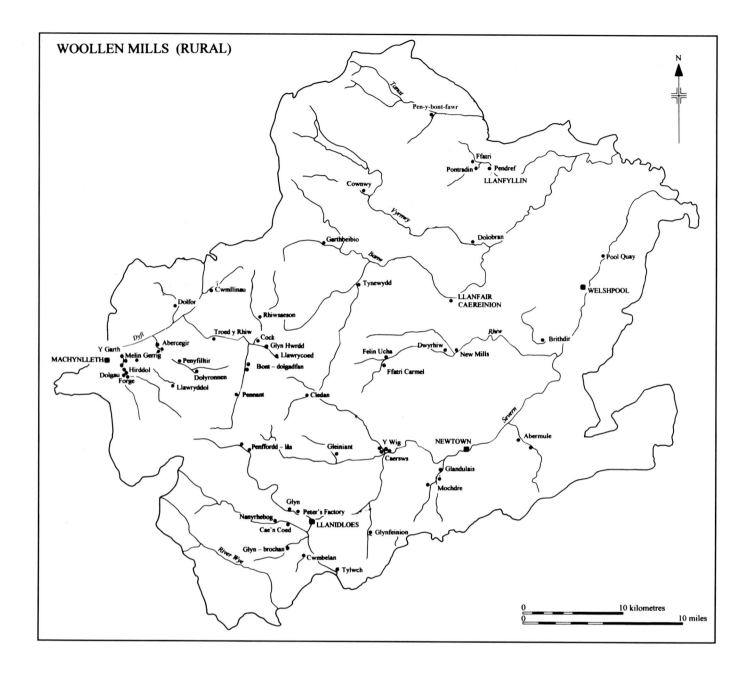

Woollen Industry

From the Middle Ages until the mid-nineteenth century, the woollen industry was one of the most important, and certainly one of the most widespread industries in Wales. Up until the beginning of the nineteenth century, it was essentially a cottage industry, with weaving and spinning being undertaken on a domestic scale supplying the demands of strictly localized markets.

From the earliest times, however, one process, that of fulling was undertaken outside the home. This process that involved the thickening of the woven

flannel was undertaken in water-driven fulling mills, known as *pandai* in Welsh. Few parishes were without at least one fulling mill, and this is reflected in the common occurrence of the term *pandy* throughout the county.

For many years, the flannel produced in mid-Wales had been sold to the Shrewsbury Drapers Company, who exercised a near-monopoly over the woollen output of the area. By the early eighteenth century, this monopoly had been undermined, with local markets being established in towns such as

Welshpool, Newtown and Llanidloes. By the end of the eighteenth century, the various processes, in particular weaving and spinning, were increasingly becoming concentrated under one roof in a 'manufactory', hence the term factory. Initially located in rural locations, they gradually became concentrated upon the towns, particularly Llanidloes and Newtown, where the three-storey weaving shops can still be seen to this day. From the 1860s onwards, steam propulsion was introduced to drive the mills in place of water power, and the tall chimney stacks of the purpose-built mills became part of the urban landscape of the county. It was during this period that Newtown acquired its title, "the Leeds of Wales".

Many of the millowners were Montgomeryshire men, some of whom had sprung from the ranks of the weavers. Their employees too were local people; the industrialization of the mills did not prompt large-scale immigration from other parts of Wales, nor from England. By the late nineteenth century, many of the mills were parts of highly capitalized companies, such as the Cambrian Co. Ltd. or the Montgomeryshire Flannel & Tweed Co. Ltd. Competition from larger, more cost-effective mills in the north of England undercut their business however, and many closed in the years following the First World War. Nevertheless, some small mills, such as that at Mochdre, continued to work into the 1950s.

By today, there is no woollen mill in Montgomeryshire, though there is still evidence of the industry of yesteryear, particularly in the weaving sheds of Llanidloes and Newtown; one of the latter houses the Textile Museum. Decaying weirs and crumbling riverbank buildings testify to the intensity of the industry in rural areas, but the great steam-driven mills of the latter stage of the development of Montgomeryshire's woollen industry have all disappeared.

E. R. MORRIS

The Welsh Woollen Manufacturing Company, Newtown.

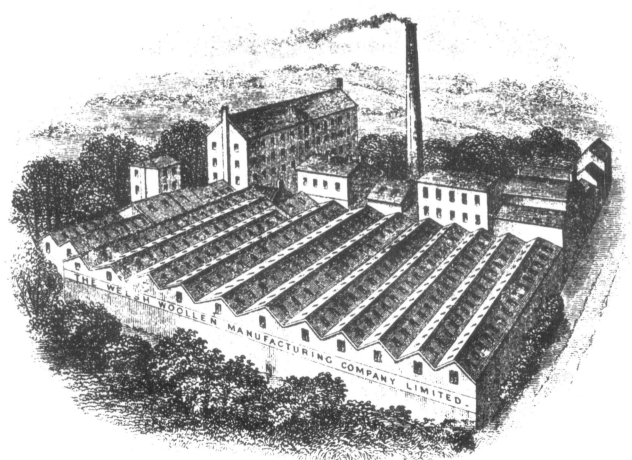

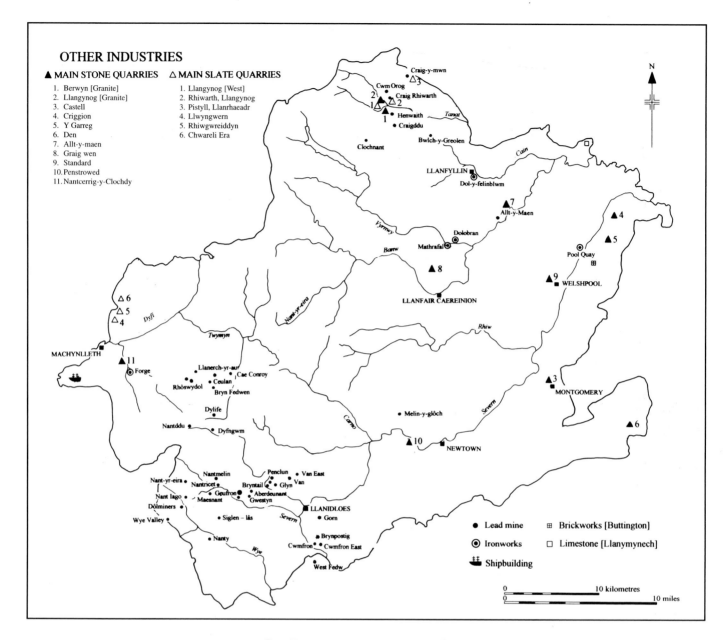

OTHER INDUSTRIES

▲ MAIN STONE QUARRIES △ MAIN SLATE QUARRIES

1. Berwyn [Granite]
2. Llangynog [Granite]
3. Castell
4. Criggion
5. Y Garreg
6. Den
7. Allt-y-maen
8. Graig wen
9. Standard
10. Penstrowed
11. Nantcerrig-y-Clochdy

1. Llangynog [West]
2. Rhiwarth, Llangynog
3. Pistyll, Llanrhaeadr
4. Llwyngwern
5. Rhiwgwreiddyn
6. Chwareli Era

● Lead mine
◉ Ironworks
⚓ Shipbuilding
⊞ Brickworks [Buttington]
□ Limestone [Llanymynech]

0   10 kilometres
0   10 miles

Other Industries

Lead Mining

One of the two main lead-bearing regions in North and Central Wales is that which extends from north Cardiganshire into south western Montgomeryshire, and which reappears again in the north east of the county. Lead mining was well-established in the county before the age of the Industrial Revolution: for centuries mining had been carried on in the Pumlumon and Berwyn ranges, dating in some cases from Roman times.

During the seventeenth century, the greatest lead working was at the foot of the Berwyn in the village of Llangynog. The veins were discovered in 1692 and large numbers of English immigrants arrived in the area to work the mines. In 1725 the mine became the property of the Earl of Powis, and his smelting at the former forge near Pool Quay was attacked as a source of environmental pollution even at that time! Nevertheless it was worked steadily until 1745, yielding an estimated profit of £142,000 to the Powis estate. Activity lapsed for some years before being revived in the latter half of the nineteenth century. Mines in the Llangynog area such as Craig-y-mwyn were worked with considerable success for some

100

years before the industry collapsed under the stress of foreign competition. The last working at Llangynog was closed in 1916.

It was during the nineteenth century that two locations in the southwest of the county, Dylife and Fan, became inextricably associated with lead mining. Developments at both locations had been handicapped by inadequate transportation; lead ore from Dylife had to be carried over rough mountain roads to Montgomeryshire's only seaport, Derwenlas, whence it was transported to Swansea or Bristol. By 1851, first the Dyfngwm, and later the nearby Llechwedd and Esgairgaled workings were in operation, These mines became known as Dylife, and in 1859 a new parish was created with a church, a school, chapels, a public house and numerous cottages for the growing workforce. Dylife's golden era was from 1858-1873 when the works were operated by the two great radical politicians, Cobden and Bright. Such was the profitability of the enterprise that they were able to sell it for some £73,000 in 1873. By 1896, however, the working of lead had all but ceased at Dylife.

In the meantime, there had also been a considerable explosion of activity at Fan. After much prospecting a rich vein was struck here in the 1860s. Managed by Captain William Williams, the mines expanded rapidly. By 1871 they were linked by rail to the main Cambrian line at Caersws and at the time of Williams's death in 1879 the Fan mines were the greatest enterprise of their kind in the British Isles.

Almost 7,000 tons of ore were produced in 1876 and 700 workmen were employed there, many of them living in the village that grew around the operation. Other works such as East Fan and Bryntail were also thriving.

By 1896, however, the boom had come to an end and the total number of lead mines in the county had fallen from some 3,000 at the height of the boom to about 400. Some small mines in the Tywyn valley, such as Llanerch-yr-aur and Cae Conroy, continued in production for a short period. Some of the spoil heaps at Fan were worked to obtain railway ballast, and there have been some recent proposals to revive mining there, but today little evidence remains of the once booming industry.

The Iron Industry

Plentiful supplies of timber and fast flowing streams made Montgomeryshire attractive for the forging of iron in the seventeenth century, and pig iron was imported into the county in barges that traversed the upper Severn, discharging at Llandrinio and Pool Quay. The first forge was established at Mathrafal near Meifod during the 1650s by Sir Charles Lloyd of Moel-y-garth. In the 1670s a further forge was opened by the Earl of Powis at Pool Quay. In 1698, the forge at Mathrafal was taken over by the Quaker Charles Lloyd of Dolobran who worked it until 1717 when a new forge was built closer to Dolobran. The detailed diary of Lloyd's clerk who managed the forge, John Kelsall, provides a fascinating glimpse of the industry in the county at that time. This forge was worked until 1727 when the Lloyds went bankrupt, though it would appear that the forge was worked by the Earls of Powis for some years afterwards.

Slate Quarrying

Although the quarrying of slate has never been of great importance in Montgomeryshire, there are two districts in the county where the industry attained some significance in response to the need for housing in Britain's industrialized areas. In the west of the county along the border with Meirionnydd were a number of quarries that produced slabs rather

The water wheel at the Nant Iago lead mine.

Lead miners from the Van lead mine.

A model of the wooden sailing ship Mary Evans, built at Derwenlas in 1867.

the Dyfi, later to the trans-shipment sidings at Machynlleth. Llwyngwern was the last quarry worked in the area, closing in 1950.

The other main slate quarrying area was at Llangynog, where roofing slates had been extracted as early as the 1530s. Quarries such as Rhiwarth were developed more intensively from the 1770s, though poor transport facilities up the Tanat valley hampered growth, and it was not until 1904 that the railway reached Llangynog. As many as 265 quarrymen were recorded in the village in the 1881 census, but by the mid-twentieth century the quarries were struggling to survive in the face of competition from artificial tiles. By the late 1930s fewer than thirty quarrymen remained, and the industry barely survived the Second World War.

Minor Industries

Stone quarries were once numerous in the county, though only a few, such as those at Llangynog, Penstrowed and Crugion/Criggion have seen substantial development. By today, quarries at Crugion/Criggion and at Tan-y-foel near Cefn Coch are still worked, producing high quality granite roadstone. Spar was once mined at Tregynon and sent by canal to the Potteries. The limestone quarries at Llanymynech on the Shropshire border were of vital importance to agriculture in Montgomeryshire, though the only quarry within the county boundary closed in 1914. Shipbuilding was once important on the Dyfi at Derwenlas and some forty small wooden sailing vessels were built there up until the late 1860s.

than roofing slates. There were three quarries around the hamlet of Esgairgeiliog, but the largest was at Llwyngwern, where 35 men worked in 1893, producing over 900 tons of slate. All these quarries depended on the Corris Railway, opened in 1859, which took their output initially to the Cei Ward on

DAVID JENKINS,
with a contribution on the slate industry by
Dr D Roberts

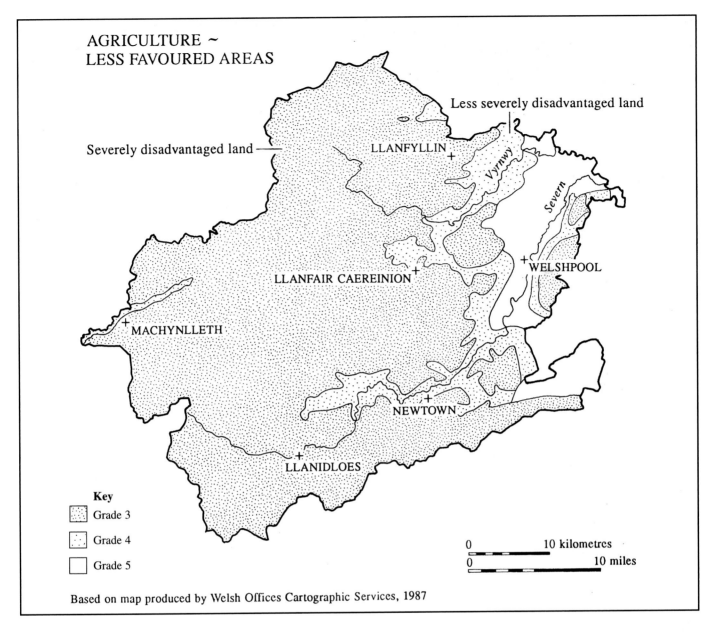

Less severely disadvantaged land

Severely disadvantaged land

LLANFYLLIN

Vyrnwy

Severn

WELSHPOOL

LLANFAIR CAEREINION

MACHYNLLETH

NEWTOWN

LLANIDLOES

Key

Grade 3

Grade 4

Grade 5

| 0 | 10 kilometres |
| 0 | 10 miles |

Based on map produced by Welsh Offices Cartographic Services, 1987

Agriculture

It is instructive to start with a modern measure, agricultural land for planning purposes is graded from 1 to 5. There is no grade 1 and virtually no grade 2 in the county. The eastern lowlands and the wider valleys are mostly grade 3 which is valuable for a wide range of purposes. The grade 4 is the disadvantaged upland areas while grade 5 is severely disadvantaged with very restricted use. These current planning grades fit very closely to the farming history because there are two farming areas; the hill areas remained culturally strong within the Celtic influence while the lowland border areas were subject to Saxon influence and systems were different.

Information until the eighteenth century can be gleaned from literature and artefacts but little would have been documented for accurate primary research. Cattle and sheep have always been important; the Welsh Black cattle are still in our uplands but the eastern, smoky-faced Montgomery breed had been absorbed into the Hereford and was virtually extinct by 1900. Upland sheep breeds such as the Kerry and the Welsh Hill Speckled Face still remain important.

Up to the eighteenth century sheep farming was the most important enterprise; some cereal crops were grown for local need but yield was low. However, in some places on the eastern fringes, the emphasis became different. During the Middle-Ages the influence of arable farming and manorial systems spread over from the lowlands of Shropshire. During the 1630s, Leland noticed that oats had been grown around the Welshpool and Montgomery area. The contrasts are not new and still pertain between the lowland drier more fertile east and the wetter less fertile uplands where the margin changes shift from one economic period to another.

Gradually communities increased the percentage of land under grazing and cropping, thus reducing that of forest. Trees also became managed and oak plantations remained extensive and famous for ship building. Tree cover for both commercial forests and amenity remains an important land use today. Until this century apple orchards were also very important for cider along the border with around 600 acres in 1900.

As population increased, more cereals were grown. The Montgomeryshire Agricultural Society was formed in 1796 and this reflected the better ways of farming and like similar societies in Wales it helped to publicize the improved systems. It also left, for posterity, written records. It quickly gained momentum in the lowlands and slowly spread into the uplands. Lime from Llanymynech came to be widely used, despite transport difficulties, but became more widespread once the canal opened in 1821 and the transport costs fell. Lime also came in by sea through the port of Derwenlas in the west of the county.

In 1801, the Home Office asked local clergy to collect details of land set aside for different crops in their parishes. The results showed that the majority bred stock although there was a higher percentage of arable land with some cereals being sold in the eastern part of the county. To the east of Llanfechain, Llangynyw and Abermule, wheat was the most important cereal, but to the west, oats was the most important crop. Rye was also fairly common on the acid less fertile soils and some was used to make bread. Swedes and turnips became associated with land improvement and were popular crops through the nineteenth century. At the end of the Napoleonic Wars in 1815, the Corn Laws encouraged farmers to continue with arable farming and, between 1801 and 1845, land under the plough increased especially along the eastern boundary; by

1845 the contrast between lowland and upland was more marked. In 1846, with the repeal of the Corn Laws, there was no longer a tariff on imported grain.

By 1870, arable farming was decreasing and the importance of stock rearing was increasing. The industry experienced trading difficulties which remained until the Second World War. With the improvement of rail and sea transport opening up the grain belts of North America, the Argentine and Australia, it became cheaper to import grain than grow it locally. Such was the expansion in horse transport for local delivery from rail heads, urban transport etc., that it would have been unlikely that we could have grown enough grain anyhow. The horse was very important until the First World War. The area was well known for high quality brood mares supplying partially broken young horses for the cavalry, other military duties and those necessary for urban delivery, horse drawn trams and hackney carriages.

During the nineteenth century, standards of stock breeding started to improve based on scientific experiments and better husbandry. New breeds of sheep were pioneered and cross breeding became popular. In many districts Dairy Shorthorn and Hereford Cattle became popular and crossbred with local breeds. John Naylor created a model farm at Leighton with buildings with hot air for drying and irrigation from farm sewage. Many of the buildings remain and some have been restored. In the twentieth century, the introduction of the Friesian led to it quickly becoming the dominant dairy breed. Montgomeryshire farmers have always sent many of their animals to England; the drovers routes such as the Kerry Ridgeway may go back to Roman times. Before the railways the drovers played a very important part in the agricultural business of the county. By today, lorries have replaced the railways and it would be rare to see cattle being driven to markets. As in the past many of the animals sold move from the uplands to the lowlands both within and outside the county. There is still a practice of sending ewe lambs for away wintering to the Cardigan coast or to Shropshire.

The twentieth century has witnessed great change. Until 1940, farming was in recession except for the period of the First World War. The resulting death of so many young men radically altered the whole of rural Britain. The great estates were often broken up and many farmers changed from being tenant to owner-occupiers. The Small Holdings Act of 1908 led to Montgomeryshire County Council becoming a large landowner and the County Council Smallholdings have since then given many young families their opportunity to commence in agriculture.

The emphasis remained on pasture and stock rearing. There was a decrease in crops requiring manual labour. As the use of internal combustion engines increased so the importance of the horse and the horse fair declined. In 1940, the horse would still have been common on the farms; by 1960, it would have been virtually replaced by the tractor. Many people in the hill farming areas would have lived lives of poverty and many chose to leave for other areas of Britain or emigrate. One hill farmer, Captain Bennett Evans (adviser on sheep to the Archers) farming on the edge of Pumlumon became well known throughout Britain for his pioneering systems of upland farming. One food item was not easy to import; milk had become more important in the urban diet and the advent of the Milk Marketing Board in 1933 gave a regular income in the recession and, as a result, became very popular expanding until the 1950s. Dairies were established at Forden and Four Crosses and the farming economy of the North East of the county and the Severn Valley became heavily dependent upon milk production.

During the Second World War, the government was determined to produce as much food as possible to counter the U-boat threat; farming was controlled by the War Agricultural Committees. The Women's Land Army played an important role as this increased food production was mainly met by traditional methods requiring much extra labour.

Raking silage.

The various Farm Acts after the Second World War established the basis of the modern industry with guaranteed prices for given quantities; any extra was discounted to move the surplus. This gave the opportunity for companies to research mechanized systems, chemical control, plant breeding and both government and private research stations developed new concepts. Many improvements such as drainage and new building investment occurred and advice, training and education were free or heavily subsidized. It was a consumer subsidy to ensure that

A lowland farm in the Severn Valley.

basic temperate foods were available to all. The various Hill Farming Acts provided a socio-economic subsidy to ensure that both the community and its infrastructure remained in the uplands as well as producing the esteemed beef and lamb.

A pattern of farming could clearly be seen following its historic role. Most of the grade 3 land is now in various combinations of cereal growing, milk production, beef finishing and some lowland fat lamb production. Cereal yields have increased due to better winter varieties, faster cultivations, fertilisers and low volume foliar sprays with herbicides and fungicides. Milk production has changed from churns, hay, cowshed and bucket units, to bulk tanks, silage and automated parlours. Artificial insemination is now widely used including beef semen on the lower yielding cows. 1600 registered milk producers in the 1950s are now down to 300 in the 1990s but the cow number is still similar so the average herd size has gone from 20 to over 80.

The beef and sheep systems occur within all areas of Montgomeryshire. The terminal bull has changed to the continental breeds, the Charolais being the most important. Beef is mainly finished on the lowland farms, being winter fed on silage and rolled cereals to give very fast growth rates. The grade 4 and 5 land will carry suckler cows with the calf being sold at the suckler sales for lowland finishing. The pure Welsh Black cow will still be common on the grade 5 land. Virtually all cattle are now winter housed, whilst many of the sheep are now housed in late pregnancy. The stratified structure of sheep farming still remains; the lowland farm will have half bred ewes or older hill ewes using a Suffolk or Texel Ram to sell fat lambs, whilst the upland farm will usually have a nucleus of pure breeds such as the Kerry or Speckled Face selling fat lambs and ewe lambs. The grade 5 land will have Welsh Mountain or Speckled Face selling draft ewes, store lambs and some finished lamb. Upland and hill land can now be renovated or reclaimed by new techniques of seeding with hardy strains of grass and white clover responding to application of lime and phosphate.

In all sections of ruminant production, dairy, beef or sheep, the main winter diet has changed from hay to silage. Larger machines, often on contract, have allowed fast filling of larger silage bunkers to get good fermentation while the big bales enable the use of 400 kg packs which are ideal for many upland and hill farmers. Veterinary skills, vaccines and drugs ensure the health of the stock.

An upland farm near Llanwddyn.

In the 1970s, changes were made once the UK joined the Common Market. Farmers could market at the best price but there was a threshold price. If average prices fell below this, produce was taken into intervention store to be released later if there was a shortage. Countries outside the EEC faced a tariff barrier. Intervention led to mountains of grain, beef, butter, milk powder and lakes of wine and edible oils. The cost became unacceptable and complex systems of reducing production came in. The first was milk quota, then there was set-aside for arable crops and this has been followed by ewe, suckler cow and male beef quotas. The huge increase in agricultural output had altered the environment so that we now have an increasing range of environmental schemes including "Environmentally Sensitive Area" grants used in the west of the county to maintain features such as heather moors.

These changes have had results not fully foreseen. Schemes to protect the smaller family farm business often helped the larger unit. The great difficulty at the time of writing this article is that of BSE and its effect upon the beef industry even though the problem is with older dairy cows. Whatever the trigger factor, the main suspect being the change of processing of meat and bone meal with lower temperature and more solvents, the disease is declining, albeit at a cost. The link between BSE and CJD is still not clear.

Ever since the Corn Laws, farming has been influenced by circumstances beyond its own control. Yet in our county, the differences of topography, climate and soil, together with attitudes of individual farmers, have given wide variations in farming practices. In recent years many facets of change have been outside local control. The price of food, both at the farm gate and in the shop, in real value has fallen, yet quality has improved. Farmers, processors and retailers have restructured their businesses into larger units using every form of technology. This has seen the growth of the larger supermarket and local butchers and milk retailers struggle to maintain their market share. Better roads and lorries with refrigerated or cooled trailers have broken the centuries old pattern of local foods. The closure of the smaller egg packing stations and the demise of the weaner groups means that neither poultry nor pigs are important in this area.

There have been many changes to the life of the

Quad-bike trailing, representing diversification in modern agriculture.

farmer in recent years. Community activities such as threshing and hand sheep-shearing are consigned to the past; machinery and contract services make work easier and many now have more leisure time. Yet income is still heavily dependent on government support and there may be some long term changes facing the industry. It is always difficult to restructure a business, especially for older people, yet many within the farming families are seeking supplements through diversification such as pony trekking, farm guesthouse and quad-biking. Some work outside the industry or work to the highest possible quality within such themes as organic beef and lamb. It would be brave to guess the future but these people maintain some of the most beautiful countryside in Western Europe. Even the wind farms are becoming part of the landscape. The economics of the future will create a balanced use of the countryside for production, recreation and the environment to fit future decades.

BRIAN POOLE

A modern silage grab.

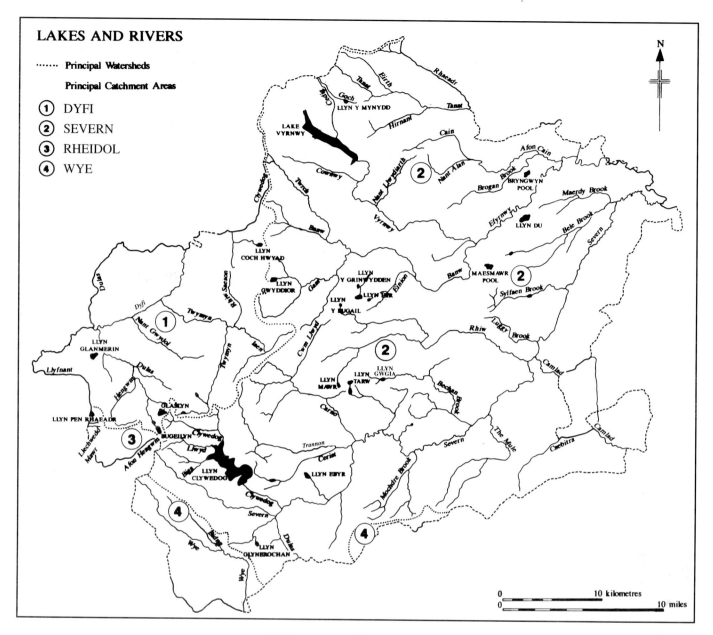

Water Supply

It was the recognition in the middle of the nineteenth century that contamination of drinking water supplies with human wastes was a major cause of disease and death, which marked the beginning of modern water supply and sewerage engineering. Local authorities were given new powers to invest in water supplies and sewerage schemes and this had a twofold impact on Montgomeryshire. In the first place, the authorities in the county, while not having the problems of the larger urban areas, had to provide for their own populations and, in the second, those larger conurbations looked to sparsely populated and high rainfall areas such as Montgomeryshire for the large sources that they needed.

To chronicle the development of many small supplies for local consumption in Montgomeryshire would take far too long and be of limited interest, but a synopsis of the development of just one would serve as an example.

In Welshpool, towards the end of the 19th century, the Borough Council negotiated a lease with the then Earl of Powis for the use of the Black Pools, about one and a half miles north of the town, to provide a water supply. These had sand filtration and, later, chlorination as a means of treatment and continued to supply Welshpool and its needs until after the Second World War. With the growth both in population and in per capita consumption, due to the clearance of poor quality houses without bathrooms and replacement with modern houses, this supply then became inadequate and it was necessary to bring a new source into use. This was achieved by running a supply from the Trinity Well on the Long Mountain and this was a good source which required chlorination but did not need filtration. These two sources together supplied the needs of Welshpool up until the 1960s.

In about 1960, there were ten boroughs and district councils in Montgomeryshire, having a total of around fifty sources serving forty distribution systems with a mixture of springs, wells, stream intakes and boreholes. Some of the installations dated back to the 1870s and the whole scheme needed rationalisation. The Montgomeryshire Water Board was formed in 1961 to take over the water supply functions from the ten authorities and after a two year period, assumed full operation in 1963. Two new schemes at Machynlleth and Llansantffraid were started in 1965 and the largest of all, the Severn Valley scheme in 1967, aimed at supplying the whole of the Severn Valley in Montgomeryshire from boreholes at Llandinam. As these schemes came into operation and their mains spread out across Montgomeryshire, many of the former supplies were

closed down. Further schemes were commenced by the Montgomeryshire Water Board in the Tanat Valley and the Banwy Valley early in the 1970s.

In 1974, the new Severn Trent Water Authority took over all water supply and sewerage functions for the whole of Montgomeryshire, amongst other areas. By that stage there were only fourteen supplies ranging from the major Severn Valley scheme to a number of small ones which had not at that stage been replaced. In addition, a number of small areas on the boundaries were served by obtaining bulk supplies from neighbouring authorities. The process of rationalization continued and, currently, there are three schemes serving Montgomeryshire.

The Llansantffraid scheme proved to be not entirely satisfactory, and water for part of north eastern Montgomeryshire is actually pumped up from boreholes in Kinnerley in Shropshire. This scheme even extends to Llanwddyn on the shores of Lake Vyrnwy, something of an irony, as Lake Vyrnwy is the biggest reservoir in Montgomeryshire and one of the largest in the country.

The history of the use of Montgomeryshire sources for conurbations outside the county is limited to two major examples, but it is interesting to consider both in more detail because they differ in almost every respect, and exemplify the differences of water supply technology between the last quarter of the nineteenth century and the third quarter of the twentieth. Liverpool Corporation had first drawn water from outside its area of supply in 1847 when it began to develop eight small reservoirs on a catchment area of eleven thousand acres at Rivington near Chorley in Lancashire, about twenty eight miles from the city. The piecemeal development of this catchment barely kept pace with the growth of demand and, in 1866, the city began to look at both the Lake District and North Wales for a major source.

Water is a plentiful natural resource in Montgomeryshire.

Right: The extraction tower at Lake Vyrnwy, through which water begins its journey to Liverpool.

In 1880, after many surveys and increasing problems in the city due to inadequate supply, they obtained statutory powers for the construction of a reservoir on the headwaters of the River Vyrnwy, a tributary of the Severn, in north Montgomeryshire. The dam, constructed in the 1880s, and yielding its first water to Liverpool in 1892, was a notable example of late Victorian engineering. It is a gravity dam (resisting the pressure of the water by its sheer mass) built of masonry using rock from a quarry, opened specially, close to the dam. All other materials had to be brought by horse and cart from the nearest railhead at Llanfyllin, ten miles distant. The maximum dimensions of the dam are 1172 feet long, 120 feet thick at the base, 144 feet from foundation to overflow crest and surmounted by a roadway. It contains 260,000 cubic yards of masonry and impounds a lake of 1121 acres, containing 13,125,000,000 gallons of water. This can supply 45,000,000 gallons per day throughout a severe drought and more at normal times. This water is piped direct to Liverpool, 68 miles away. The catchment area, amounting to 23,000 acres, was all purchased by Liverpool Corporation in order to control any activities which might pollute the water,

and this water, being relatively pure, required minimal treatment, which consisted of slow sand filters at a treatment plant at Oswestry on the aqueduct. The flow to Liverpool was originally entirely by gravity, but in the 1950s, booster pumps were installed to increase the capacity of the aqueduct. The dam and catchment area were taken over by Severn Trent in 1974. In addition, there is a management regime, which allows a measure of flood regulation and of releases of water to support abstraction from the Severn downstream. It still supplies a large part of Liverpool's water supply, but this was supplemented in the 1960s by the construction of the Llyn Celyn reservoir near Bala and the associated abstraction works from the Dee at Huntington above Chester.

Feeder stream at Lake Vyrnwy

In the early 1960s, a totally different scheme was conceived for the Clywedog, another tributary of the Severn, joining it at Llanidloes. To start with, the promoters were a consortium of authorities rather than a single one. Secondly, it is designed almost entirely for river regulation, mainly to release water so that abstracters from the Severn could be certain of sufficient water in the river to support their requirements, and also to retain some spare capacity in the reservoir to absorb a major flood from this part of the Severn catchment. The third major difference is that it is a concrete buttress dam. It has dimensions of 237 feet high, 750 feet long and it contains 254,000 cubic yards of concrete. It impounds a reservoir 615 acres in extent, containing 11,000,000,000 gallons when full. The catchment area is about 11,500 acres. It also was taken over by Severn Trent Water Authority on the reorganization of the water industry in 1974.

The final part of the story is that Severn Trent Water Authority was privatized, in respect of its water supply and sewerage functions, at the end of the 1980s, but the regulatory and river management functions passed to the National Rivers Authority and subsequently to the Environment Agency.

D. W. L. ROWLANDS

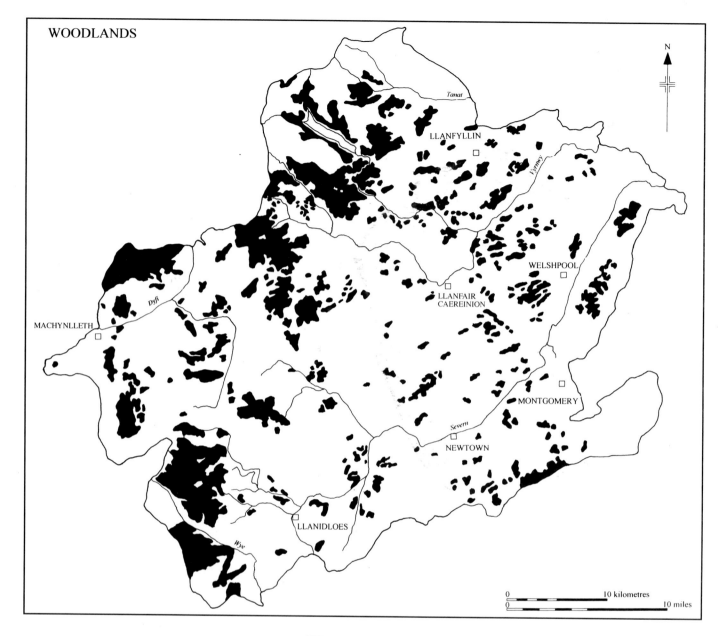

WOODLANDS

Tanat

LLANFYLLIN □

Vyrnwy

WELSHPOOL □

LLANFAIR □
CAEREINION

Dyfi

MACHYNLLETH
□

MONTGOMERY □

Severn

NEWTOWN □

LLANIDLOES □

Wye

N

0   10 kilometres
0   10 miles

Forestry

Leaving aside the vegetation of geological times, the story of forests in Montgomeryshire begins with the end of the last Ice Age and the disappearance of the ice-cap about 12,000 years ago. The progression through the first few thousand years would be rather like taking a journey today, south from the north polar ice-cap into temperate regions: tundra, followed by scrub birch, willow and Scots pine, then better forests rather like the remains of the Caledonian forest of today and, finally, oak, alder and the other species which now form the lowland forests. Some species, such as Norway spruce, did not cross from Europe before the English Channel was formed and were absent until introduced by man.

Over the last few thousand years the climate has varied, sometimes being warmer than today and sometimes colder. With these changes of climate there have been corresponding changes of vegetation. It is probable, however, that Montgomeryshire was almost entirely covered with trees for several thousand years until man began to have an impact on the landscape.

The first people here after the Ice Age would have been Mesolithic hunter-gatherers. To begin with these would only have been summer visitors, retreating south again with the onset of winter and having virtually no impact on the environment.

Then came the first farmers and gradually, by the use of fire and tools, first stone and later bronze and iron, forests were cleared and replaced by grassland and, to a lesser extent, arable. This has not been a continuous process. There have been periods when, due to political, social or climatic change, the process was reversed and farmland was abandoned and reverted to forest.

It had long been thought that before the Roman conquest it had not been possible to clear the heavy forest of the Severn valley. Modern archaeological findings now show that there were settlements there as long ago as the Bronze Age, which indicates that woodlands were in retreat here, as well as in the uplands. A major factor in the disappearance of woodland has been the effect of grazing by livestock, especially sheep which, although they do not affect mature trees, eat off the seedlings so that when the trees become aged and die there are no replacements. Montgomeryshire has been an exporter of timber for many centuries. The earliest method of transport over long distances seems most likely to have been by water. Logs were lashed together into rafts and floated down the Severn and, as long ago as 1285, there is a record of damage to Montford Bridge caused by such a raft. Lord Burleigh's plan of Shrewsbury of 1575 shows a raft of timber by the Welsh Bridge. In 1742, Sir Richard Corbett sold oak from the Leighton estate, said to be the finest navy timber ever felled in Montgomeryshire, so that trade was clearly well established by that date. A little later there is a record of 26 individual trees felled at Vaynor, Berriew ranging from 1000 cu ft to 2500 cubic feet. By 1808, transport was improving and the advertisement for a sale at Trefnant Hall refers to the proximity of the Canal, the River Severn and the turnpike road. The Reverend Walter Davies, writing in 1810, refers to Montgomeryshire timber being much used in naval dockyards as far afield as Deptford and Plymouth. Despite the tremendous scale of the fellings he still refers to Montgomeryshire as the best wooded county in north Wales.

Another major cause for the felling of timber was the production of charcoal, particularly for the smelting of iron. By the middle of the seventeenth century, the felling of forest in the Weald, long the traditional area for iron smelting, led the government to ban its use in that area for the production of charcoal. It was not surprising, therefore, that the trade moved to Montgomeryshire where, in addition to the plentiful sources of timber, there were good flows of water to power the mechanical bellows which were then coming into use.

The first forge in Montgomeryshire was set up by Sir Charles Lloyd near Mathrafal in 1651 and by 1722 the manager was having to travel as far as Llandinam, 24 miles away, to obtain timber for charcoal, at considerable cost in transport at that time.

Important ancillary industries were the production of bark for tanning and the development of estate sawmills. A notable example of the latter is the Powis Estate Sawmill which is still operating today. Many of the owners of these woodlands were concerned to replant, either from considerations of good estate management or from the belief that oak for warships would always be the first line of defence for the country, but not all were so prudent. Sadly it was often the case that timber was felled to pay off debts, to provide extravagant dowries or to build palatial mansions. It is recorded that £100,000 worth of timber was felled to pay for the building of Garth. However when owners got into financial difficulties and sold, the new owners were often interested and enterprizing people who were prepared to spend a lot of the money made in commerce to improve their estates, which works often included extensive planting.

The 1914-18 war brought the forests of Britain to their lowest ebb and in 1919 the Forestry Commission was formed. Planting was dependent on the price and availability of land. There was some replanting of felled woodlands on private estates but the main non-Commission planting was a further 4000 acres at Lake Vyrnwy. In the 1939-45 war the inter-war planting was too small for felling but much of the remaining private plantations and 700 acres of the original Lake Vyrnwy woods were clear-felled. By the time of the Montgomeryshire County Council's structure plan of 1951 the Commission owned 25,775 acres of which 10,093 were planted. There were 35,130 acres of other woodland. Of this, 5000 acres were at Lake Vyrnwy but a good deal of the remainder was described as devastated by wartime fellings.

In the late 1940s the government of the day recognised that financial incentives were needed to enable owners to replant and they introduced substantial tax concessions for planting. This greatly encouraged replanting and also stimulated the growth of private forestry companies, which operated by enabling wealthy people outside the countryside to invest in forestry. This concession was abolished in the Budget of 1988 when forestry was taken completely out of the taxation system.

The present position is that, from a low of about 6% of Montgomeryshire forested, there has been a recovery to about 14%. It is estimated that there are about 22,000 acres of hardwood, of which about half is oak and about 48,000 acres of conifers, of which rather more than half is Sitka Spruce, with substantial areas of Douglas Fir, Norway Spruce and Japanese Larch. This has led to the current fad of decrying 'alien conifers' but anyone who knows the beauty of Lake Vyrnwy, where the slopes surrounding the Lake are almost entirely clad in these species, will recognise that, if sensibly planted, these can actually enhance the landscape. They have interest and value as a wildlife habitat as well, providing living space for a variety of species and in particular a refuge for the last surviving populations in Montgomeryshire of the native red squirrel. They are also the only economically viable forestry crop on the uplands, which otherwise could only produce scrub hardwoods.

In addition there are over a million trees growing in copses, hedgerows, riverbanks and as individuals and these are predominantly hardwoods with oak, ash, birch and alder the most common.

The market for Montgomeryshire timber has also changed. New sawmills, designed specifically to handle home-grown softwood, and pulp-mills to convert the smaller timber into paper and building board, have been established but, sadly, most of the timber grown here is processed outside the county, thus failing to make the contribution to local employment which it might have done. Because of economies of scale, wood-processing facilities have to be large to compete in a world market.

Employment within the forest has also declined due to mechanization but is still probably greater than it would have been were the land still rough grazings, as most of it had been. Much of the work, however, is done by mobile gangs, often based in towns, which do not form a stable part of the rural community as the regular staff used to do. The effect of this is illustrated by the fact that the forest village of Llwyn-y-Gôg has been sold off by the Commission and few, if any, people employed in forestry now live there.

The prospect of world demand for timber exceeding supply by an increasing margin for the foreseeable future indicates that the forests of Montgomeryshire should continue to thrive and to form an important part of our landscape and our economic life.

D. W. L. ROWLANDS

Forestry alongside the Llanwddyn-Bala road.

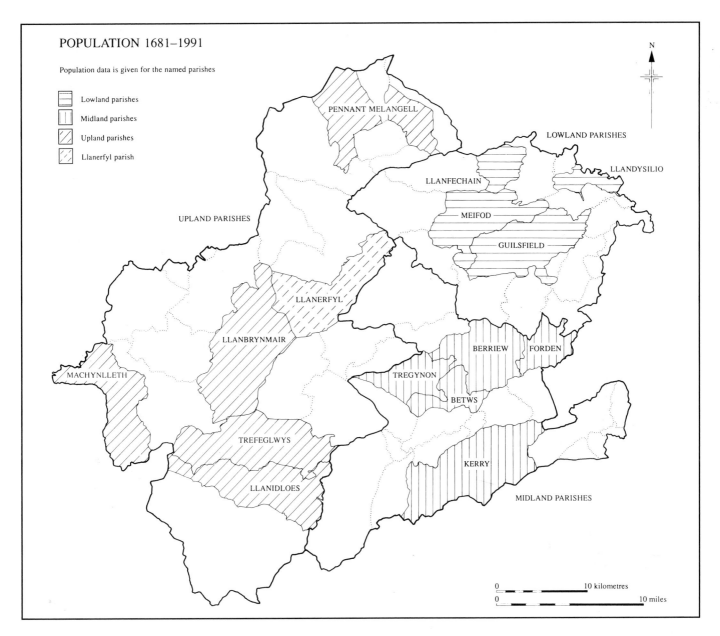

POPULATION 1681–1991

Population data is given for the named parishes

Lowland parishes

Midland parishes

Upland parishes

Llanerfyl parish

N

PENNANT MELANGELL

LOWLAND PARISHES

LLANFECHAIN

LLANDYSILIO

MEIFOD

GUILSFIELD

UPLAND PARISHES

LLANERFYL

LLANBRYNMAIR

BERRIEW   FORDEN

TREGYNON

MACHYNLLETH

BETWS

TREFEGLWYS

KERRY

LLANIDLOES

MIDLAND PARISHES

0   10 kilometres

0   10 miles

Population

The first ten-year national census was held in 1801, and before that date any figures of population therefore have to be estimates, calculated on the basis of such sources and statistics as are available. For Montgomeryshire, fortunately, there are sources from which useful data can be extracted, such as the Hearth Tax returns of 1671-4 and the St Asaph Notitiae (a census carried out by clergymen and returned to the Bishop) of 1681-6. These offer information on estimates of population and, where they overlap, mutually consistent figures can be provided for the latter part of the seventeenth century. In particular, the two sources offer a starting point for an informed estimate of the county's population some one hundred and thirty years before the first National Census.

This county is particularly well blessed with surviving ecclesiastical parish registers of baptisms, marriages and burials in the pre-census period, and they can provide additional valuable information. For example, by adding baptisms and deducting burials, the population trends up to the beginning of the national decennial censuses in 1801 can be deduced. This method is, of course, subject to error. There was always a degree of under-recording in the parish registers, particularly of baptisms and marriages. Furthermore, many Nonconformist and

Roman Catholic registrations will have been omitted. This can result, in particular, in errors in calculating the ratio of births to deaths, a key factor in making population estimates. The other factors, which cannot be taken into account, are emigration and inward migration. It is likely that emigration was already taking place in the eighteenth century and it seems probable that emigration exceeded immigration. While this might in turn counter the under-recording of births, the sense in which the registers must be used with qualified caution is all the more apparent.

A study was conducted some years ago by Dr Melvin Humphreys, on this basis, of fifteen parishes in three groups representing the lowland, midland and upland areas of Montgomeryshire for the period 1685-1801. These sample parishes enabled Dr Humphreys to provide population estimates for the whole county by comparison with neighbouring parishes where registers had not survived. His study also made comparisons with the population history of England, as researched by Professor E.A. Wrigley and Dr R.S. Schofield. In the present essay, this study has been extended, using the census data, to 1991. It has long been held that there is under-recording in the censuses of 1801 and 1811, and the figures for those two years need to be viewed with some caution.

In the present study, there are also errors caused by boundary changes in the nineteenth and twentieth centuries. Such changes may well serve to cancel each other, and in some cases their effects are mitigated by the grouping of parishes. Even so, in the case of the lowland cluster of parishes the figures for 1981 and 1991 have been omitted; Guilsfield forms a large component of this group and the community was the subject of far-reaching boundary changes in 1987.

The map which accompanies this study shows the three areas into which the county has been divided and the sample parishes.

It can be seen that demographic trends in Wales largely mirrored England, although with slower growth, until 1921, when industrial and agricultural depression hit Wales harder than England.

The population of Montgomeryshire shows a similar increase until 1841. The county exported food, woollen products and lead to the rest of Britain, and it was only when the challenge of food imports from the colonies and elsewhere and the expansion of the South Yorkshire woollen industry began to have an effect that the trends began to diverge.

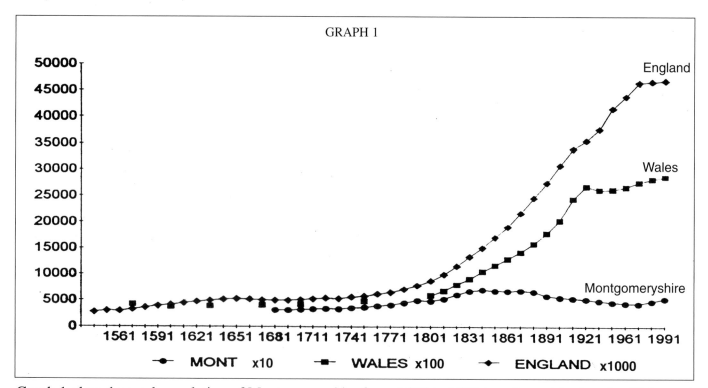

Graph 1 plots the total population of Montgomeryshire from 1685 to 1991 together with plots for Wales and England to scales which enable the trends to be compared.

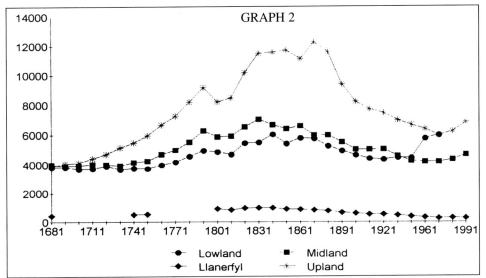

GRAPH 2

Legend:
- ● Lowland
- ■ Midland
- ◆ Llanerfyl
- ＊ Upland

Graph 2 demonstrates the population trends in the three groups of sample parishes showing the variation of demographic experience in the different parts of the county. Since some of the upland parishes were affected to some extent by mining, quarrying and industry, the statistics have been included for one parish, Llanerfyl, which was not affected either by these factors, or by boundary changes, throughout the whole of the period under review.

A noticeable feature of the regional demographic evidence is the relative stability of the population in the lowlands and midlands of Montgomeryshire from 1685 to 1991 compared with the rest of the county. It is the uplands which show the most dramatic population growth before 1871 and subsequently the greatest decline.

In part, this growth may have been sustained initially by enclosure and improvement of land which had formerly been used only for summer grazing. There may, however, have been other factors at work. Llanidloes, for example, which is included in this area, enjoyed considerable growth due to its vigorous woollen industry, and there was also active mining and quarrying in other parts of the upland zone, such as at Llangynog. The much earlier decline of Llanerfyl's population, in a parish remote from either activity, and which relied very largely on agriculture, more accurately indicates the difficulties of communities with a purely upland, agrarian economy.

From the middle of the nineteenth century a marked decline in population is observable in Montgomeryshire and elsewhere in rural Wales and

England. This decline is all the more noticeable when compared with the growth taking place elsewhere in Wales and in the United Kingdom as a whole. The trend continued until the middle of the twentieth century, and was finally reversed between 1971-1981. The reasons for this turn around have included the improvements made in communications, the general drift of people to rural areas in quest of a non-urban lifestyle, the activities and investments made by both national and to a lesser extent local government agencies, and the activities of a few exceptional entrepreneurs. In particular, the designation of Newtown as the venue of a modest new town development project has had a significant effect on the population in the Severn Valley. Although the reduction in the population of most upland communities has been arrested in the last couple of decades, there has been no significant growth, and one or two communities have continued to show a decline.

There remains a perception in Montgomeryshire of an outward movement of people in the 18 to 35 age group and a slightly larger inward movement of those over 35 years of age. A proportion of the county's immigrants clearly move to the area to retire, arriving at or acquiring property a few years before their retirement from work. Employment in agriculture has steadily declined since the middle of the last century and, while the trend was arrested during both World Wars, it otherwise continues. Indeed, there is little likelihood of this long-term trend being reversed across Great Britain. During much of the twentieth century depopulation has been a major concern in Montgomeryshire and to its community leaders and local politicians. This concern has faded in the last couple of decades of the century. However, in an increasingly globalized economy, where there is a strong downward pressure on both labour and food costs, it is easy to imagine that Montgomeryshire will find difficulty in sustaining the vibrant economy that has always been one of the key determinants of a vigorous demographic base.

D. W. L. ROWLANDS

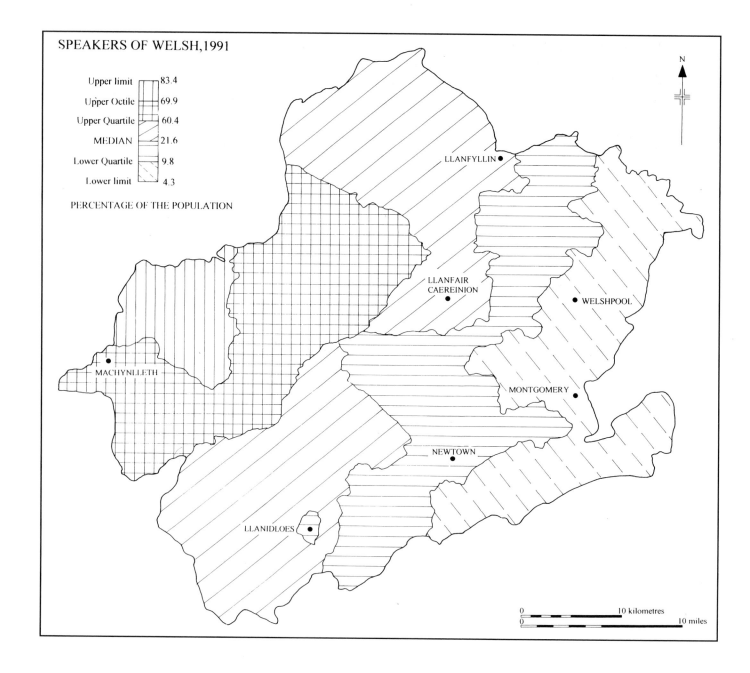

SPEAKERS OF WELSH,1991

Upper limit — 83.4
Upper Octile — 69.9
Upper Quartile — 60.4
MEDIAN — 21.6
Lower Quartile — 9.8
Lower limit — 4.3

PERCENTAGE OF THE POPULATION

LLANFYLLIN •

LLANFAIR
CAEREINION •

• WELSHPOOL

MONTGOMERY •

NEWTOWN •

• MACHYNLLETH

LLANIDLOES •

0 — 10 kilometres
0 — 10 miles

Changing Language Geographies of Montgomeryshire, c.1749-1991

Montgomeryshire has often been described as a 'border county'. Presumably this designation dates from past times when the shire area was often grouped with the lands and territories of the Marcher Lordships. Yet, in cultural and linguistic terms (both closely intertwined in terms of meaning and practical realities) the county embraces a range of communities that have been - indeed, continue to be - either distinctively Welsh or quintessential English in speech and outlook. Despite the very significant

language changes that have occurred in Wales as a whole, this is a very distinctive, long standing and enduring feature in the cultural geography of the county. The fact that these have remained constant for more than two centuries can be linked directly to factors of place and regional location, to the nature of economic growth and development, to local differences in terms of historical demography, to resultant long-term patterns of population decline in some parts of the county and growth in others.

In this chapter we trace the successive language geographies from the first clear evidence on which we can draw, that of 1749, through to the last population census taken in 1991. This time span, approaching two and a half centuries, embraces, in south Britain generally, periods of very considerable social and economic change: it starts with the so-called 'pre-industrial' era, includes the industrial revolutions of the nineteenth and early twentieth centuries, profound and widespread urbanization, two major world wars (each of which brought significant major social changes), and the post-industrial society of our own times with increased emphasis on social and cultural pluralism. Although Montgomeryshire did not always experience immediate and direct impacts, each of these major change-events was to be the start of long-running processes that were to have a strong impact on the survival of Welsh-speaking communities.

The first detailed picture of linguistic conditions in Montgomeryshire in the mid-eighteenth century is based on analyses of ecclesiastical documentary sources that, to us today, might seem to be somewhat of a surprise, namely the extant reports from rural deans and the parochial 'queries and answers' prepared for the visitation of Anglican bishops. Although even by that date an anglocentric outlook seems to have pervaded much of the upper echelons of the Established Church, there exists strong evidence that church officials still took considerable trouble to ensure that the language of worship was in accordance with local needs. Often, at parish level, these objectives were met through the employment of Welsh-speaking surrogates as curates and assistant ministers. Considerable care seems to have been taken to make regular surveys, inspections and written reports to monitor local conditions and practice so that these statutory obligations could be observed. In addition, the final reports of the Royal Commission on the Church and Other Religious Bodies in Wales, which reported in 1910, include invaluable information, in particular the detailed survey data compiled for official purposes by Sir John Williams in 1905 and 1906. These relate to local churches and chapels in every denomination and record much specific detail as to local linguistic conditions, including assessments and comments on the validity of specific arrangements to meet local needs. Drawing on all these sources we are able to build detailed maps that depict local conditions and summarise the broad changes that were to diffuse through eastern Montgomeryshire between 1749 and the early 1900s.

The three major language areas - Welsh, bilingual, English speaking parishes - are all represented in eighteenth-century Montgomeryshire. All the evidence indicates that parishes in the north and west were virtually monoglot Welsh in speech and outlook: those in the east, including communities within the wide flood plain of the Severn and the flanking hills and countryside were completely English. The much narrower, sinuating, intermediate bilingual zone, where both Welsh and English were used in the church services, marked the zone of transition between these two major culture provinces. In all likelihood, at this date the majority of the population living in these communities spoke either Welsh or English; only a minority would have been fully bilingual in today's meaning of the term. These assessments were personal and had been formulated by the parochial clergy - men with a close knowledge of their own localities.

Much insight as to the processes of language change over time can be obtained by focusing on the nature and extent of this most interesting bilingual zone. There is considerable evidence that, in reporting to their bishop in 1749, the rural deans were fully aware of local conditions within this bilingual zone. Thus, from Llanfyllin, we are informed ' . . . most of ye Town People understand Engl. well enough & some of ym. rather better than W; at Trefeglwys the use of both Welsh and English in public worship was a long standing arrangement [with] no change now from the past'. The bishop also received a number of reports that, as at Aberhafesb and Llanllwchaearn (Newtown), services in Welsh were ' . . . more intelligible & more agreeable to the major part of the Congregation' but, as at the latter, the dropping of Welsh services had been curtailed not by the curate but to meet the whims of the leading men of the Parish. A century later, the return dated 1832 shows that attitudes seem to have changed, following the development of a 'flannel manufy.' Now, according to the rural dean, who seems to have accepted the appropriateness of these arrangements, all the services were in English.

In north-east Montgomeryshire the bilingual zone seems to have been significantly wider than in the central districts of the county due, in part, to the existence of the Tanat valley as a traditional route way which links the communities of the upland interior with the Shropshire Plain, serving as a major diffusion route for English-language based culture into upland Wales. Yet, it is very interesting to note that this same bilingual zone passed through the borderland parish of Llansantffraid-ym-Mechain into the Oswestry district where, the mid-eighteenth century rural deanery reports recorded that several churches, despite their location in England, continued to use Welsh. In 1809, from Llanyblodwel, Salop, we are informed that the two Sunday services are in '. . . Welsh and English alternately, observing your Lordship's direction. . .'. Although Welsh was to disappear from most of the neighbouring parishes, and from the services of Oswestry parish church, this arrangement was to continue throughout the nineteenth century.

By the early nineteenth century a number of parishes which formerly, in 1749, lay in the dominantly Welsh speaking areas, had introduced a greater use of English, so joining the bilingual zone. In 1809, the arrangements at Manafon included an additional English service on Sunday evenings '...for encouraging Sunday scholars to respond to the psalms...'. At nearby Llanfair Caereinion, although Welsh seems to have remained the language most widely used, English had been introduced for evening services; and all the prayers, at all services, were said in English. Clearly, these arrangements echoed emergent growing aspirations amongst Welsh people that a knowledge of the English language was necessary for progress. In consequence, Anglican Sunday schools placed a growing emphasis on the use of English among the rising generation so that they would be better 'fitted' for the future.

The 1847 Education Report - despite its opinionated anglocentric stance - does offer us some very relevant insights as to the linguistic situation in mid-nineteenth-century Montgomeryshire. From many different locations came reports that confirmed the overwhelming Welshness of western districts. Thus, less than half of the pupils at Cemais, in the Dyfi valley, understood any English; at Darowen the local school master had great difficulty in answering 'simple questions on his school'; from Llangadfan, in the upper Banw valley, it was reported from the Church School that 'the children understood scarcely a word of English'; whilst at nearby Llanllugan the majority of pupils 'were ignorant in the extreme, unable to understand a word of English and ill mannered'! But, the changes that we have noted were beginning to make their appearance, especially

in towns which were beginning to function as reception points for English attitudes and new ideas. Here, as at Machynlleth, it was noted that English was understood at the National School and that children were '... speaking English in the streets ...during play hours'.

But the Education Reports also confirmed the overwhelming Englishness of eastern parishes: at Berriew it was reported that the '... inhabitants are employed in agriculture, and, except a few in the remote parts of the parish towards Llanfair, speak English only'; at Betws Cedewain the school children 'all spoke English as their mother tongue'; at Buttington, east of Welshpool, 'all classes speak English'; at Churchstoke 'they are all English [sic] children , there being no Welsh spoken in the parish', the majority of the farmers and the farm labourers at Guilsfield '. . . understand English only'. Similar reports came from every parish throughout the Severn valley and beyond, including the interesting observation that whilst everyone speaks English at Ceri (Kerry), immediately southeast of Newtown, here the English spoken by the local people as their 'mother tongue' was 'very inferior [to that spoken] in the remoter districts of west Wales'!

In addition to the substantial and very significant statistical data on the language/s used in Sunday schools (the most popular form of education, which were much better attended than day schools), the 1847 Education Reports contain descriptive information that helps us to understand the distinctive nature of the linguistic milieu at specific locations within the bilingual zone. Thus, whilst farmers are described as 'remarkably illiterate and ignorant of English' at Aberhafesb, it was reported to the commissioner that '...the English language has recently spread widely along the left bank of the Severn, and is spoken by the greater part of the inhabitants...' At Castle Caereinion, where, it was estimated, still only one half of the population had a spoken knowledge of the English language in addition to Welsh, most of the Church School pupils knew English 'better than Welsh' though their master himself only spoke English with 'difficulty'.

All these local observations, together with the rounded estimates of English speakers tabulated in Appendix E of the 1847 Education Report, concur with the linguistic milieu as recorded in the church visitation documents. But, in addition, Appendix H of the Report contains very unusual and specific language statistics based on actual surveys that had been conducted by leading members of the various nonconformist chapels in the parishes of Llanfair Caereinion, Castle Caereinion, Manafon and Llanwyddelan. These tabulations, identified in the Report as the 'Memorials from Dissenters . . . respecting the want of education' not only give specific details as to the numbers speaking Welsh, English, or both languages, but also provide insights as to national affiliation ('Welsh', 'English'), population numbers, and statistics of those who 'can' and who 'cannot' read, write, do arithmetic, 'grammar', do 'geography', and/or 'singing'. These comprehensive surveys included information on Sunday school attendances and religious affiliation, township by township within each parish. In short, these Dissenters' 'Memorials' provide considerable detail on a whole range of educational and linguistic features that were characteristic of a contiguous group of parishes within the bilingual zone at this date.

It is clear that the Established Church did place considerable emphasis on the need for the young to acquire a working knowledge of English but it is very important for us to remember that this was a priority widely shared by most people. Despite the prevailing drive for a much wider acquisition of the English language it is of considerable interest to us today, that, as a close study will reveal, beyond marginal changes along its edges, between 1749 and the early 1900s, the bilingual zone remained fairly static in terms of regional location.

The static and enduring nature of this bilingual zone is in marked contrast to the significant shifts in the language divides that have been analysed, for the same time periods, in both north-east Wales and in south Wales. Within these major industrial regions in-migration and the mushrooming of new urban communities in the nineteenth century ushered in, and speeded up, the processes of anglicization. Throughout the nineteenth century, although the population of Montgomeryshire grew, the upland communities of the west continued to lose people. In 1801, 42 per cent of the population were living in areas which, according to the church visitation returns, were Welsh/mainly Welsh in speech - more, in relative terms, at the time of the first population census than in the dominantly English-speaking communities. By 1881 (the last date for which, because of subsequent parochial boundary changes,

we are able to compile comparable statistics), the Welsh areas accounted for less than a third of the population in contrast to the English areas which then stood at 60 per cent. Between these dates, the proportions living in bilingual parishes declined from 21 per cent in 1801 to less than 8 per cent in 1881.

What do these broad statistics tell us about the processes of language change?

First, we can recognize that for reasons of regional location in the wider context of the country of Wales, the old Welsh-speaking communities in Montgomeryshire occupied, as has been stated, the western upland areas. Because of their low agricultural potential these continued to lose people throughout the nineteenth century. Conversely, from Llanidloes and Newtown downstream within the Vale of Severn and also within the flanking parishes - all dominantly English-speaking communities - the population continued to grow. In part the pervading Englishness of these areas was due to matters of a particular regional location that locked these communities into direct contact with Shropshire. But to a considerable degree, also, these districts had their own intrinsic dynamics, linked to their agricultural and economic development, and which attracted new people. By the third quarter of the nineteenth century, as E.G. Ravenstein noted, from his famous 'statistical surveys' of the Celtic languages, although 'still largely employed in the religious services of the dissenters and occasionally even in the Established Church ... Welsh is gradually being forgotten'. Here, it was noted in 1882 that whilst the original Welsh names of places and houses still survived, English had become overwhelmingly dominant as the everyday speech of the people and if the 'constant migration of Welsh-speaking people from the hill country to the north into the more fertile valley lands' had not occurred, 'the Welsh language would have died out much faster'.

The bilingual zone straddles both these major language provinces. In a very real sense this seems to have functioned as the key agent of language change. Once a parish became bilingual in speech, under the social attitudes prevailing in the nineteenth-century this was accepted as a one-way intermediate status in the process of change towards anglicization: in nineteenth-century Montgomery-shire we find that no bilingual parish reverted to a 'mainly Welsh' at a later date. Bilingual status was merely a stage in the general anglicization process. So, although some questions remain as to the general validity of the church data after the mid-nineteenth century (when, increasingly, in many different parts of Wales the Church became identified as the chief promoter of Englishness), there are clear signs that only 10 per cent of the county's population (accounting for 7.5 per cent of parishes) retained a bilingual status. For most parishes in direct contact with the Englishry of east Montgomeryshire, the social and educational aspirations towards English had been achieved: their former bilingual status was only ever of a temporary nature - a cultural Trojan horse that led, inevitably and in a decided manner, towards fuller and eventually complete integration with the English-speaking zone. Although imposed by the religious and educational establishment of the day, all these changes were accepted by the ordinary people and a knowledge of the English language was accepted as a highly desirable acquisition by successive rising generations. In the end, rather than looking west towards the hills they all looked 'down country' towards the rich agricultural lands of Shropshire, the land that offered a prosperous future but one that could only be shared through the medium of the English language.

Left behind, though, were the decidedly Welsh parishes of the west. The different regional context meant that here it was much easier to maintain direct everyday cultural links with the wider Welsh-speaking Wales that flourished outside the county. All these western parishes have retained a deep, intense Welshness that has continued, unquestioned, in many localities into our own times. Only a very few, such as the small urban community of Machynlleth, showed any inclination to adopt English and then often this turned out to be temporary in nature. In all these western communities, all integral parts of a distinctively major Welsh culture area, there was no need for bilingual services in the parish churches until much later in the twentieth century.

Further light on the broad patterns of change through much of the nineteenth century can be gleaned from an examination of population dynamics with each of the major language change categories. The main contrasts were between those parishes moving towards a full English status (including those recorded as 'consistently English') and those that retained their Welshness during these decades. As can be seen from the table, greatest population changes were recorded where the most significant linguistic changes had occurred and some interesting differences occurred both before and after 1841. Regional location, in the context of a wider Wales or an adjacent position with the English plain, and the internal dynamic that can be linked to differential patterns of economic development go a long way to help us to understand the language geography of Montgomeryshire as it had evolved by the end of the nineteenth century.

Overall trends between 1901 and 1991 are revealed by maps (a) to (g) and the main map on page 118, though numerous problems arise when we draw on the official census returns starting in 1901 and subsequent enumerations in attempting to work out details of long-term trends. Although successive changes in local government boundaries do give rise to a number of statistical problems, in Montgomeryshire these do not pose the same difficulties as elsewhere. Indeed, as can be seen from the maps displayed, despite changes of name, specific changes of local government boundaries were minimal until the extensive reorganization of local government in 1974 when new so-called 'Ward areas' replaced the territorial units of urban and rural district councils. Between 1901 and 1971, the census authorities only published language information consistently, census by census, for urban and rural district council areas. Whilst the administrative urban districts cover relatively small discrete areas, the rural districts (because they needed to relate to a minimum population base) were much more extensive, embracing a large number of different language communities, with considerable changes from place to place in the ratio of Welsh and English speakers. In consequence, language maps that incorporate these latter administrative units are very generalized in nature and fail to reflect the significant local differences that, for example, are evident from the analyses of the church visitation data.

Nevertheless, if we are to trace changes over time, of necessity we have to use the data available despite their shortcomings from ideal methodological considerations. The decline from some 47% of Montgomeryshire population able to speak Welsh in 1901 to 23% in 1991 closely reflects changes within Wales in general but, except for 1901,

Montgomeryshire has retained a higher proportion of its population as Welsh speakers - especially from 1921 onwards. The differences in the proportions of Welsh speakers living in the county and in the country of Wales becomes greater (over 6% points) between 1951 and 1971 when the county's total population numbers dipped down to the low of 41,230 in 1971 before the population recoveries recorded in the 1981 and 1991 censuses.

Montgomeryshire seems to have retained a slightly higher proportion of Welsh monoglots than in the nation generally. But, as larger numbers acquired fluency in English, and, also, perhaps, due to the passing of an elderly generation of native Welsh people, these minor differences disappeared after the 1951 census. By 1991 the numbers of Welsh monoglots was thought to be of no significance and, in consequence, the census authorities did not attempt to collect this information.

It is clear that the high proportions of Welsh speakers in the census wards of north and west Montgomeryshire are, in reality, extensions into the county of the dominant Welsh milieu of the belt of countryside that includes the small towns of Llanfyllin and Llanfair Caereinion but with lower ratios of 20% and over in the vicinity of Llanidloes. As we move further east and south-east through the county the proportion of Welsh speakers falls rapidly to less than 10% of the population east of Newtown and in the Severn Valley, including Montgomery town and Welshpool. Clearly in terms of cultural geography, this belt of countryside, where Welsh speakers are a minority, is an integral part of the long-standing zone of culture transition or borderland that has long existed between England and Wales. The remotely peopled communities of north Radnorshire are an integral part of the long-established Englishry. This, then, is the situation recorded by the last census taken in 1991 but these very distinctive territorial differences have long been in existence.

The census information relates to the numbers, and to the numbers and proportion, of Welsh speakers in the normally resident population. When we examine the proportions of Welsh speakers recorded as having been born in Wales, a number of localities recorded significantly more Welsh speakers than in the population generally: at Machynlleth 64 per cent in the population were returned as Welsh speakers but the proportion rises to 71 per cent of Welsh born people. Similarly, Caersws and Llanidloes; (21 per cent Welsh speakers in the total population as opposed to 25% of those born in Wales), Llansantffraid-ym-Mechain (19 as opposed to 21 %), Welshpool (11 as opposed to 15%), Llandysilio (8 as opposed to 14%) and Churchstoke (5 as opposed to 9% of people born in Wales) recorded similar differences. These results tend to suggest that in-migration from England has contributed to the dilution of Welshness in these particular areas. But there may be other explanations. For example, unlike previous censuses, in 1991 details were recorded of 'absent households'. This significant change means that persons who worked away but still maintained a home (perhaps a parental home?) in their native locality were also recorded - so creating what might be a statistical anomaly that has inflated the actual numbers of Welsh speakers who live and work in Montgomeryshire on an everyday basis. Clearly, the 1991 census results are not fully comparable with those collected in previous years and their analysis calls for much vigilance and care if meaningful results are to be achieved.

Much more significant in the context of our understanding of conditions in the twentieth century is the fact that whilst retaining Welsh speakers in the majority in 1971, the western and the northern rural communities seem to have become much less intensely Welsh in 1971 than they had been in the decades leading up to 1931. Nevertheless, whilst maintaining the overall contrasts of English in the east and Welsh in the west, it is plain that the clear regional contrasts that had existed in the eighteenth century seem to have been maintained through to our own times. The main differences now, however, seem to be that whilst still overwhelmingly Welsh in speech and outlook, in the rural west and in the communities of northern Montgomeryshire, Welshness as such is much less intense as a distinctive culture indicator in the 1990s than it was in the 1930s.

W. T. R. PRYCE

continues on next page

For explanation of the hatchings - see main map on page 118.

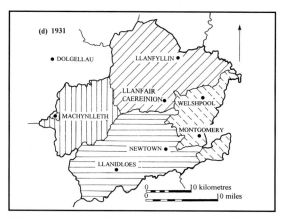

(d) 1931

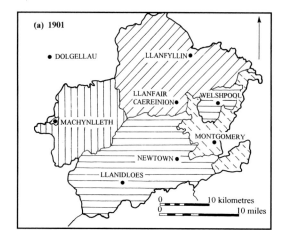

(a) 1901

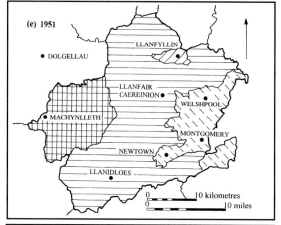

(e) 1951

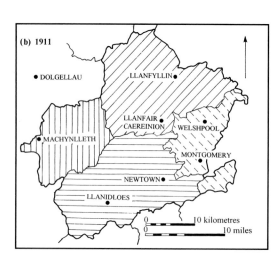

(b) 1911

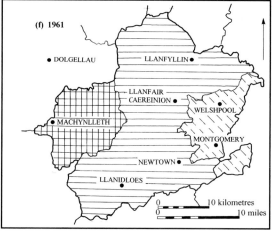

(f) 1961

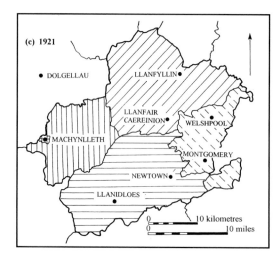

(c) 1921

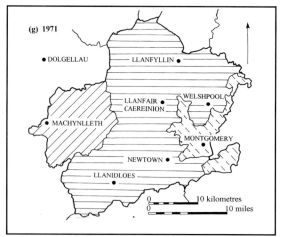

(g) 1971

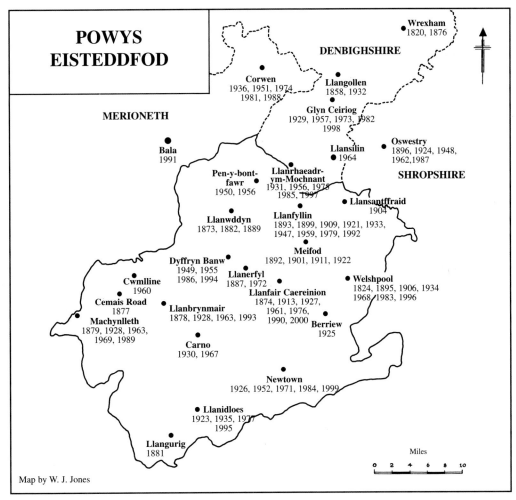

MERIONETH

DENBIGHSHIRE

SHROPSHIRE

Wrexham
1820, 1876

Corwen
1936, 1951, 1974
1981, 1988

Llangollen
1858, 1932

Glyn Ceiriog
1929, 1957, 1973, 1982
1998

Oswestry
1896, 1924, 1948,
1962, 1987

Bala
1991

Llansilin
1964

Pen-y-bont-fawr
1950, 1956

Llanrhaeadr-ym-Mochnant
1931, 1956, 1975
1985, 1997

Llansantffraid
1904

Llanwddyn
1873, 1882, 1889

Llanfyllin
1893, 1899, 1909, 1921, 1933,
1947, 1959, 1979, 1992

Meifod
1892, 1901, 1911, 1922

Dyffryn Banw
1949, 1955
1986, 1994

Llanerfyl
1887, 1972

Welshpool
1824, 1895, 1906, 1934
1968, 1983, 1996

Cwmlline
1960

Llanfair Caereinion
1874, 1913, 1927,
1961, 1976,
1990, 2000

Cemais Road
1877

Llanbrynmair
1878, 1928, 1963, 1993

Berriew
1925

Machynlleth
1879, 1928, 1963,
1969, 1989

Carno
1930, 1967

Newtown
1926, 1952, 1971, 1984, 1999

Llanidloes
1923, 1935, 1977
1995

Llangurig
1881

Miles

0 2 4 6 8 10

Map by W. J. Jones

The Powys Provincial Eisteddfod

Originally, the term eisteddfod was used for an assembly of people; later for a congress of bards held to formulate rules in connection with their craft and, eventually, to denote an event or festival which embraces not only literature, but also other cultural activities which are arranged as competitions. The tradition can be traced back to the fifteenth century and, perhaps, to an event held at Cardigan in 1176 under the patronage of Rhys ap Gruffudd (Lord Rhys). According to Brut y Tywysogion (The Chronicle of the Princes), this eisteddfod was proclaimed a year in advance, and two chairs were awarded as prizes, one for poetry and the other for music. It is interesting to note that the Welsh National Eisteddfod and the Powys Provincial Eisteddfod are also proclaimed one year in advance.

Several eisteddfodau were held in late medieval times. The most important were those held at Carmarthen in 1451 and at Caerwys, Flintshire, in 1523 and 1567. During the seventeenth and

eighteenth centuries the eisteddfod declined in popularity, but the bards still held competitive meetings, for their own amusement, in taverns and ale houses.

There was a revival, however, in the early nineteenth century, and east Montgomeryshire occupies a unique place in this renaissance and in the evolution of the eisteddfod in Wales. In August 1818, a number of influential clergymen gathered at the Rectory, Kerry, the home of the Reverend John Jenkins (Ifor Ceri) to consider the future of the eisteddfod as an institution and how it could be developed as a force in the cultural life of the Principality. The following clergymen were present at Kerry on this occasion: David Rowlands (Dewi Brefi), Carmarthen; Walter Davies (Gwallter Mechain), Manafon; W. J. Rees, Cascob, Radnorshire; Rowland Williams, Meifod; David Richards (Dewi Silin), Llansilin; and his brother Thomas Richards, Berriew. Also present was Thomas Burgess, the bishop of St David's at the time.

It was these men, and especially W. J. Rees, who organized the so-called Provincial Eisteddfodau.

The pattern envisaged was to partition Wales into four provinces, namely, Gwent, Dyfed, Powys and Gwynedd. Each province, in its turn, was to hold an eisteddfod, and if a profit was made to use part of it to publish Welsh literature. The first of these Provincial Eisteddfodau was held at the Ivy Bush, Carmarthen, in 1819. Present at this eisteddfod was one of the most enigmatic Welshmen ever born, Edward Williams (Iolo Morganwg), 1747-1826; he was a stone mason by trade yet with a vast knowledge of Welsh literature and well-acquainted with most of the important Welsh MSS in private collections at the time. The Gorsedd of Bards was a creation of his fertile imagination, and it was at this eisteddfod at Carmarthen that the Gorsedd was first associated with the eisteddfod.

The first Provincial Eisteddfod held in Powys was at Wrexham on 13 and 14 September 1820. The eisteddfodic province on this occasion included the counties of Denbigh, Flint and Montgomery, and the president was Sir Watkin Williams Wynn. The second Powys Provincial Eisteddfod was held at Welshpool on 7, 8 and 9 September 1824. In the evening, English concerts were held to entertain the non-Welsh patrons of the festival. The most lasting feature to emerge from this eisteddfod was the ode 'Dinistr Jerusalem' (The Destruction of Jerusalem) by Ebenezer Thomas (Eben Fardd), a young man who had just reached his 22nd birthday that year.

This provincial arrangement lasted less than a decade, but during the following years several eisteddfodau were held in various districts in Powys, although they cannot be termed provincial in the original meaning of the term, e.g. between 1824 and 1913 Llanfair Caereinion and Corwen (especially the latter) became the venue of several eisteddfodau.

The concept of Cadair Powys (The Chair of Powys) was not forgotten either, and in some districts the Cymreigyddion societies held eisteddfodau in the name of Powys, like the one held at Llanwddyn in 1873. From 1877 to 1879 a series of eisteddfodau called 'Eisteddfod Gadeiriol Maldwyn' were held at Glantwymyn, Llanbrynmair and

Machynlleth, and it is obvious that these were scions of the traditional Powys Provincial Eisteddfod.

By 1913 the literati of Powys felt that a sort of controlling body was necessary to direct and supervise the eisteddfod, and at a meeting held at the County Library, Newtown, on 6 September 1913, this was accomplished and Cymrodoriaeth Cadair Powys was created. The districts which were included in the Cymrodoriaeth this time were Mechain, Caereinion, Cedewain, Llanerch Hudol, Cyfeiliog, Mochnant, Mawddwy, Arwystli, Deuddwr and Oswestry. Owing to the outbreak of the Great War (1914-1918), however, the first eisteddfod of this Provincial Series was not held until 1921. From 1921 until the present day, with the exception of the years 1937-47, the eisteddfod has been held regularly with an occasional gap of a year or two.

The Powys Provincial Eisteddfod, today, can not only claim to be descended in a direct line from the eisteddfod held at Welshpool in 1820, but can also boast to be the only one that has followed the pattern envisaged at Carmarthen in 1819. Gorsedd Talaith Powys, under the leadership of a Presiding Druid, who is elected under present rules every three years, was also formed during the reorganization of 1913. As well as adding colour and pageantry to the eisteddfod, the Gorsedd can also bestow honours upon those persons who have given sterling service in support of Welsh culture in their own neighbourhood and often beyond.

E. D. JONES-EVANS*

The second Powys Provincial Eisteddfod was held at Welshpool in 1824.

126

Boroughs, Urban Districts and Rural Districts

Civil Parishes

1 Llanwddyn
2 Llangynog
3 Llanrhaeadr-ym-Mochnant
4 Pennant
5 Hirnant
6 Llanfihangel
7 Llanfechain
8 Llansantffraid Pool
9 Carreghofa
10 Llandysilio
11 Llandrinio
12 Llansantffraid Deuddwr
13 Meifod

14 Guilsfield (Without)
15 Llangynyw
16 Llanfair Caereinion
17 Llanerfyl
18 Llangadfan
19 Garthbeibio
20 Cemais
21 Caereinion Fechan
22 Llanwrin
23 Isygarreg
24 Uwchygarreg
25 Penegoes
26 Darowen

27 Llanbrynmair
28 Carno
29 Llanllugan
30 Manafon
31 Llanwyddelan
32 Tregynon
33 Betws
34 Aberhafesb
35 Llanwnnog
36 Trefeglwys
37 Llanidloes Without
38 Llangurig
39 Llandinam

40 Penstrowed
41 Mochdre
42 Kerry
43 Llanmerewig
44 Churchstoke
45 Llandysul
46 Berriew
47 Castle Caereinion (Rural)
48 Forden
49 Trelystan
50 Middletown
51 Bausley

Local Government until 1974

By the 19th century the government of the counties by the magistracy, and that of the old boroughs by corporations whose make up and powers had been fixed by charters granted in the Middle Ages, were very largely out of date and inadequate. Great economic and social changes had occurred in the country which necessitated a reorganization in local government to help it serve the needs of the modern age. The first important reform came in 1834 when the administration of the Poor Law was taken from the parishes (which had been responsible for it since 1601) and vested in Poor Law Unions controlled by Boards of Guardians elected by ratepayers. This was the first great inroad on the powers of the county magistracy and was much resisted by them. Montgomeryshire was divided into four Poor Law

Unions whose boundaries (with the exception of those of Machynlleth Union) were arbitrary and cut across the age old boundaries of the successive cymydau, cantrefi, lordships and hundreds which had remained much the same and given some continuity to local units.

The 1835 Municipal Corporations Act, by standardizing government in every borough in the country, swept away the bewildering variety in administration which had characterized the ancient self-governing towns. In two of the county's four boroughs - Montgomery and Llanfyllin - this reform was delayed until a later Municipal Reform Act, that of 1882.

In 1888 the Liberal administration of Gladstone put through the great local government Act which created elected County Councils with chairmen, aldermen and councillors to replace the rule of the county magistracy in Quarter Sessions.The County Council was empowered to set up committees to deal with such matters as finance, highways, education.

The two ancient towns of Newtown and Machynlleth had for many years ceased to be boroughs and so were not affected by the Acts of 1835 and 1882. They had continued to be governed by the local magistrates but in 1894 another important local government Act was passed which made them Urban Districts with powers similar to those of the four boroughs.

There remained the rural areas, and the same 1894 Act subdivided the county (excluding the four boroughs and two Urban District Councils mentioned above) into four Rural Districts to be administered by elected rural district councils. Here again there was a break with tradition for the boundaries of these new units followed those of the Poor Law Unions of 1834 and not those of the older Hundreds. The same Act stated that the Rural Districts should consist of parishes, each of which was given the right to elect a parish council. These parishes are known as civil parishes and were the smallest units in local government; their boundaries, by and large, follow those of the old ecclesiastical parishes with certain exceptions; such as Churchstoke, whose civil parish corresponds to the four ecclesiastical ones of Churchstoke, Snead, Hyssington and Sarn, while Machynlleth ecclesiastical parish provided three civil ones, Machynlleth, Isygarreg and Uwchygarreg.

Until 1984 the territorial extent of the Municipal Borough of Welshpool took in a great deal of the adjacent rural area and included within its bounds two parishes and portions of others. This was due to the extensive Charter granted to the old borough in the Middle Ages by the feudal lords of Powis. On the other hand the almost equally ancient borough of Llanidloes embraces a very small area.

The boundaries of Llanfyllin and Montgomery boroughs were those of their respective parishes. Newtown Urban District embraced the parishes of Newtown and Llanllwchaearn but Machynlleth Urban District covered only a very small area.

Certain minor points may be noted - that part of the ecclesiastical parish of Llanymynech which was transferred from Denbighshire to Montgomeryshire was constituted the civil parish of Carreghofa. The two pieces named Caereinion Fechan had maintained a peculiar separateness since the 13th century, having always been attached to the large cwmwd of Caereinion.

E. R. MORRIS

The Town Hall Welshpool.

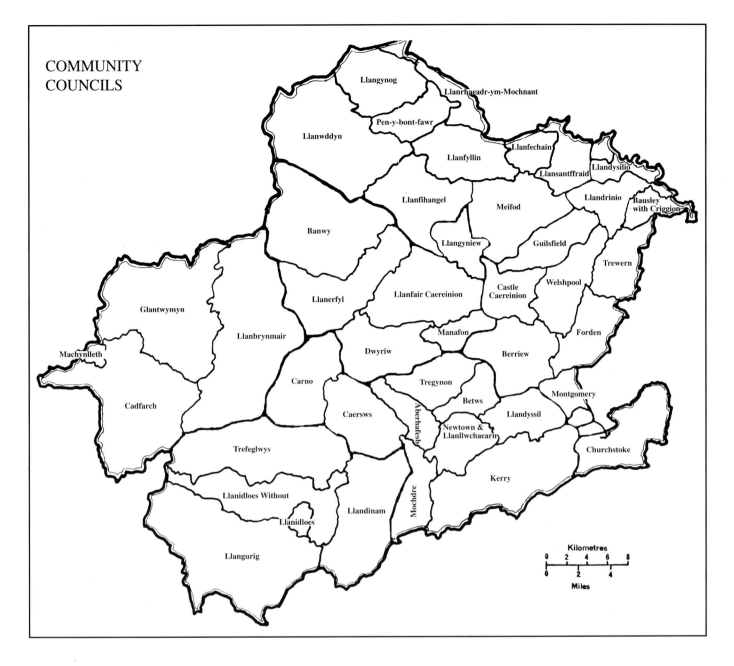

Within the map: Llangynog, Llanrhaeadr-ym-Mochnant, Pen-y-bont-fawr, Llanwddyn, Llanfyllin, Llanfechain, Llansantffraid, Llandysilio, Llanfihangel, Meifod, Llandrinio, Bausley with Criggion, Banwy, Llangyniew, Guilsfield, Trewern, Glantwymyn, Llanerfyl, Llanfair Caereinion, Castle Caereinion, Welshpool, Llanbrynmair, Manafon, Forden, Machynlleth, Dwyriw, Berriew, Carno, Tregynon, Montgomery, Cadfarch, Betws, Caersws, Aberhafesb, Llandyssil, Newtown & Llanllwchaearn, Churchstoke, Trefeglwys, Mochdre, Kerry, Llanidloes Without, Llandinam, Llanidloes, Llangurig

Kilometres
0 2 4 6 8
0 2 4
Miles

Local Government since 1974

Prior to 1974, with the exception of the ancient boroughs of Llanfyllin, Llanidloes, Montgomery and Welshpool which were established by Charter in the Middle Ages, local government structure in Montgomeryshire has existed since 1888 when County Councils were created, followed in 1894 by Urban and Rural District Councils.

As from the 1 April 1974 the thirteen County Councils in Wales were replaced by eight larger ones of which the new Powys County Council covered almost the entire areas of the former Brecknock,

Montgomery and Radnor Counties, while the four boroughs and six district councils in Montgomeryshire were replaced by one district council extending over the whole of the old county. At the same time Parish Councils were re-named Community Councils which themselves were subsequently subjected to a Special Review by the Local Government Boundary Commission for Wales, resulting in a reduction in their numbers from 57 to 45. Many of the former Parish Councils continued unchanged so far as their areas were concerned but some had extensive boundary alterations while in several others existing Communities were amalgamated to form new Communities. There were minor alterations in the boundary between Montgomeryshire and Glyndwr District Councils concerning a slight change at Llanrhaeadr-ym-Mochnant and Llanwddyn, a technical adjustment at Llangurig when one property was transferred to Radnor District Council and at the boundary with Meirionnydd District Council when part of the Community of Caereinion Fechan was transferred to Meirionnydd. The Special Community Review became operational on the 1 January 1987. Similarly a review of the electoral arrangements for Montgomeryshire resulted in a reduction in the number of members from 49 to 46 and in the number of wards from 41 to 39.

The first meeting of the Montgomery (later to be re-named Montgomeryshire) District Council was held at Welshpool on the 23 May 1973 under the provisional chairmanship of Mr Ion Trant, High Sheriff of the County when Councillor J E Jones, Berriew was elected chairman of the new council and Councillor H H Bennett, Llangurig appointed its vice-chairman. One of its first resolutions, in the event of Powys County Council declining to delegate Small Holding Functions to the District Council (Montgomeryshire prior to 1974 was one of the largest Small Holding Authorities in Wales) was to apply to the Secretary of State for Wales for an agency which was subsequently granted in March 1974 for a period of five years. The agency was however in the light of Powys County Council's refusal to continue delegation terminated on the 31 March 1979. Similarly Montgomery District Council accepted the agency for Motor Vehicle Licensing until it also was revoked and the duties transferred first to Shrewsbury and eventually to the Driver and Vehicle Licensing Department in Swansea.

The Council decided not to present a petition to her Majesty the Queen for the grant of a Charter conferring Borough Status on the District with the accompanying style of Mayor and Deputy Mayor to its leaders. The Council also resolved that Welshpool should be the centre of administration.

The main functions of the new (Powys) County Council were Education including Libraries, Highways, Social Services, Structural Planning i.e. dealing with the main strategic policy for the County, Probation Service, Consumer Protection, Traffic Management, Police, (jointly with other County Councils) Fire Service and Leisure Services.

The District Council became responsible for Environmental Health, including Refuse Collection and Disposal, Planning, (local plans), Housing, Collection of rates (including Precepts issued by County Councils) and Building Regulations.

With the passing of the Water Act 1973 Sewerage and Sewage Disposal became the responsibility of the new Water Authority which in the case of Montgomery were Welsh Water Authority and Severn-Trent Water Authority.

Montgomery District Council inherited some 3,500 dwellings and 800 garages from its predecessors in 1974 and during its first year of office spent £1,068,540 on new construction and adopted a capital programme of £2,225,894 for 1975-76. In addition £186,070 was spent on improving existing dwellings in 1974-75 whilst for 1975-76 this latter figure had increased to £1,048,402. The Council also advanced moneys on mortgage to enable persons to buy their own homes and included £350,000 in its estimates for 1975-76 for improvement grants to private houses. Traditionally local government has seen its own role as being the provider of local services with its main concern being delivery and quality of those services rather than the cost effectiveness and the generation of profit. But in the last few years the housing situation has changed radically. The provision of new dwellings is now the responsibility of Housing Associations while housing mortgages have become largely the function of Building Societies.

In 1994 Montgomeryshire District Council submitted a bid to the Welsh Office of £1,006,000 in respect mostly of Renovation Grants (Mandatory and Discretionary), Specific Grants and general improvements in the Llanfyllin Renewal Area. No sum for new construction by the Council was included in the total bid.

Since the introduction of the Right to Buy Scheme over 1,450 dwellings have been sold in Montgomeryshire.

Local authorities are no longer the prime providers of new social housing. New capital funding is being channelled through the Housing Corporation and

Housing Associations, making local authorities the enablers rather than providers of housing services. Instead local authorities' strategic role is seen as reviewing and improving the quality of their housing strategies, as well as identifying housing needs and demands, encouraging innovative methods of provision by others and working closely with housing associations, private landlords, building societies and other providers of finance.

As far as other services are concerned the Local Government Planning and Land Act 1980 required local authorities to first subject building and highways construction and maintenance work to competition from outside contractors if they wished to carry it out by direct labour. The Local Government Act 1988 has - subject to certain exemptions- extended this requirement to a number of "defined" activities namely, refuse collection, street cleaning, schools and welfare catering, buildings cleaning, vehicle maintenance, grounds maintenance and the management of sports and leisure facilities. Among these exemptions are the de minimis rule applicable where the gross expenditure of an activity does not exceed £100,000 or where the authority's labour force does not exceed 15 in number as well as other exemptions. The introduction of Compulsory Competitive Tendering has had a significant impact on the internal organization of authorities, including staff, necessitating changes in Committee systems, in departmental structure and the need to separate clients' functions from contractors' functions. Clients are those members and officers responsible for the specification and monitoring of services, while contractors including the Council's Direct Services Organization are those working for the authority who are responsible for providing and delivering the services required.

The traditional role of local authorities as a provider of services has changed to that of enabler - limiting their own work to monitoring services provided by others. The aim of compulsory competitive tendering is to restrain public expenditure and so ensuring that local authorities use their resources to secure maximum possible value for money in the belief that the private sector can carry out those services efficiently and more cost-effectively than by in-house methods. It is possible that legal and financial services may also in the future be let to successful bidders from outside private firms.

Government subvention is inevitably accompanied by financial control and the 1980s introduced a system to curb excessive expenditure. Central Government rate limitation or rate-capping where actual expenditure exceeds a prescribed level (with in 1990 the Business Rate or Non-Domestic rate set and distributed by Central Government itself) was introduced. In the same year the government replaced the former rating of property system with the Community Tax or Poll Tax which made each person over the age of 18 liable for paying his/her share of the new form of local charges. The new tax was found to be so unpopular it was replaced in 1993 by the Council tax - a revised form of the old rating system.

A real appreciation of the economic development of Mid Wales cannot be made without mentioning the immense contribution made by the Mid Wales New Town Corporation and its successors the Mid Wales Development Corporation and the Development Board for Rural Wales. These organisations were established primarily to stem the depopulation of the region, which had gone on unabated since 1841, so that by 1961 the number of inhabitants had decreased to 44,165. They were charged with doubling the population of Newtown from 5,500 in 1961 to the present day estimate of 12,000, providing industrial units to rent and the development of social facilities and supporting the tourist related enterprises. The Board's industrial development has been substantial with investment concentrated in a few locations, with Newtown and Welshpool identified as "Growth Areas" with smaller scale development at the "Special Towns" of Llanidloes and Machynlleth. To supplement the DBRW's efforts Montgomeryshire District Council has developed industrial estates such as Banwy Industrial Estate and Llanfyllin, and in 1988 set up its own Economic Development Unit responsible for overseeing the village workshop programme, business advice and tourism development. In addition the Council in partnership with the DBRW has established a Business Centre that provides free business advice to any person wishing to establish a business in the area, also support for existing small businesses as well as running successful courses.

Notwithstanding the success of the Board and the increase that accompanied it in the District's population from 44,165 in 1961 to the present figure of 53,000 and the campaign in favour of a unitary authority, the Secretary of State for Wales announced that as from 1 April 1996 Montgomeryshire was not to be a unitary authority but would merge with Brecknock and Radnor District Councils to form a new unitary authority covering the whole of present day Powys.

IDRIS WYN WILLIAMS

Above: The Maldwyn Leisure Centre, Newtown, developed by Montgomeryshire in the 1980s in partnership with Powys County Council.

Right:
The Council Offices, Welshpool. Built by Montgomeryshire County Council these offices served as the headquarters of the District Council from 1974.

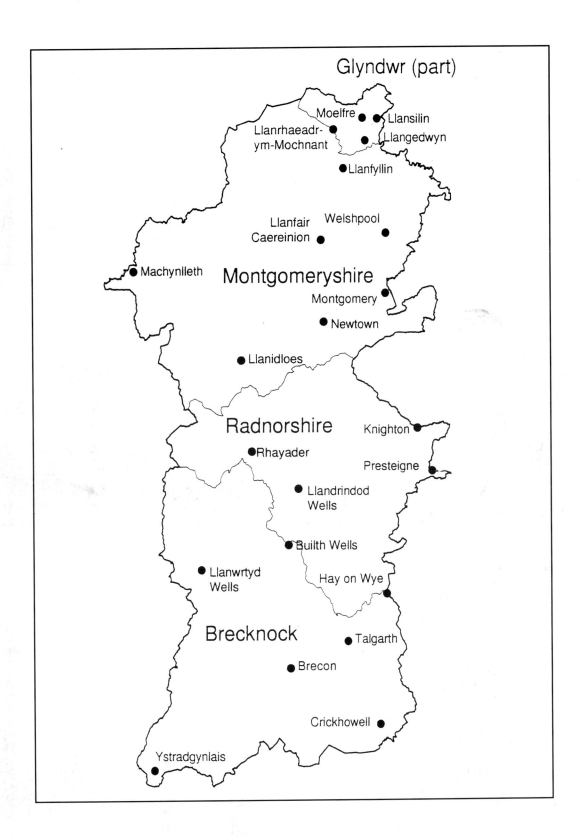

Glyndwr (part)

Moelfre
Llansilin
Llanrhaeadr-
ym-Mochnant
Llangedwyn
Llanfyllin

Llanfair
Caereinion
Welshpool

Machynlleth
Montgomeryshire

Montgomery

Newtown

Llanidloes

Radnorshire
Knighton

Rhayader
Presteigne

Llandrindod
Wells

Builth Wells

Llanwrtyd
Wells
Hay on Wye

Brecknock
Talgarth

Brecon

Crickhowell

Ystradgynlais

Powys County Council

The new County of Powys came into being on 1 April 1974. Created under the 1972 Local Government Act, it consisted of all of the historic counties of Montgomeryshire and Radnorshire and the greater part of the former county of Breconshire. Stretching from the southern flanks of the Brecon Beacons, in

133

the upper Swansea Valley, to the Dyfi River and the Berwyn Mountains in the north, it was a large area. Despite this large area much of the land was hilly or mountainous and the total population at the time was only just over 100,000. Changes in local government had been under consideration for many years before 1972 and several different proposals had been made for the amalgamation of the old shires to form new larger units. By the time of the 1972 legislation there was widespread acceptance that change would come and the proposal to create the new county of Powys did not meet with strenuous opposition. The creation of the new Montgomeryshire District Council, by the amalgamation of all of the existing Borough, Urban District and Rural District Authorities was of course part of the same 1974 changes.

Given such a large unit with comparatively poor internal communications, the incorporation of three ancient Shires and the considerable distances, the creation of any sense of community and of common interest would never be easy. Despite these difficulties the new County did have the advantage of a degree of homogeneity in terms of economic and social structure. The problems created by a hundred years of rural depopulation were to be found in virtually all parts of the new county.

It was intended by government that the changes of 1974 would also involve changes in local government management, particularly a move to a more corporate approach signalled by the replacement of the Clerk of the County Council by the new post of Chief Executive. Although the change was made by Powys County Council, the new Authority was set up on strongly departmental basis. Each department and departmental committee determined the structure it would develop and the extent to which the old counties, as units, would continue to be used as basis for the activities of the new County Council. It was decided to locate the headquarters of the new council in Llandrindod Wells. This decision permitted the release of the former County Council Offices in Welshpool to the Montgomeryshire District Council for its headquarters. As far as the new County Authority was concerned, it established Area Offices for Montgomeryshire in Newtown, in premises in the Park formerly occupied by the Newtown Urban District Council and Newtown and Llanidloes Rural District Council and premises in Broad Street and

nearby, formerly occupied by the old County Council. Nearly all Departments set up administrative arrangements for the old counties, some such as Highways also in due course created area sub-Committees based on the old counties, others such as Education and Social Services favoured more local management bodies at school or centre level.

The initial problems faced by the new County Council were largely administrative, including a shortage of appropriately trained and experienced staff. Within a couple of years the financial position began to deteriorate, marking the start of a trend which would continue for the remainder of the life of Powys County Council (until 1996). These financial difficulties were created by two different factors. Firstly the determination of successive national governments to reduce local authority expenditure. In 1974 the newly formed County Council took over responsibility for a whole range of services including Agriculture, Consumer Protection, Fire Service, Libraries, Museums etc. It also took over responsibility for the three major local authority services that consumed the greater part of local authority revenues, i.e. Education, Highways and Transportation and Social Services. Any government wishing to reduce local authority expenditure was going to look to these services and therefore the County Council's budget for the largest contribution to the savings.

Secondly the three former county councils had been in receipt of exceptionally high levels of National Government Rate Support Grant. In 1920s and 1930s it had become apparent that the income of small rural Welsh county councils, from local taxation, was insufficient to maintain services at the standard expected. After 1945, through the Rate Support Grant, arrangements were made to rectify this situation. By the early 1970s counties such as Montgomeryshire were receiving such a high proportion of their income from the Rate Support Grant (over 90%), that national government became seriously concerned. The changes introduced under the 1972 legislation had been designed, in part, to permit the shifting of a greater part of the burden to the local tax payer. Powys County Council therefore had in its earlier years not only to bear the general pressure to reduce expenditure, but also a more targeted drive by national government, to shift some of the burden in Powys through local taxes and through charges for services on to the local tax payer and residents.

The new government, elected in 1979, was to remain in power for the whole of the remainder of the life of Powys County Council. As time went on its policy towards local government changed from one of short term cuts to one of pressure for sustained change and reform. To deal briefly with these changes is not easy. Perhaps reiterating some of the slogans and catch phrases used is the easiest way to describe the direction of the new policies. Terms were used such as 'the need to ensure that value for money' and that there was 'public accountability', the need to change local authorities 'from providers to enablers', the need to inject 'the discipline of the market into local authorities' and to ensure local government services were customer orientated and not provider dominated.

The most visible effects of these changes were in the education field, in finance and in the introduction of compulsory competitive tendering for certain activities.

During the 1980s and early 1990s a series of Education Acts were passed the most important being those of 1986, 1988 and 1991. Under this legislation local management of schools was introduced, with financial delegation, and the responsibility for the operation of the Further Education Sector was substantially removed from the county councils, to a new Welsh Office Funding Council. The composition of school governing bodies was altered to provide for more representation of parents and teachers and less for local authorities. Governing bodies were then given very considerable budgetary and other powers. A concept of opting out was also introduced under which, through a parental ballot, a school could remove itself from local authority control.

In the field of finance, as the County Council's core budget was reduced, a multitude of new opportunities were created, by central government, for bidding for special funds. These were usually for short term projects or for capital projects. To achieve success, under many of the programmes, cross-departmental or cross-authority bidding was essential. New mechanism had to be created to permit the preparation and administration of these bids and the grants subsequently secured.

Some local authorities, for political and other reasons, decided to resist many of these changes. Powys County Council decided to prioritize making the new education system work. Over a period of about five years the necessary changes were introduced culminating in a major reorganization of the Education Department in 1992/3, designed to facilitate a new role as provider of support services to schools and the creation of a new Community Department. As far as Montgomeryshire was concerned in 1990 the Montgomeryshire College of Further Education was merged with its Radnorshire and Breconshire equivalents, to form Coleg Powys and in 1993 this became a corporate independent body. Only one school ever held a ballot in Montgomeryshire to opt out of local authority control, the small village school at Llanerfyl, which had been threatened with closure. It was subsequently permitted by the then Secretary of State for Wales to set itself up as a Grant Maintained School.

The other major change as already mentioned was the introduction of Compulsory Competitive Tendering for certain services, under the Local Government Act of 1988. As far as the County Council was concerned the services initially affected were largely manual and included the cleaning of premises, highways, building and grounds maintenance, and catering. The council decided that it wished to win the contracts to deliver these services so as to protect local employment. To do this a new Direct Services Organization and Board were created on a cross-departmental basis. Very considerable success was achieved in gaining the contracts concerned.

The nature of these and the many other changes introduced resulted in fundamental changes in the organization and structure of the Authority and in the way it was managed. The role of and effectiveness of the Policy and Resources Committee in providing leadership was the key to the making of changes and for creating an effective corporate management structure for the authority through the Chief Executive and his management team, composed of departmental chief officers.

The way the former Powys County Council responded to the many challenges of the later 1980s and early 1990s is believed to have had a considerable influence in the decision of the Welsh

Office to set up a unitary authority based on Powys rather than on the pre-1974 County Councils. It has also had a considerable influence on the way the new unitary authority has been set up with its emphasis on a common structure recognizing the three old counties as key administrative areas.

During the period of the existence of Powys County Council many major construction projects were completed in Montgomeryshire. These included the new college of further education and theatre in Newtown, new primary schools buildings in six communities, a new leisure centre at Llanfair Caereinion and three joint sports centres projects in other towns built with Montgomeryshire District Council, a second river bridge and new fire station at Newtown, four new library buildings and a new museum in Welshpool, and four new residential homes for the elderly. In addition many schemes of extension and adaptation were carried out to buildings such as schools. The Authority also actively continued the old Montgomeryshire policy of supporting rural provision through community centres and halls. In addition to many schemes for improvements to village halls and village playing fields supported by Powys County Council between the 1st April 1974 and the 31st March 1996 fifteen new halls were built and opened. Perhaps in the long run it is for these kinds of policies the Council will be remembered.

DAVID HALL

The new Churchstoke Community Hall, built on a site adjacent to the village school and recreation field.

The new Powysland Museum, Welshpool, located in converted premises, which were originally a canal-side warehouse.

Growth/Key Towns

Village Workshops

LLANGYNOG

LLANWDDYN

LLANFYLLIN

FOUR CROSSES

LLANERFYL

WELSHPOOL

LLANFAIR CAEREINION

GLANTWYMYN

LLANBRYNMAIR

MACHYNLLETH

TREGYNON

CAERSWS

NEWTOWN

MELLINGTON

LLANIDLOES

0   10 kilometres

0   10 miles

Modern Industrial Development

Over a century ago any traveller from old Montgomeryshire would have been justifiably proud to see the produce of the region liberally distributed throughout the world. Woollen and leather goods, lead, slate and stone not only clothed and housed the people of Wales but were exported to the four corners of the earth. Industrial giants like David Davies of Llandinam were busily transforming the economy of Great Britain. Today, as we enter the new millennium, that tradition stands proud. To reflect on this, one cannot but marvel at the total transformation of the industrial base of Montgomeryshire over the last forty years. The need for change was simple.

Agriculture, the very bedrock of the economy and society of rural Wales, simply no longer had the same demand for labour.

A new employment base had to be created if Montgomeryshire was to take its right and proper place in the economic make up of Wales. Moreover, it had to be created if the area was to reverse the massive haemorrhage of its youngest and brightest talent. The population figures make for stark and ugly reading. From its peak of 67,623 in 1871 the population fell to its lowest point of 43,119 in 1971. Worse, the biggest inequalities started to show amongst those who were categorized as economically active who led the exodus in search of new employment opportunities.

Radical thinking was needed if the area was to reverse this trend. In the post war era, which saw manufacturing and industry grow to unprecedented levels, radical, and indeed visionary individuals grasped on this as the future for Mid Wales. Cardiganshire County Council as it was then, had initiated a move to form a regional development body for Mid Wales. The initial concept was to attract industry and jobs to the area and far sighted individuals such as Clement Davies and George Hamer, along with Montgomeryshire County Council, joined in the call for what would ultimately prove to be the turning point of the economic history of Mid Wales.

The Mid Wales Industrial Development Association, itself the forerunner of other rural development bodies in the UK, was formed in 1957. Led by Professor Arthur Beacham, Professor of Economics at the University of Wales, Aberystwyth, the Association represented the then County Councils of Brecon, Cardiganshire, Merioneth, Montgomery-shire and Radnorshire. The five Councils financed it, with modest help from the Development Commission, an arm of government concerned with the well-being of the rural areas of England and Wales.

Throughout the 1950s the pattern for growth, which remains even today, was set in train. A succession of engineering firms provided substantial employment opportunities in Newtown. Giants of engineering brilliance such as the Mills' foundry of Llanidloes exported their produce throughout the world. Many Idloesians can still recall exotic foreign journeys to install and maintain the famous Mills presses.

The first firm to come to Montgomeryshire as a result of the Association's work was a clothing firm from Stockport. Following a pilot scheme in Llanfyllin, the company took over a derelict old Church School in Machynlleth in 1958. Not only did the company expand that operation but it established new ventures in Lampeter and Cardigan. Despite troubled times, who in the area does not know of the developments which built on the area's textile tradition and gave rise to the household name of Laura Ashley, one of Montgomeryshire's biggest

success stories. A string of small scale developments fed the regeneration process until a major breakthrough was achieved in 1964 when the Association made a successful application to the Government for the new concept of building 'advance factories' in Mid Wales. These were initially factories of 10,000 sq.ft. built to a standard specification and suitable for most light industrial needs. The first was built in Welshpool in 1966.

Whilst encouraging, these initiatives were not in themselves sufficient to stem the tide of depopulation. Between 1951-61 the population fell from 46,000 to just over 44,000.

In retrospect, it is extremely difficult to comprehend the importance of one piece of work which was to transform the economic fortunes of Montgomeryshire. 'Depopulation in Mid Wales', a report by a Government committee chaired by the aforementioned Professor Beacham, argued that depopulation was as significant a factor of economic disadvantage as unemployment. It was a crucial factor in winning coveted 'Development Area' status for Mid Wales which meant that for the first time, government financial aid was available to new industry on similar terms to areas of high unemployment. From 1966 to this day, this aid has been a cornerstone of Montgomeryshire's economic success story. The mid 1960s witnessed the steady growth of both a factory and housing programme based on Newtown, and it was at this time that history again intervened to great effect.

As far back as 1948, Montgomeryshire's County Architect and Planning Officer had suggested the building of a new town in the Severn Valley. The Association had taken forward the argument with the momentous result that in 1966, the first Secretary of Wales, the Rt. Hon. James Griffiths, MP, commissioned a study into the development of a 'New Town in Mid Wales'. The controversial report which emerged proposed the building of a New Town for 70,000 people at Caersws.

On reading the proposals today it is impossible not to admire the vision and thinking of the time. Development on any scale in such a majestically beautiful environment remains a highly controversial issue. It was this very controversy however, which fuelled the engine of growth. The economic development of Mid Wales was firmly on the agenda and, whilst the report itself was rejected, a more modest plan to expand Newtown itself was accepted.

In 1967 the Mid Wales Development Corporation was formed under the powers of the New Towns Act. The primary purpose was to double the size of Newtown to a population of 11,000 within 10 years. In the event, it was finally achieved in the early 1990s.

The interim story however, was a far cry from the conventional concept of a sleepy rural idyll. By the time the Corporation's vision was achieved Montgomeryshire had attained, and still enjoys, international status.

Modern factory units at Newtown.

In 1977 the Development Board for Rural Wales was formed to unite the strengths of the Mid Wales Industrial Development Association and the Mid Wales Development Corporation. Despite its many and vociferous critics (it was once referred to as the Destruction Board for Rural Wales) as well as its name changes through Mid Wales Development to its now merged status as the Welsh Development Agency, DBRW transformed the wealth-creating capacity of Montgomeryshire.

The major thrust of its policy throughout Mid Wales was based on the concept of Key, or 'growth towns'. The thinking was clear and unequivocal — by expanding nominated settlements this would provide prosperity and opportunities for surrounding towns and villages. This philosophy was supported by the Board's additional capacity to build houses and provide for social and community facilities.

Modest marketing campaigns to attract business to the area (the *Exchange & Mart* magazine boasted adverts for advance premises of 750 sq.ft. and a house) grew into international marketing ventures. Working closely with the area's local authorities the scope of DBRW's work expanded into a range of business support measures which covered everything from the provision of business premises to specialist business start-up services, an Education Industry awareness programme, business finance, export assistance through the Mid Wales Export Association and a dedicated business advisory service. A successful joint programme with Montgomeryshire District Council also provided a network of small workshops in villages throughout the county from Glantwymyn to Llanwddyn.

Whilst the concept of 'advance build' had proved extremely successful throughout Mid Wales, growth patterns from the late 80s were determined more and more by a switch to a 'bespoke build' programme, particularly in the Severn Valley. The programme was driven by client demand and the late 80s and 90s saw the creation of a range of custom built premises for household names.

Probably the best known is the giant Laura Ashley Texplan facility on Mochdre in Newtown. This was followed by many more, some of the most recent examples being the award winning Control Techniques facility on the Gro in Newtown, the European Headquarters of the Fisher Gauge Company of Canada at Welshpool, Grayman's Pressings at Llanfyllin and several units for overseas companies at Welshpool.

If one reflects on the Board's first annual report for 1977 — 78 the scale of the work becomes clear:-
'The Board now owns and manages a stock of 104 factories (throughout Mid Wales) — Factories totalling 190,000 sq.ft. have been let at Aberystwyth, Blaenau Ffestiniog, Dolgellau, Penrhyndeudraeth, Brecon, Hay on Wye, Newtown, Welshpool and Llandrindod Wells. The tenants of these factories will employ in total between 500-600 people.

Furniture producers have come to Dolgellau, Hay on Wye, Newtown, a well-known pottery manufacturer from Stoke-on-Trent to Penrhyndeudraeth and to Brecon a supplier of nameplates to the motor industry. A Welshpool factory will house the expansion of an existing printing business and new factory tenants at Newtown manufacture carpets, office equipment and toiletries.'

As we enter the new millennium Montgomeryshire alone boasts a stock of 245 industrial work units covering a floor space of 2,036,597 sq.ft. Whilst the once mooted airport at Caersws has not materialized Welshpool now hosts a regional facility. Schools within the county have won national business awards. Japanese, Canadian, Finnish, American and French firms have found a successful home for their businesses. Where lead from the area helped roof houses and cotton clothed all nationalities, car components, hydraulics, office equipment, furniture, plastics, electrical components, printed material and much more find their way into a global economy. The successful mix of inward investment and indigenous business growth has meant that without exception virtually every settlement in Montgomeryshire proudly holds up its own unique business success.

In 1996, the Board confidently published its Annual Report under the title *From Rural Market Towns to International Market Places* and Mid Wales was hailed as 'A Place Whose Time Has Come'. Llanfair Caereinion, Welshpool, Montgomery, Machynlleth and Newtown featured prominently in that publication. Two Montgomeryshire men had also held the Chair of the organization.

Whilst unemployment figures in themselves are not a sufficient measure of wealth and prosperity, they allow the reader an insight into the major structural changes that had taken place. Between 1987 and 1999 unemployment fell from 11.7% to 3.9%. Indeed, throughout the 90s the figure hardly ever rose above 7%.

From its low population point of 43,119 in 1971, the last Census of 1991 had seen growth to 52,692. The pioneers of the Association would surely be pleased.

Within a global economy it is almost impossible to forecast change, such is the pace of development. New technologies will bring new opportunities and further change is inevitable. The advent of the Internet and e-Commerce makes business location more flexible and this offers both threats and opportunities to Montgomeryshire. Its idyllic environment will always attract those who seek a splendid quality of life but international market forces dictate that no area will be immune from global competition.

The so called 'information society' is a revolution even bigger than that forged by people like David Davies. Montgomeryshire should be proud of its capacity to play a full role in this revolution of revolutions.

The Development Board for Rural Wales ceased to exist as a separate entity on 28th February 1999. Mid Wales is now one of four regions of the Welsh Development Agency. The region remains unique in that it is entirely rural, relying still on its agricultural base. Europe, and European Structural Funds in all their complexity offer the next great challenges and opportunities for the new millennium.

The author is greatly indebted to Mr Peter Garbett Edwards OBE of Llandinam, who scripted the original version of this chapter. Peter himself was a leading figure in the story of Montgomeryshire's regeneration and an inspiration to many who sought to build on his work.

GERAINT DAVIES

Llanerfyl Village Workshops.

140